Max Beerbohm and
The Act of Writing

Self-caricature drawn on cardboard, with sealing-wax buttonhole

Max Beerbohm and the Act of Writing

LAWRENCE DANSON

CLARENDON PRESS · OXFORD

1989

Oxford University Press, Walton Street, Oxford OX2 6DP

Oxford New York Toronto
Delhi Bombay Calcutta Madras Karachi
Petaling Jaya Singapore Hong Kong Tokyo
Nairobi Dar es Salaam Cape Town
Melbourne Auckland
and associated companies in
Berlin Ibadan

Oxford is a trade mark of Oxford University Press

Published in the United States
by Oxford University Press, New York

British Library Cataloguing in Publication Data
Danson, Lawrence
Max Beerbohm and the act of writing
1. English literature. Beerbohm, Max,
1872–1956—Critical studies
I. Title
828'.91209
ISBN 0–19–812863–0

Library of Congress Cataloging in Publication Data
Danson, Lawrence.
Max Beerbohm and the act of writing / Lawrence Danson.
Includes index.
1. Beerbohm, Max, Sir, 1872–1956—Criticism and interpretation.
2. Persona (Literature) 3. Self in literature. I. Title.
PR6003.E4Z63 1989 824'.912—dc19 88-21083
ISBN 0–19–812863–0

Set by CentraCet, Cambridge
Printed in Great Britain
at the University Printing House, Oxford
by David Stanford
Printer to the University

Acknowledgements

MANY people helped me in writing this book—more than I'll remember to acknowledge. My debts to Sir Rupert Hart-Davis are partially recorded in the footnotes; for his personal good offices I thank him here. Those footnotes also record my many gleanings from the late Robert H. Taylor's collection of books, manuscripts, and drawings; but they cannot say how generous Bob Taylor was in sharing his own knowledge, or recall the wit and unfailing good humour of the lender. To him and to our mutual colleagues in the Princeton University Library—Nancy Coffin, Charles Green, William Joyce, Richard Ludwig, Patricia Marks, Mark Farrell, Alexander Wainwright—my deepest thanks. At Merton College, Oxford, it was a pleasure to renew acquaintance with Roger Highfield and John Burgass. N. John Hall and Mark Samuels Lasner shared the fruits of their own work and gave welcome advice. Rodney Dennis at the Houghton Library, Harvard, and John O. Kirkpatrick at the Harry Ransom Humanities Research Center, University of Texas at Austin, helped with my enquiries. R. H. McCall, CBE set me right on an interesting point; the Revd B. F. Price found books. My colleague A. Walton Litz gave generous encouragement and advice, from beginning to end. My wife, Mimi Danson, helped invaluably at every stage, as always. Thanks to all.

I am happy to acknowledge the generous support of the Princeton University Humanities Research Board and the Department of English, Princeton University, and its Chairman, Emory Elliott, who helped with the cost of acquiring and reproducing the illustrations.

Grateful acknowledgement is made to Eva Reichmann and the Estate of Sir Max Beerbohm for permission to reproduce Beerbohm's words and drawings; and to the following owners of Beerbohm's drawings for permission to reproduce work in their collections: Ashmolean Museum, Oxford (Plates 23, 32); The Burgunder Shaw Collection, Cornell University Library (Plate 12); N. John Hall (Plate 5); Houghton Library, Harvard University (Plates 2, 14); Mark Samuels Lasner (Plates 4, 16, 20, 26); The Warden and Fellows, Merton College,

Oxford (Plates 6, 7, 13); Newberry Library, Chicago (Plate 31); Princeton University Library and the Robert H. Taylor Collection, Princeton University Library (Cover, frontispiece, and Plates 1, 3, 5, 8, 9, 10, 18, 19, 25, 28, 30, endpiece); Tate Gallery, London (Plates 17, 21, 24, 27); Harry Ransom Humanities Research Center, University of Texas at Austin (Plates 11, 29); Yale University Library (Plate 22).

Parts of Chapter 8, and a few paragraphs in Chapter 1, appeared originally in the *The Princeton University Library Chronicle* and are printed here by permission.

Contents

List of Illustrations

Parenthetical numbers refer to the description, where included, in Rupert Hart-Davis, *A Catalogue of the Caricatures of Max Beerbohm* (Cambridge Mass: Harvard Univ. Press, 1972).

Self-caricature drawn on cardboard, with sealing-wax buttonhole. Taylor Collection, Princeton University Library. (no. 1422) *Frontispiece*

[Tipsy Max]. Taylor Collection, Princeton University Library. (no. 1400A)
page 253

Note on Texts

IN quoting from Beerbohm's work I have used the edition that came most conveniently to hand—usually, what I could find on the open-stack library shelves. Though I have also consulted first editions, as well as many manuscripts, I have taken my cue from Beerbohm himself and treated those 'firsts' as pleasing but not as sacred objects. (The Collected Edition published by William Heinemann, 1922–8, has two disadvantages: it is not complete, and it is extremely rare.) I list here the editions from which I have quoted—some of them 'firsts', some not—and for convenience I give in parenthesis the work's original publication date:

And Even Now (1920) (New York: E. P. Dutton, 1921).

Around Theatres (1924) (New York: Simon and Schuster, 1954).

A Christmas Garland Woven by Max Beerbohm (1912) (London: William Heinemann, 1912).

The Happy Hypocrite, a Fairy Tale for Tired Men (1896) (New York: John Lane Company; London: John Lane, The Bodley Head, 1906).

Last Theatres 1904–1910 (1970), introd. by Rupert Hart-Davis (New York: Taplinger Publishing Company, 1970).

Letters to Reggie Turner, ed. Rupert Hart-Davis (1964) (London: Rupert Hart-Davis, 1964).

Mainly on the Air (1946) (New York: Alfred A. Knopf, 1958) [expanded version of the 1946 edition].

Max in Verse (1963), collected and annotated by J. G. Riewald (Brattleboro, Vt.: Stephen Greene, 1963).

More (1899) (London: John Lane, The Bodley Head; New York: John Lane Company, 1921).

More Theatres 1898–1903 (1969), introd. by Rupert Hart-Davis (London: Rupert Hart-Davis, 1969).

A Peep into the Past and Other Prose Pieces (1972), collected and introd. by Rupert Hart-Davis (Brattleboro, Vt.: Stephen Green Press, 1972).

Rossetti and his Circle (1922), ed. N. John Hall (New Haven, Conn., and London: Yale Univ. Press, 1987).

Seven Men (1919) (New York: Alfred A. Knopf, 1924).

A Variety of Things (1928) (New York: Alfred A. Knopf, 1928).

The Works of Max Beerbohm (1896) (London: John Lane, The Bodley Head, 1921).

Yet Again (1909) (New York: Alfred A. Knopf, 1923).

Zuleika Dobson or an Oxford Love Story (1911), illustrated ed. with introd. by N. John Hall (New Haven, Conn. and London: Yale Univ. Press, 1985).

The various publishers of these books used several different systems of punctuation to indicate direct quotation—single or double inverted commas, stops inside or outside the quotation marks. I have taken the liberty of regularizing these conventional pointings.

I.

Max the Essayist and Mr Beerbohm the Man

MAX BEERBOHM was an elusive—I would say 'author' if that were not to beg the question. Was he essentially a writer or a visual artist? He won't stay put. His essays turn into fiction as we read them, his fiction turns into parody, his parody into criticism, his criticism into caricature, his caricature into essays. Yet all this shifting takes place against the ground of as seemingly immutable a shape as ever an artist assumed. He is the incomparable, impeccable Max. The dandy's dress of the 'nineties phase—top hat and tails—is less important to the overall effect of his self-representations than the arresting impassivity of the face. The unresponsive eyes under their heavy, sloping lids are in surprising contrast to the round playfulness of the high forehead, small chin, and infantile button-mouth. In later years Beerbohm gave Max a moustache and grey hair, but the face remains essentially unchanged, its composure still hard to distinguish from terminal bemusement (Plate 1). Unchanging, too, is the delicate body with its tiny feet, mere points tenuously connected to the ground on which the figure stands. It is usually a small figure, elegant in its first appearances and tidy later, making up in self-contained perfection what it lacks in muscle or mobility (Plate 2). The reader or viewer may not always recall precisely what this figure did, but we know he did it well, and suspect that he never sweated while doing it. The work fades into the image of its author. Of all his literary caricatures, this one of Max, which fixes its subject in our minds while it contributes to the conundrum of his definition, is Beerbohm's most ingenious misrepresentation.

To have imposed himself as a personality is an odd achievement for one who carries tactfulness to a point of high art. The lapidary perfection of his style seems to assure the reader that here we will stumble over no embarrassing outcroppings of idiosyncrasy; that the way has been smoothed by an artist who 'seems still to be saying, before all things, from first to last, "I am utterly purposed that I will not offend"'. (That, from the epigraph to his first and most aggressively self-advertising book, turns out to be more an ironic warning than an apology. It is the good intention of the habitual offender.) His collections of caricatures make similar pretences of self-effacing concern; so, in a prefatory note to *Rossetti and his Circle* (1922): 'Anxious to avoid all occasion of offence, I do hope this little book will not be taken as a slight to men of the moment'—where the only slight is that 'men of the moment' may feel left out for not having been made to look foolish or grotesque.

The pretence of self-effacement extends most interestingly to that slippery variety of forms in which he chose to work. He was a marginal genius: I use the adjective literally, to suggest his place at the edges, looking in—yet by the same token capturing space shunned by authors more central to the canon. It is part of his equivocal triumph that he subverts the formal boundaries established by our departments and faculties of literature; his improvisations are inimical to canon-making. His fictions cloud the categories by posing as autobiography. In them, 'a riter ov th time, naimd Max Beerbohm, hoo woz stil alive in th twentieth senchri', may inhabit the same fantastic space as 'an immajnari karrakter kauld "Enoch Soames"'. And his autobiographies pose as fiction, in the same way that Max is his own caricature. His parodies, including but not limited to those in *A Christmas Garland*, disturb our standards for originality in art, and complicate the notion that what art should imitate is life.

The chameleon-coloured parodist ought to be the least distinct of artists, merely the shadow of a true original—except that a Beerbohm parody creates something distinctly new, and arguably as original as the text it parodies. Subject and object jostle for priority, as Max creates his own authorial image in an act of erasure ostensibly designed to recreate the image of another author. We have scant vocabulary to describe originality which confesses its basis in the imitation of a prior original. The idea of mimetic originality seems, at first glance, a contradiction in terms. But the paradox is a daily reality: we become and maintain ourselves through the imitation of others, who are similarly constituted in endless acts of imitation. Beerbohm's parodic art demonstrates a similar fact about the creation of a virtual personality in the act of writing.

He threatens to dissolve the category 'book' itself, as he plays vertiginously across boundaries that are presumed to separate author and reader, or to join writer and work. Again, parody is at the centre of this dissolving motive. Whom do we read when we read 'The Mote in the Middle Distance'—Henry James? Max Beerbohm? or the asterisked original H*nry J*m*s? The so-called 'improvements' he made in his private copies of other writers' books was literally a marginal artistry; with mock-frontispieces and other satiric adornments, he could turn whatever he touched into a Beerbohm original. The perfect surface of his own books is repeatedly agitated by acknowledgements of our readerly presence. The essayistic calm may be shattered by a comic fit of authorial bad manners: 'Here I am trying to entertain you, and you will not be entertained. You stand shouting that it is more blessed to give than to receive. Very well. For my part, I would rather read than write, any day. You shall write this essay for me.'[1] The book threatens, for a finely controlled moment, to dissolve into the confusions of life.

His current, fragmented reputation reflects the conditions of his art. To some readers he is the author of a single strange comic novel, *Zuleika Dobson*. Some know him as a caricaturist, others as a parodist, or a theatre critic, or an essayist in the tradition of Lamb, Thackeray, and Stevenson. In the merest matter of chronology he is elusive. He is indelibly associated with the *Yellow Book* and the 1890s; but the book that established that association—the very slim volume mockingly called *The Works of Max Beerbohm* (1896), with its essays on King George the Fourth and the dandies of the Regency—begins a career of relentless retrospection. That his best work is very much of this century—is even, I will argue, related to the movement called modernism—may therefore surprise readers who place him in the vaguely distant past. That a writer who announced his retirement during 'the Beardsley period'[2] was broadcasting on the BBC in the 1950s seems uncanny.

For many readers Beerbohm exists more as a cultural rumour than

[1] 'Hosts and Guests', in *And Even Now* (New York: E. P. Dutton, 1921), 128–9. The title-page 'improvements' are discussed and generously illustrated by N. John Hall, 'A Genre of his Own: Max Beerbohm's Title-page Caricatures', *English Literature in Transition 1880–1920*, 27 (1984), 270–88.

[2] 'I shall write no more. Already I feel myself to be a trifle outmoded. I belong to the Beardsley period.' 'Diminuendo', in *The Works of Max Beerbohm* (London: John Lane, Bodley Head, 1921), 160.

as a first-hand experience. Partly this is the result of physical circumstance. Of the more than 2000 items listed in Sir Rupert Hart-Davis's *Catalogue of the Caricatures of Max Beerbohm*, only 341 were published in Beerbohm's ten volumes of caricatures.[3] And those volumes are themselves rare books. The 'Collected Edition' of his writing 'was limited to 780 sets, of which 750 were for sale and 30 for presentation'.[4] To know Beerbohm well, one must track him into private collections and rare book rooms: the elitism implicit in his demand for an exceptionally sophisticated audience has become explicit in the work's material rarity. Partly the rarity was a commercial choice; in that area, too, he knew the value of his elusiveness, though it actually benefitted the dealers and collectors more than it ever did the author.[5] But it is only one of the ways in which he managed his knowledge that self-effacement can be a powerful imposition when what is effaced is sufficiently interesting.

I am interested in Beerbohm—by which I mean not so much the man as his writing and (to a lesser extent, because of my own limitations in the subject) his drawing; I am especially interested in what his work says about an area roughly described by three words I will often use, parody, personality, originality. But the clear distinction I have just tried to make between author and product is exactly the sort of thing his work obscures. In this book I have made some effort to use the name 'Beerbohm' for the man who wrote and to reserve 'Max' for the created figure inside the writing and drawing, as well as

---

[3] Hart-Davis, *Catalogue of the Caricatures of Max Beerbohm* (Cambridge, Mass.: Harvard Univ. Press, 1972). The number 341 comes from J. G. Riewald's introduction to his collection of *Beerbohm's Literary Caricatures* (Hamden, Conn.: Archon Books, 1977).

[4] J. G. Riewald, *Sir Max Beerbohm Man and Writer* ('s-Gravenhage: Martinus Nijhoff, 1953), 214.

[5] Beerbohm's attitude toward the collectors is expressed in a letter he wrote in 1922 to a Mr Hall: 'I know very little about first editions—even my own—and care very little about them—even my own (of which I possess but few, and haven't the faintest desire to fill the gaps). Perhaps if I were a bookseller I should be keener on the presentments of my work. I gather from this or that "catalogue" that they are lucrative. Would that they were so to me! However, I don't grudge the vendors their pelf, nor greatly blame the purchasers for their folly. I can sympathize with avarice on the one hand, and with any kind of collector's mania, on the other. And indeed, of all forms of collector's mania, the mania for first editions—even mine—seems to me the nearest to the borderline of sanity.' Typed letter Rapallo 1922, in the Humanities Research Center, Austin, Texas. And see the story 'Not That I Would Boast', which I discuss in Chapter 7.

for the actual signature on the drawings. At times both can be distinguished from 'Max Beerbohm', the literary-historical figure. But I have not been consistent, partly because it is often impossible to distinguish between the man and his creation. Still, nomenclature matters. Whole attitudes can be conveyed in the choice of name. 'Sir Max Beerbohm' implies a figure of achieved reputation, safely *hors de combat* yet still at the centre of his national culture: the name signifies something venerable. 'Max' is a playful name, ironical but also cosy: it signifies the figure in the caricatures who became indistinguishable from the old man on his balcony overlooking the Mediterranean. 'Beerbohm' signifies, I think, a tougher figure than either of these, an artist who deserves to be treated with critical rigour.

As he was born, however, he was Henry Maximilian Beerbohm. In view of the elusiveness I claim for him, it might be useful to begin in the conventional style with a brief recounting of biographical facts— and afterwards to notice some of the questions the facts raise about the man and his art.[6]

The Beerbohms were a typical Victorian middle-class family—that is to say, an incomprehensible mixture of rectitude and eccentricity. Max's father, Julius Ewald Edward Beerbohm, was born in 1810 in Memel on the Baltic, in what is now Lithuania. Julius Beerbohm lived for a time in Paris where his impressive manners won for him the nickname 'Monsieur Superbe Homme'. In London he became a corn-merchant and publisher of trade-papers (*Beerbohm's Evening Corn Trade List* and *Beerbohm's Morning Shipping List*). In 1849 he married Constantia Draper, the daughter of a bank clerk. They had three sons and a daughter. Constantia Beerbohm died in 1856, and Julius married her younger sister, Eliza (born 1831). Such a marriage, between a surviving husband and the deceased wife's sister, was, strictly, illegal; but no one seems to have objected. Eliza and Julius had four daughters and, on 24 August 1872, a son, their last born, Henry Maximilian, called Max by the family.

[6] The authorized biography is David Cecil, *Max* (London: Constable, 1964). Its great value is diminished by the absence of any documentation. S. N. Behrman's *Portrait of Max* (New York: Random House, 1960; pub. in England as *Conversation with Max*) adds to the Beerbohm canon a wealth of anecdote, doing for Max (in suitable miniature) what Boswell did for Johnson. Riewald's compilation of biographical and bibliographical facts (see n. 4 above) is still useful, but his bibliography will be superseded by Mark S. Lasner's, forthcoming in the Oxford Bibliographies series. The bulk of Beerbohm's family correspondence and other papers is at Merton College, Oxford.

His father was sixty-two when Max was born; the three sons of his father's first marriage were eighteen to twenty-one. So Max was in most ways closer to his mother and sisters than to the men whose very distance nonetheless exerted a proportionately powerful fascination. Max's oldest half-brother became a sheep farmer in South Africa. The second son became one of the leading actor-managers of his day under the stage name Herbert Beerbohm-Tree; he was already one of the most famous men in England when his little brother began staking out his own, more oblique claims to fame. The third half-brother, Julius, nicknamed 'Poet', never achieved Herbert's fame, but he must have seemed at least as spectacular in the eyes of a school-bound sibling. He was an impecunious bon vivant and an energetic dandy; he could draw as well as write; he was an adventurer whose travel book, *Wanderings in Patagonia, or Life among the Ostrich-Hunters*, was published when Max was seven years old.

The home-dwelling part of the family—the old man, the women, and Max—lived in Kensington, off the Bayswater Road. From 1881 to 1885 Max went to school at Mr Wilkinson's in Orme Square. From 1885 to 1890 he was at Charterhouse, where he was encouraged in, among other things, extracurricular drawing and the writing of comic verse in English and Latin. And in 1890 he went up to Merton College, Oxford.

It was a time, especially at Oxford, when a person could become famous for a pose. It was the heyday of personal publicity, the time of Whistler and Wilde. Max worked harder at his pose, his caricatures, and his prose style than at his studies, with the result that he left Oxford without a degree but in possession of a reputation. His pose was recorded shortly after he went down from Oxford by the young artist Will Rothenstein in his collection of *Oxford Characters*. In the letterpress accompanying Rothenstein's portrait of 'Mr Max Beerbohm', he is described as 'A dandy' famous for 'His use of curious and obsolete words' and for the 'boot-buttons in his cuffs':

His brilliant caricatures which were the joy of his friends at Oxford, where they were eagerly passed from hand to hand, have since given him the well-deserved reputation of our only caricaturist. Suave, smiling, polished, and cynical, we can but wish him the successful career which should accompany talents of so precious an order.[7]

---

[7] Rothenstein, *Oxford Characters* (London: John Lane: New York: R. H. Russell, 1896).

By the time Rothenstein's book appeared, in 1896, Beerbohm had already published the essays (including 'The Incomparable Beauty of Modern Dress', 'Dandies and Dandies', '1880', 'A Defence of Cosmetics', and 'A Note on George the Fourth') which were revised for publication later that year in *The Works of Max Beerbohm*. Before year's end, he had also published *Caricatures of Twenty-Five Gentlemen*. He was twenty-four years old, and famous.

He had left Oxford to play the dandy, but on slender means: the family was not wealthy, and even Max had to earn a living. So while he was writing and drawing he also took the first of the only two jobs he ever held. He became his brother Herbert's press-secretary on a tour of America. And on that tour he met and courted a young actress, Grace Conover (whom he nicknamed 'Kilseen'). Their engagement dragged on for several years. In 1903 she was succeeded in his affections by another of Herbert's actresses, the more accomplished and famous Constance Collier. It was a briefer affair than the first. And in 1904 he met the American actress Florence Kahn who specialized in Ibsen. Since 1898 Max had been the regular drama critic for the weekly *Saturday Review*, a job he carried on until 1910. In that year he married Florence Kahn, quit his job, and moved to a small house, the Villino Chiaro, in Rapallo, Italy. He lived there the rest of his life, returning to England only during the two World Wars and for brief visits to organize exhibitions of his caricatures. The elegant immobility of his long expatriation created a wonderful effect; it made him, on the rare occasions of his reappearance, as striking a personality as he had been in the socially dandified days of the 1890s.

To the Anglo-American audience who saw him so rarely he seemed immutable. It was not indeed a life fraught with incident. But neither was it artistically static nor (as the caricatures make obvious) was it detached from political or professional affairs. His best work both as a writer and cartoonist was published in the Italian period, after his reputation seemed set. Still, the appearance of a long diminuendo is not without basis: some of this work had in fact been begun earlier, and almost all of it was over by the late 1920s. The *enfant terrible* whose drawings of royalty had once caused scandals was knighted in 1939. Occasionally after the 1930s he broadcasted on the BBC, self-consciously posing as what in fact he had become, a voice from the past. Florence died in 1951. Shortly afterwards, Elisabeth Jungmann, who had been Gerhart Hauptmann's personal secretary, became

Max's companion in the Villino. He married her in 1956, a month before his death on May 20.

The strangeness of Max Beerbohm, this aloof combatant and dignified comedian, combines with his more immediately obvious qualities of attractiveness, approachability, even (to use the word he used, with all its ironies on its head) 'cosiness', to make his work, at its best, tough and enduring. He is a type of the artist as egotistical enigma, enticing with his absence, puzzling in his elusive presence. Returning to some questions suggested by my brief biographical survey, I begin with the strange name. It will sound 'foreign' to most ears and Jewish to many. It sounded that way to George Bernard Shaw. Shaw could ruffle Beerbohm's incomparable calm better than anyone. In a letter to Beerbohm in 1903, he refers to 'your Jewish genius'; and Beerbohm rejects the imputation with a surprising lack of humour:

I am *not* a Jew. My name was originally Beerboom. The family can be traced back through the centuries in Holland. Nor is there, so far as one can tell, any Hebraism on the distaff side. Do I *look* like a Jew? (The question is purely rhetorical.)[8]

Beerbohm's biographers follow suit, mentioning the putative Jewishness only to deny it: Lord David Cecil denies it on his second page.[9] But the rumour clings. In print, of course, his contemporaries seldom mention the matter. Ezra Pound's poem 'Brennbaum' is in every sense exceptional:

> The sky-like limpid eyes,
>   The circular infant's face.
> The stiffness from spats to collar
> Never relaxing into grace;

[8] Shaw to Beerbohm 15 September 1903, and reply by Beerbohm quoted in Bernard Shaw, *Collected Letters 1898–1910*, ed. Dan H. Laurence (London: Max Reinhardt, 1972), 372.

[9] Cecil quotes Beerbohm, without further attribution: 'I would be delighted to know that the Beerbohms had that very agreeable and encouraging thing, Jewish blood . . . but . . . there seems no reason for supposing it.' According to Cecil, there could not have been any 'Jewish blood' in any Beerbohm for several generations back, because they 'belonged to the cream of Memel's upper bourgeoisie' (*Max*, p. 4). Behrman quotes Beerbohm, 'I am not Jewish . . . I cannot claim that' (*Portrait*, p. 280).

The heavy memories of Horeb, Sinai, and the forty years,
Showed only when the daylight fell
Level across the face
Of Brennbaum 'The Impeccable.'[10]

Pound was a neighbour in Rapallo; they knew each other reasonably well. (Max drew at least three caricatures of Pound to this one by Pound of Max.) Pound was an anti-Semite; but what the full-time anti-Semite says, other people often think.

Edmund Wilson, in a superb 'Analysis of Max Beerbohm', writes about 'the alien element in Max' which contrasts with 'the Englishman' in him.[11] In a later essay Wilson recounts his visit to the elderly Beerbohm at the Villino Chiaro. He describes two

portraits of Max's grandparents on the continental side ... They had a recognizable resemblance to Max, but seemed so much like the idealized characters of an eighteenth-century opera that I almost suspected Max, with his inveterate love of hoaxes, of having invented these grandparents himself; but when I met him the moment after, I felt that he must indeed have behind him a tradition of wit and elegance.[12]

This published account was based on an earlier journal entry which contained another detail about the portraits: 'only one thing suggesting Jewish stock the somewhat flat nose of the grandfather'.[13]

The question is not whether Beerbohm was actually Jewish, in any parental proportion—only whether contemporary readers *thought* he was Jewish. And that question matters insofar as Beerbohm's self-creation, in person and print, seems to deny their assumption. For an Englishman of his time Beerbohm had an unusual number of Jewish associates: both his wives were Jewish, as were the two best friends of his early manhood, Reggie Turner (the illegitimate son of a member of the Lawson—originally Levy—family) and Will Rothenstein, and the friends of his old age, Siegfried Sassoon and Sydney Schiff. Beerbohm's rumoured Jewishness casts an interesting shadow across his lived self-portrait as the perfect English Gent.—and turns it into

[10] From *Lustre* (1915), in *Personae: The Collected Poems of Ezra Pound* (New York: New Directions, 1926), 193.
[11] Wilson, *Classics and Commercials: A Literary Chronicle of the Forties* (New York: Farrar, Straus, Giroux, 1950), 434.
[12] Wilson, 'A Miscellany of Max Beerbohm', in *The Bit between my Teeth: A Literary Chronicle of 1950–1965* (New York: Farrar, Straus and Giroux, 1965), 42.
[13] Wilson, *The Fifties*, ed. Leon Edel (New York: Farrar, Straus, Giroux, 1986), 194.

a caricature. He is so perfectly the Englishman that Shaw and Pound (among others) assume a pretence—or as I will prefer to call it, a parody—in his very posture. In the 1890s he posed as an aesthete, and later he posed as the Englishman famous for perfect self-containment and control. These poses are not deceitful; they do not necessarily cover a very different reality. They are poses because they strike us as willed, and they are parodies because they mock the text of their own being.

There is another rumour which, like this one, is significant to the degree it is assumed rather than spoken. Malcolm Muggeridge had the unique bad taste to say it: 'Beerbohm ... was in panic flight through most of his life from two things—his Jewishness and his homosexuality.'[14] It is not easy to imagine Beerbohm 'in panic flight'. And insofar as Muggeridge claims anything about sex in that sentence it is only a truism: most people who do not engage in homosexuality fear its attractions for them. In a future chapter I will discuss Beerbohm's personal and literary relations with Oscar Wilde and Reggie Turner. Here I only want to say that Beerbohm's letters to Turner and his conduct during the Wilde affair show that Beerbohm kept clear of what he later called the 'Sodomitic cesspool ... that was opened in 1895'.[15] He made his literary debut, in Lord Alfred Douglas's Oxford magazine *Spirit Lamp* and then in the *Yellow Book*, under circumstances guaranteed to arouse suspicion; but it was the debut of an ironist, even a hoaxer.

It is useful to have the common suspicion voiced since Max, the model of personal rectitude, is also the author of his readers' question. The very perfection of his self-creation solicits an interrogation to which it refuses to respond. His polished form is expressive yet comically enigmatic at every turn. And critical responses to him hinge in part on the critic's attitude toward the kind of complex pose I am trying to describe. To some it seems a delightfully civilized act—the raising of old-fashioned upper-middle-class English good manners to

[14] Malcolm Muggeridge, 'A Survivor', *New York Review of Books*, 25 January 1965, p. 33. On the matter of religion he carries his assertions beyond the outrageous (Beerbohm 'desperately wanted to substitute Burke's *Landed Gentry* for the family Talmud ... Behind Beerbohm's facade of Yellow Book aestheticism there lurked a frightened Rabbi') to the obscene (the assimilation of wealthy Jews into upper-class British society 'is our version of Dachau').

[15] Letter 7 August 1920 to John Middleton Murry, refusing to review Frank Harris's biography of Wilde. Taylor Collection, Princeton University.

the status of actual art; and to others it seems (by the same tokens) frivolous and evasive, an art reflecting a life of mere surface, even morally or politically reprehensible. On the record, most responses belong to the first camp. (But recent English critics tend to be hard on Beerbohm than Americans: Max's evasive pose of willed triviality both exemplifies and mocks a tradition of amateurism from which English dons are eager to be dissociated.[16]) W. H. Auden exaggerated only slightly when he wrote that 'in literary and artistic circles, from the start of his career until his death, he was a sacred cow. Never once, so far as I know, was he attacked by any critic worth listening to, and this is not a healthy sign.'[17]

One exception to Auden's rule was Rebecca West, and she is worth listening to because she raises the question of Beerbohm and women. It is a question any reading of Beerbohm's work ought to raise: In *Zuleika Dobson* the entire male undergraduate population of Oxford University commits suicide for love of a babbling female magician, and in one of his best-known essays, 'The Crime' (1920), Max literally burns a book by a woman author. (But *The Happy Hypocrite* is about the redemptive powers of a good little woman's love.) Beerbohm's art, in the life and the work, requires for its success an audience willing to be included in his charmed circle. But every circle defines an outside as well as an inside, and Rebecca West, as a feminist, found herself excluded. Her brief article 'Notes on the Effect of Women Writers on Mr Max Beerbohm' (1929) ingeniously and angrily turns the inside out.

Often in this book I will be reading prismatically, finding Beerbohm's image through his parody of another author's image. Rebecca West's satirical portrait of Beerbohm is a reversed instance of this literary triangulation. West had some personal reasons for antagonism. She had been H. G. Wells's lover, and Wells had been both parodied and caricatured by Beerbohm. And she herself had been caricatured

---

[16] The most significant recent studies are by Americans: see John Felstiner, *The Lies of Art: Max Beerbohm's Parody and Caricature* (New York: Knopf, 1972); Ira Grushow, *The Imaginary Reminiscences of Sir Max Beerbohm* (Athens: Ohio Univ. Press, 1984); Robert Viscusi, *Max Beerbohm, or the Dandy Dante: Rereading with Mirrors* (Baltimore, Md.: Johns Hopkins Univ. Press, 1986); and *The Illustrated Zuleika Dobson* and *Rossetti and his Circle* ed. N. John Hall (New Haven, Conn.: Yale Univ. Press, 1985 and 1987).

[17] Auden, 'One of the Family', in J. G. Riewald, ed., *The Surprise of Excellence: Modern Essays on Max Beerbohm* (Hamden, Conn.: Archon, 1974), 173.

by him. This in itself was a dubious distinction since Max's caricatural world is almost exclusively male. Out of more than two thousand caricatures in Hart-Davis's *Catalogue* I count barely twenty real (as opposed, that is, to imaginary) women. These include eleven actresses—a special category in terms of the represented human figure, three artist's models in *Rossetti and his Circle*, royalty, and Mrs Humphry Ward as a child with her uncle Matthew Arnold.[18] Some-time around 1917 he caricatured Rebecca West dressed in trousers as a female George Bernard Shaw. In a letter surrounding the drawing, he explains to Shaw that 'It was the result of my having read in the *Star*, now and again, some very brilliant articles by Miss West. I had marvelled at her skill in catching your tone of mind and the hang of your sentences. Very wonderful it all seemed to me, and not quite sufferable—rather a monstrous birth.' He tells Shaw that he has not kept up with West's career but that he has 'little doubt that in the past year or two she has been strenuously shaking off her likeness to you, and becoming her own self'. Shaw's praise for her recent novel, however, 'gives me to fear that perhaps after all she is still very Shavian—cool, frank, breezy, trenchant, vain, swift, stern, frivolous, incorruptible, kind, accurate, and all the rest of it!'[19]

I don't know when West first saw this drawing, but in Hart-Davis's *Catalogue* she is listed as its owner. The combination of flattery and hostility Beerbohm directs at Shaw is typical of the men's relationship. (I discuss that relationship further in Chapter 4.) Both the drawing and the explanatory letter include Shaw in the circle where it is a privilege to be satirized—or at least a penalty against which it would seem cranky to complain. West's inclusion is more ambiguous: she is drawn because she is a woman who writes like a man, which makes her formidable but 'monstrous'; Beerbohm's hope that she has now become 'her own self' implies the hope that she has ceased writing like a man—and by that token removed herself from the category of people worth satirizing.

[18] Among the actresses, one was a girl-friend (Cissie Loftus: see Chapter 3), one his fiancée Constance Collier, and one his wife, Florence Kahn. Unlisted by Hart-Davis are some lovely water-colours of Florence, now at the Humanities Research Center, Austin, Texas.

[19] Hart-Davis, *Catalogue*, no. 1761 gives the title 'Miss Rebecca West as I dimly and perhaps erroneously imagine her' and the conjectural date 1917, along with the text of the letter to Shaw (23 June 1918) that surrounds the drawing. It is reproduced in *The Young Rebecca: Writings of Rebecca West 1911–1917*, ed. Jane Marcus (New York: Viking Press, 1982).

In her 'Notes on the Effect of Women Writers on Mr Max Beerbohm' West gives her own verbal caricature of Max's lived self-caricature. She discomposes certain elements of it—his connoisseurship, his polish, his disengagement—and makes *them* literally monstrous:

He presented himself ... looking extraordinarily like one of those little Chinese dragons which are made in the porcelain known as *blanc de Chine*. Like them he has a rounded forehead and eyes that press forward in their eagerness; and his small hands and feet have the neat compactness of paws. His white hair, which sweeps back in trim convolutions like one of these little dragon's manes, his blue eyes, and his skin, which is as clear as a child's, have the gloss of newly washed china. He is, moreover, obviously precious, and not of this world, though relevant to its admiration: a museum piece, if ever there was one.[20]

The occasion is a dinner given in honour of the American authors of *Porgy*, a play about another group, like women, excluded from the Beerbohm world. And because the party is composed mainly of 'literary ladies', 'Mr Beerbohm' is ill at ease and wishes 'himself back again in his rightful home in the Ceramics Department of the South Kensington Museum'. More ladies arrive and West describes Beerbohm's supposed discomfort: 'I perceived that on this tide Mr Beerbohm was beginning to bob like a cork. It seemed a pity he had come.' Hypnotically affected 'by the delicate, fixed perfection of his personality', West finds herself thinking back to the days of Max's 'nineties, and to her own parents, and especially her mother, 'magnificent ... in her complete dedication to beauty and uselessness'. Such beauty and uselessness are what Mr Beerbohm wants in women. Instead he gets Rebecca West and her literary friends. West's account of the awkward occasion descends to the moment when one of the literary ladies, G. B. Stern, turned 'to the most famous living caricaturist and asked him in accents so clear that there could be no possible mistake about what she said, "Did you ever learn to draw, Mr Beerbohm?"'[21]

---

[20] West, *Ending in Earnest: A Literary Log* (Garden City, NY: Doubleday, Doran, 1931), 66–74. (A revised version of the article originally published as 'A London Letter: Mr Beerbohm and the Literary Ladies', *Bookman* [New York] (June 1929), 417–22.)

[21] G(ladys) B(ronwyn) Stern (1890–1973), the prolific author of a popular series of novels about Jewish matriarchy, tells the anecdote very differently. Her account of meetings with Max can be found at Merton College, Oxford in a 24-page typescript

The whole anecdote is as unfair as a good anecdote by Beerbohm himself. Its essential tactic is the excluding of the exclusive Mr Beerbohm from a circle dominated by women (and by implication Americans and blacks). Its motive is to humiliate him, which it can do by inverting the social and gender hierarchies on which Beerbohm's own satire, caricature, and parody are grounded.

Rebecca West's satire on Beerbohm is worth comparing with a more nuanced and sympathetic portrait by another great feminist writer, Virginia Woolf. In her *Diary* Woolf describes a dinner-party in 1928, very close to the time of the literary party Rebecca West attended. Where West found a little porcelain lion with child-like skin, Woolf found 'a thick set old man . . . No freakishness, no fancy about him . . . a red veined skin, heavy lines; but then his eyes are perfectly round, very large, & sky blue . . . well groomed & decorous in the extreme . . . brushed, neat, urbane.' West takes satirical revenge for being excluded from Beerbohm's professional respect; but Woolf is 'half flattered half saddened' to be treated by him as '*equal*':

> Am I on that level? Virginia Woolf says—V. W. thinks—how do you write? & so on: I was one of his colleagues & fellows in the art of writing; but not I hoped quite so old. Anyhow he asked me how I wrote. . . . Indeed he was nothing if not kind; but looked long and steadily. . . . And he said he was so pleased by the praise of intelligent people like ourselves.[22]

Beerbohm's collegiality half-saddens Woolf, I think, because the acceptance implies complicity in various things she is ambivalent about. It places her in the world of 'charming' literary things. It suggests that literary success may deprive her of the edgy, outsider status Rebecca West clings to. It ages her toward the 'immortality' she

---

(unpublished? n.d.). It is fulsome in his praise. Her version of West's story begins: 'It must have been one of my lucky periods because I kept on finding myself seated beside him at small intimate dinner-parties . . .' (p. 15). In *Another Part of the Forest* (London: Macmillan, 1941), she writes about a dinner-party she gave (as she told a newspaper reporter) '. . . in honour of Mr Max Beerbohm's return to England from Italy'. On that occasion she disagreed with Beerbohm about the merits of an artist they both knew. She defended the artist, but later apologized to the 'Master' 'for perhaps having appeared too overheated'. '"No", said Max Beerbohm, "if two people cannot agree upon a third person whom they both know, the one who likes him is right, always."' Stern writes, without apparent irony, that 'Truth flashed like lightning, as it must have flashed throughout the Sermon on the Mount' (pp. 61–2).

[22] 18 December 1928. *The Diary of Virginia Woolf.* vol. 3: *1925–1930*, ed. Anne Olivier Bell (New York and London: Harcourt Brace Jovanovich, 1980), 212–13.

claims for Beerbohm in her *Diary*. It suggests that even the accomplished Max is not entirely sure of his own status, and needs, like Virginia Woolf, reassurance. It is sexless.

With these versions of him we can compare the self-portrait. As Beerbohm invented him, Max emerged from Merton College a dandiacal boy-man in a state of perpetual precocity.[23] He assumed the privileges both of infancy and old age. Until about 1910 he emphasized the youthful side; later he emphasized the age. He erased the transitions. Max's calendrical immunity is related to the idea of his smallness. In his drawing 'Genus Beerbohmiense' (n.d) he poses himself next to his older half-brother, the actor-manager ('Species Herbertica Arborealis'); Herbert is a towering, pompous figure, and 'Species Maximiliana'—who barely reaches Herbert's enormous chest—seems smaller still for his awkwardly self-conscious attempt to imitate the larger man's imperious posture (Plate 3). The caricature works a double pretence, as Beerbohm represents Max imitating the larger species of mankind. In the drawing, Max's face is hard to read: embarrassment, perhaps—but if so, as much for Herbert as for himself; and if embarrassment, then also self-consciousness, self-restraint, and a dignity that is also decency. The caricature idea of Max is present in the drawing, but so too is Beerbohm who created him, the sophisticated artist whose presence is manifest in all his writing.

In his early essays, the infant Max is always shadowed by his mature self; guiding the presentation is Beerbohm's ironic awareness of the whole compound figure. His self-portrait in 'A Cloud of Pinafores' (1896), for instance, transfers Max's creation from the artist to the audience; he becomes the gratification of their sentimental desires:

Had I not been *parmi les jeunissimes*, I should not have made the little success I have. The public does not, I suppose, care greatly whether I write well nor whether my premises and conclusions be correct. But it knows me to be a child-author, and likes to picture me at my desk, dressed in black velveteen, with legs dangling towards the floor. (*More*, pp. 175–6)

---

[23] F. W. Dupee, 'Max Beerbohm and the Rigors of Fantasy': '. . . the public and the private man, the insider and the outsider, the precocious child and the preternaturally youthful ancient oddly combine to form . . . [Beerbohm's] intricate singularity of mind'. In Riewald, *Surprise of Excellence* p. 180.

The image gives ineffaceable evidence of Max's astonishing youth, but also, because it is verbal caricature, keeps us aware of the other, ageless side of Max, who knows all about authors and their readers.

Sometimes the early essays take the opposite approach, implying precociousness by seeming to emphasize the aged part of the compound. But from that direction, too, the doubleness emerges. In 'Going Back to School' (1897), a series of contrasts between a suffering school boy and the successful author is simultaneously a series of parallels:

Were I to meet, now, any one of those masters who are monsters to you, my boy, he would treat me even more urbanely, it may be, than I should treat him. When he sets you a hundred lines, you write them without pleasure, and he tears them up. When I, with considerable enjoyment and at my own leisure, write a hundred lines or so, they are printed for all the world to admire, and I am paid for them enough to keep you in pocket-money for many terms. (*More*, p. 157)

The mock-vindictiveness gives away the schoolboy in the twenty-five year old author. He is so eager to set distance between himself and the schoolboy that he claims to write 'with considerable enjoyment'— a claim as intentionally laughable as the rest of his pose, with hat 'tilted at a gay angle' and 'smoking *la cigarette d'appetit*', watching the 'very small, pale boy' being shipped back to school and murmuring, 'There . . . but for the grace of God, goes Max Beerbohm!'

The portrait of the artist in these essays is verbal self-caricature; the essays themselves are self-parodies. Parody requires—in varying degrees I will discuss when I come to *A Christmas Garland*—the reader's recognition of the parodied style. *Self*-parody requires the same readerly recognition; but it elides a two-step process by simultaneously creating and imitating that style. Self-parody implies that authorial personality is something assumed rather than essential, since it can be imitated even by its possessor. Therefore we usually think of self-parody either as a bad version of the authentic original—what an author writes when he is not successfully being himself—or as a critical version that exposes something inauthentic in the original. Self-parody as a perjorative term suggests that the author is, in this deficient instance, alienated from the style through which he exists, that an embarrassing gap has opened between style and author. But Max lives precisely in that gap, creating himself by imitating his reader's knowledge of a personality that exists, vertiginously, only in the imitation. The vivid personality Beerbohm creates in his writing is always a pastiche, and one of the elements it imitates is itself.

His one *explicit* self-parody (as opposed to the covert self-parodies that make up most of his work) manipulates the aged-youthful compound. Called 'A Vain Child', it makes fun of the precociousness which at the time of writing was Beerbohm's chief claim to being an author worth parodying. It is a heavy-weight exegesis of a fairy-tale and a portrait of the sophisticated artist as he might be imagined by the author of *Struwwelpeter*. It was published, in the *Saturday Review*, within months of *The Works*, as though a book by Max Beerbohm must immediately occasion a self-parody; and it was one in a group of parodies, under the general title 'A Christmas Garland Woven by Max Beerbohm', as though there were no great difference between Beerbohm imitating (say) George Meredith and Beerbohm imitating himself. Each author in the garland has a style, each style is a personality, each personality can be worn by Max.

But 'A Vain Child', clever as it is, really has the deficiency Beerbohm ironically acknowledges in a prefatory 'Note': 'Not one of the writers [who have supposedly contributed to his 'Garland'] seems to have fallen below his or her level, and some have even risen above it,' he writes. 'Mr M*r*d*th, for example, and Mr M*cl*r*n seem to have written more clearly, I myself more sincerely, than usual.' In 1896, a sincere Max Beerbohm would have been a difficult idea to accommodate in any event; but sincerity in a self-*parody* really taxes the reader's conceptual muscle. The claim translates, partly, into the fact that the explicit self-parody confesses outright what the more typically covert self-parodies make a game of hiding. The essay is 'more sincere' because for once the author tells the truth about his intention to create an insincere self-portrait. But however heavily qualified, this 'sincerity' does imply some limiting explicitness.

So, his opening move—'How very delightful Struwwelpeter is! For all its crude translation and cheap aspect, it has indeed the sentiment of style, and it reveals, with surer delicacy than does any other record, the spirit of a German Christmas Day'—imitates almost mechanically the opening of the first essay in *The Works*: 'How very delightful Grego's drawings are! For all their mad perspective and crude colour, they have indeed the sentiment of style, and they reveal, with surer delicacy than does any other record, the spirit of Mr Brummell's day.'

Here, confessed as affectation, are 'the curious and obsolete words'—
'patulous', 'furiel', 'fugient'—that helped make him one of Rothenstein's 'Oxford Characters'. The self-parody contains its share of tag-
phrases in Latin and Greek, its syntactical inversions ('Long on the
surface of the water lay he'), its Latinate liberties with English syntax
('Hoffman guides me, as Mephisto, Faust, through all the nurseries
of that childish world').

These stylistic tricks declare the young Beerbohm's presence; they
are the exaggeration of his quiddity. Yet not one of the tricks was
invented by him. Each is derived from a big historical bag of stylistic
choices; each was at least potentially available to any writer in 1896.
Therefore the self-parody of Beerbohm's style entails a parody of the
many styles that comprise it, and in capturing his uniqueness it
declares his unavoidable derivativeness.[24] 'A Vain Child' partly hides
and partly reveals its constituent parodies, not only of *Struwwelpeter*,
but of Wildean fairy tales, Pateresque pictures-in-prose, even (with a
characteristic thump of stylistic bathos) 'the language of our rural
police'. The self-parody says that when Beerbohm imitates himself he
is imitating a world of stylistic others. And amidst this density of
cultural and historical reference is the verbal caricature of the author
as child: 'In a dream, I saw myself strutting, even as Johnny had
strutted, a creature of high and insolent carriage, bearing beneath my
arm a scarlet book, labelled "The Works of Max Beerbohm".'

The self-parody describes another real dilemma Beerbohm faced
for much of his career: he was a creature of magazines and newspapers, but he had nonetheless to separate himself, economically and
culturally, from his own world of journalism in order to re-create
himself as a 'classic'. The end of 'A Vain Child' refers to the problem:
it is a dream-vision inside a parody framed as the exegesis of a
German fairy-tale—but it is also a dark picture of a world where
writing is a form of commerce:

Before my feet lay a river that was the river of Journalism, and from the
surface of its water three inkstained fishes were gaping at me. In a tragic
instant, I had fallen among them. I awoke shivering.

Yes! Hoffman's tale had been an allegory, a subtle prophecy of my own

---

[24] Roger Lewis, 'The Child and the Man in Max Beerbohm' *English Literature in
Translation 1880–1920*, 27 (1984), 296–303, censures Beerbohm on several grounds.
The most dubious is that 'his gift for parody absolved him from having to think up new
styles of his own . . .' (p. 299).

estate. Need one clinch the parallel; I was, of yore, a haughty and remote artist, careless how little I earned in writing perfect things, writing but quarterly. Now, in the delusion that editors, loving the pauper, will fill his pockets, I write for a weekly paper, and call myself "We". But the stress of anonymity overwhelms me. I belong to the Beerbohm period. I have tumbled into the waters of current journalism, and am glad to sign my name,

MAX BEERBOHM

Oscar Wilde said that the gods gave Max the gift of eternal old age; in Rapallo he embraced the gift. As a young author need not advertise his youth, so an older author need not advertise his age—but the figure who emerges at rare intervals from his Italian retreat never lets us forget it. The BBC radio audience that discovered or rediscovered Beerbohm in the 1930s and 1940s was hearing 'what the writers of obituary notices call "an interesting link with the past"'.[25] The electronic disembodiment through space was made odder by his enactment of temporal disembodiment: the accent of the voice belonged literally to a different age. Yet even in these broadcasts, though they could approach the merely curmudgeonly, old age and infancy were still combined. The opening of 'Music Halls of My Youth' (1942) is typical:

Ladies and gentlemen, or—if you prefer that mode of address—G'deevning.

It is past my bed-time; for when one is very old one reverts to the habits of childhood, and goes to bed quite early—though not quite so early as one went to one's night-nursery; and not by command, but just of one's own accord, without any kicking or screaming. I always hear the nine o'clock news and the postscript; but soon after these I am in bed and asleep. I take it that my few elders and most of my contemporaries will have switched off and retired ere now, and that you who are listening to me are either in the prime of life or in the flush of enviable youth, and will therefore know little of the subject on which I am going to dilate with senile garrulity. (*Mainly on the Air*, p. 36)

Or, explaining the title of his talk 'A Small Boy Seeing Giants' (1936), he hastens 'to explain that the Small Boy is myself—or rather *was* myself, half a century ago' (*Mainly on the Air*, p. 24), thus acknowledging the chronological ambiguity in the title and in the situation.

[25] 'A Small Boy Seeing Giants', in *Mainly on the Air* (New York: Knopf, 1958), 29.

Beerbohm chose an early if productive retirement even before his move to Italy at age thirty-seven. From the start of his career, when he was disguised as a dandy, he was looking back to the heartier days of the Regency. His connection with the past was so insistent that, from his earliest writing, he made himself seem to *be* a man of the past. Arranging an exhibition of caricatures in 1923, he explained in a letter to the owner of the Leicester Galleries that one 'series (16 drawings) gives a conspectus of the eighteen seventies: gentlemen (imaginary but typical) of that not-as-yet-much-explored, but charming, period. These drawings profess to have been done by me *at the time*. I was born in 1872. The dates on them show that they were done when I was very young indeed.'[26]

In his unfinished manuscript *The Mirror of the Past* there are the notations: '*Charm of the Past* From moral standpoint, one isn't responsible—every decent man hates his own time in proportion to his decency. It is *filtered*, has *style*'.[27] To Holbrook Jackson, who had dedicated *The Eighteen Nineties* to him—the book in which Enoch Soames couldn't find himself mentioned—he wrote: 'It is the period one didn't quite know, the period just before oneself, the period of which in earliest days one knew the actual survivors, that lays a really strong hold on one's heart. The magic of the past begins for me at the 'eighties and stretches back as far as the 'sixties.'[28] Or, simply, there is this from his Rede Lecture on Lytton Strachey (1943): 'The past is a work of art . . .' (*Mainly on the Air*, p. 199).

Each of these statements about the past is characteristic, not least because each is potentially misleading. The irresponsibility he claims for himself is complicated by the fact that both in writing and caricature he did involve himself with aspects of contemporary society. But his topicality was selective. The 1901 series of drawings called 'The Second Childhood of John Bull' is unusual less because of its blunt satirical anger than because it is an extended comment on a current situation. The two World Wars provoked nothing like this outburst against the Boer War and jingoism. Royalty, on the other hand, was a consistent target for his satire. The Leicester Gallery exhibition in 1923, with its imaginary portraits of men of the 'seventies,

[26] Letter to Cecil L. Phillips, 17 April 1923, in the Taylor Collection, Princeton University.
[27] Taylor Collection, Princeton University.
[28] 30 October 1913, in the Taylor Collection, Princeton University.

also contained a series on the Royal Family; the caricatures were so offensive—*The Times* called them 'Teutonically brutal', other papers said 'dastardly', 'infamous', and 'scarifying'[29]—that they had to be withdrawn. Most of Beerbohm's recent readers have never seen the more bluntly angry caricatures, or can have seen them only in inadequate reproductions. These caricatures do not entirely overturn the idea of Max as a delicate small figure hiding from current reality in a fictive past; but they certainly do make that figure more complex.

The temporal limit he claims for his interest—the 1860s to the 1880s—is characteristically self-diminishing. The figures in his landscape actually include the near-contemporaries of his best-known parodies and of his dramatic criticism. He defines himself as a personality very much in relationship to these figures; but his self-defining relationships also include figures from his uncannily long-lived past, which seems to stretch back to the days of Beau Brummell through those of Thackeray, Carlyle, Rossetti, Morris, Swinburne, Pater, Whistler, and, of course, Wilde—at which point fantasy and biographical reality are hard to distinguish. What is most noticeably absent from this range of interest is an engagement with significant younger artists. 'The past is a work of art': it can be parodied, caricatured, satirized, fully recreated as a Beerbohm original; and its artists can be manipulated and appropriated. The present, however, is process: unfinished, the parodist doesn't know what to make of it. By the end of the First World War, Beerbohm had virtually stopped trying. The historical Beerbohm and the immutable Max share a fastidious disdain for the post-Edwardian world. That disdain makes Max seem not old-fashioned but chronologically stunted in growth.

Edmund Wilson was surprised that the elderly Beerbohm 'did not like [Virginia Woolf's] novels, and expressed himself contemptuously and pettishly about the stream of consciousness'. 'I should have thought', Wilson wrote in his journal, 'that for Max Beerbohm, with his exquisiteness of style, Virginia Woolf would have been the writer of her Bloomsbury generation in whom he would have been most interested.' He found it 'a little frightening that age should make it impossible to react any more to excellence in the art to which one was dedicated'.[30] A letter Beerbohm wrote to Woolf in 1927 (exactly a

[29] Riewald, *Man and Writer*, p. 26.
[30] Wilson, *The Fifties*, p. 202. In 'A Miscellany of Max Beerbohm', the comment is slightly softened: 'I was rather dismayed to discover that . . . Max Beerbohm had got to a point where he was unable to appreciate new excellence in an art he had practiced and loved' (*The Bit between my Teeth*, p. 51).

year before Woolf's *Diary* entry discussed earlier) casts light on this
particular antipathy, as well as on his more general unwillingness to
engage himself—even through satire—with the art of a younger
generation. The occasion was Woolf's essay 'Mr Bennett and Mrs
Brown', in which she draws a sharply polemical line between the art
of the Edwardians and that of the Georgians. The essay is a statement
of the modernist project for continually making it new. When it
appeared, Beerbohm had been in Italy for seventeen years; he had
fulfilled the promise of *The Works*: 'to be outmoded is to be a classic,
if one has writen well'. Woolf's interest was invested in newness,
Beerbohm's in permanency.

In the letter, Beerbohm decisively locates himself on the far side of
Woolf's 1910 divide. He associates himself, not even with the
Edwardians, but with the eminent Victorians: 'You certainly are very
like your father', he tells Leslie Stephens's daughter—opening a
rhetorical gap wider than the actual ten years' difference in their ages.
As for her writing, Beerbohm says he admires her essays, but:

In your novels you are so hard on us common readers. You seem to forget us
and to think only of your theme and your method. Your novels beat me—
black and blue. I retire howling, aching, sore; full, moreover, of an acute
sense of disgrace. I return later, I re-submit myself to the discipline. No use:
I am carried out half-dead.[31]

Beerbohm responds to Woolf with preemptive senescence: he makes
himself into a helpless old man before she and her Georgians can do
it to him.

With that letter in mind, we can compare some dates. Joyce's
Dubliners was published in 1912, the year Beerbohm published *A
Christmas Garland*; Pound's *Personae* was published in 1909, one year
before *Zuleika Dobson*; 'The Love Song of J. Alfred Prufrock' was
published in 1917, two years before *Seven Men*. And we can notice
that Joyce, Pound, Eliot—and Virginia Woolf—are the next great
parodists after Beerbohm. For all the high seriousness of their
modernist project, the parodic motive runs as deeply in their work as
(to different effect, of course) it does in Beerbohm's. And for all the
distance he sets between himself and the younger artists, Beerbohm's
parodic art is a response to similar creative dilemmas. In 'Mr Bennett

---

[31] Letter from Rapallo, 30 December 1927, in the Taylor Collection, Princeton
University.

and Mrs Brown', Woolf asks how 'character' can be freed from the
conventions which create it, how we can have 'human beings' in novels
without the periphrastic 'house'-building of the Edwardian realists.
Condemned to second-handedness by the fact of our common
language, Woolf's Georgians are trying to destroy the only tools they
have for building. 'And thus it is', she writes, 'that we hear all around
us, in poems and novels and biographies, even in newspaper articles
and essays, the sound of breaking and falling, crashing and destruction',[32] as modern authors dismantle the old narrative conventions in
their attempt to present the veritable 'Mrs Brown'.

The Edwardians whose methods Woolf rejects in 'Mr Bennett and
Mrs Brown'—Arnold Bennett, H. G. Wells, and John Galsworthy—
had all been parodied by Beerbohm in *A Christmas Garland*. Beerbohm's word for 'character' is 'personality'. Even the covert parodies
and self-parodies of his familiar essays ask, in effect, the question
Woolf's Georgians were asking: how to create 'character' (or 'personality') in a worn-out periphrastic mode? The parodies imply an answer
similar to hers: one discovers an original self in the act of rewriting
another.

In his letter to Virginia Woolf, as often in his essays and caricatures,
Max licenses his aggressive potency by making himself little and
helpless. In fact, Beerbohm was not a particularly small person. Will
Rothenstein's first impression of him in 1893 included the predictable
'A baby face', but also the fact that he was 'rather tall ... with an
assurance and experience unusual in one of his years'.[33] A lifetime
later, when Beerbohm was eighty-two, Edmund Wilson was struck by
the contrast between the immutable image and its old artificer:

... his appearance surprised me by a kind of impressiveness which I had not
expected to find. He always liked to represent himself in his caricatures with
an almost cherubic head and a frail and wispy figure, the extremities also
diminishing; but he was actually rather taller than he looks in these, and his
head was larger and stronger than I had imagined even from his photographs.

Wilson adds, 'He was a good deal more positive, also, than his writing
would have led me to believe, even a little contentious—though it may
have been I that stimulated this tendency'.[34]

[32] *The Captain's Death-Bed and Other Essays* (New York: Harcourt Brace Jovanovich,
1950), 114–15.
[33] Rothenstein, *Men and Memories 1872–1900* (London: Faber and Faber, 1931),
144.
[34] Wilson, *The Bit between my Teeth*, pp. 42–3.

From Oxford in the 1890s to Rapallo in the 1950s Beerbohm had managed a career in the arts of satire, parody, caricature, as well as other less easily defined forms of disguising. They are aggressive forms that required, as Beerbohm distinctively practised them, the ostensible erasure of self for the representation of the satirized, parodied, or caricatured other. That Edmund Wilson should have been surprised to find Beerbohm, first, not small and, second, 'a little contentious' is testimony to the strange quality of Beerbohm's success. Max had to be small to create himself from the ruined fragments of other artists' images, and from his own ruin too, when in the encounter of irony with narcissism Max himself became the text for Beerbohm's self-inscription.

Beerbohm in his writing plays with the relationships between author and audience, creator and creation, originality and influence. Without overlooking the work's carefully nurtured limitations, I find those reflections significant even when Beerbohm amusingly disclaims his serious intentions. The disclaimers of significance or offensiveness are strokes in the self-caricature that keeps Max himself at the centre of his work.

They contribute to the paradox of his style. Young and old, Max speaks a bookish vernacular: it is the way we expect someone who talks like a book to sound. His voice is native to its setting. Like a book, Max is neatly contained; he is full of arcane knowledge; he is fashioned rather than spontaneous. Like Dr Johnson's voice in Boswell's *Life*, Beerbohm's vernacular breaks down the distinction between oral and written. Beerbohm explains in a drama review (1900) why Henry James failed as a playwright:

The characters in *Guy Domville* were made to speak precisely that curious and intricate language through which Mr James reveals himself to us in his books. When Mr James makes the characters in his book speak this language, the result is a trifle disconcerting, and we tolerate it only because Mr James is a more interesting character than any character that ever he, finely creative though he is, could project for us. . . . Dialogue spoken on the stage must be composed in a natural and un-literary manner. (*More Theatres*, pp. 307–8)

That requirement is a partial explanation for Beerbohm's own scant efforts at playwriting, but it also suggests why a 'literary manner' can project an 'interesting character' in the appropriately *literary* setting.

Virginia Woolf refers to the paradox of this style in her description of Beerbohm as 'the prince of his profession': 'He has brought personality into literature, not unconsciously and impurely, but so consciously and purely that we do not know whether there is any relation between Max the essayist and Mr Beerbohm the man.'[35] Woolf's comments on 'The Modern Essay' were published in *The Common Reader* in 1925, two years before Beerbohm's letter about 'Mr Bennett and Mrs Brown'. She gracefully describes a central issue raised by Beerbohm's act of writing:

What Mr Beerbohm gave [to the modern essay] was, of course, himself. This presence, which has haunted the essay fitfully from the time of Montaigne, had been in exile since the time of Charles Lamb. Matthew Arnold was never to his readers Matt, nor Walter Pater affectionately abbreviated in a thousand homes to Wat. They gave us much, but that they did not give.

Mr Beerbohm, on the other hand, 'was himself, simply and directly, and himself he has remained'. To be in writing 'simply and directly' oneself is not an easy trick. Virginia Woolf knew that as well as anyone; hence her question about the Max who is written and the Mr Beerbohm who writes.[36] Beerbohm gives away one part of the trick in the essay 'A Pathetic Imposture' (1900): 'In a sense, every kind of writing is hypocritical. It has to be done with an air of gusto, though no one ever yet enjoyed the act of writing' (*Yet Again*, p. 77). Writing as 'himself, simply and directly', Beerbohm is by necessity 'hypocritical', but the pretence goes beyond the assumption of a persona. What Oscar Wilde wrote about the poisoner Thomas Wainewright applies to the relation between 'Max the essayist and Mr Beerbohm the man': 'A mask tells

---

[35] Woolf, *The Common Reader*, 1st ser. (New York: Harcourt Brace, 1925), 222.

[36] Beerbohm was so good at seeming to be 'simply and directly' himself that his closest friends, unlike Woolf, tend to claim a seamless relation between the essayist and the man. Thus Will Rothenstein's son John, who grew up knowing Beerbohm, says 'that to all who look at his caricatures or read his essays, his personality is fully revealed'. John Rothenstein attributes this supposed perfection of self-revelation partly to Beerbohm's mastery of technique but more to his mastery of self: '. . . of Max it may truly be said that he is conscious of *all* that is in him, and that he has expressed it so completely that others also may know all that is in him.' (*A Pot of Paint: The Artists of the 1890's* [New York: Covici, Friede, 1929], 206. Rothenstein's italics.) Rather than quibble with Rothenstein's opinion, I would wonder how an artist in the literally distorting arts of parody, satire, caricature, and criticism created so convincing an impression of immediacy—or, to use the word that appears repeatedly in this connection, 'personality'.

us more than a face. These disguises intensified his personality.'[37]
(Wilde himself gave the relation one further turn: 'When you are
alone with [Max]', he asked their friend Ada Leverson, 'does he take
off his face and reveal his mask?'[38]) About Max in Mr Beerbohm's
writing, Virginia Woolf continues

We only know that the spirit of personality permeates every word that he
writes. The triumph is the triumph of style. For it is only by knowing how to
write that you can make use in literature of your self; that self which, while it
is essential to literature, is also its most dangerous antagonist. Never to be
yourself and yet always—that is the problem.[39]

Woolf's cadences recall those of T. S. Eliot in 'Tradition and the
Individual Talent': 'Poetry is not a turning loose of emotion, but an
escape from emotion; it is not the expression of a personality, but an
escape from personality.'[40] And her phrase, 'Never to be yourself and
yet always—that is the problem', reminds us of the modernists who
recognize, with Beerbohm, the necessity for seeming in order to be.

It is a modern problem, this business of being devious in order to
be oneself in writing, but with old roots. Pater wrote of Lamb that 'the
desire of self-portraiture is, below all more superficial tendencies, the
real motive in [his] writing at all—a desire closely connected with that
intimacy, that modern subjectivity, which may be called the *Montaignesque* element in literature'; and Pater on Lamb is very similar to
Woolf on Beerbohm: 'What he designs is to give you himself, to
acquaint you with his likeness; but must do this, if at all, indirectly,
being indeed always more or less reserved, for himself and his
friends'.[41] And saying it of Montaigne and Lamb, Pater covertly
suggests that he too gives us himself in his imaginary portraits and
critical essays. Montaigne, Lamb, Pater, Beerbohm stand in the
tradition of essayists who stamp an original likeness on a palimpsest of
quotations and misquotations. The *Montaignesque* writer gives us

[37] 'Pen, Pencil and Poison', in *The Complete Works of Oscar Wilde*, (London: Collins, 1948), 995.
[38] In Ada Leverson's 'Reminiscences', in *Letters of Oscar Wilde to the Sphinx*, rpt. in Violet Wyndham, *The Sphinx and her Circle* (London: Andre Deutsch, 1963), 119.
[39] Woolf, *Common Reader*, p. 222.
[40] Eliot, 'Tradition and the Individual Talent', in *The Sacred Wood* (London: Methuen, 1928), 58.
[41] *Appreciations*, in *Walter Pater: Three Major Texts*, ed. William E. Buckler (New York: New York Univ. Press, 1986), 464.

'himself' in a language that flaunts its second-handedness. And the claim that his writing is permeated with 'personality'—to use Woolf's phrase again—is itself a conventional claim that enacts the unassuageable desire to be immediately present in language. Lamb's Elia is the nostalgist of that essayistic tradition as Mr Beerbohm's Max is its comedian.

Seeming follows being as parody follows writing—except that often in Beerbohm's writing the order is uncannily reversed. In its narrow sense, parody is the imitation of a style, usually with satiric intention and humorous effect. Beerbohm himself, typically, deprecated what he called his 'rather dreadful little talent for "parody"'.[42] And taken in the narrow sense, parody is indeed a very specialized skill; 'a subsidiary art', Beerbohm called it, bearing to literature the relation that mimicry bears to acting, and like mimicry 'a speciality of youth' (*Last Theatres*, p. 66). But the more one thinks about parody the harder it becomes to distinguish it from the larger phenomenon, literature, of which it is supposedly a subsidiary member. Parody, the marginal art, threatens to usurp the centre whenever we think about originality in art, for it is only by creative deformation, a violence of imitation, that new art makes itself out of old. 'Every writer is a parodist' says a recent critic, 'in love with what he mimics, who fancies he can decide where parody will stop and writing commence, but whose efforts to exhibit the decision taking place only show that it never does.'[43] His evidence is the prefatory 'Note' to *A Christmas Garland*: Beerbohm says that he had acquired when young 'the habit of aping, now and again, quite sedulously, this or that live writer', but that this book of parodies 'may be taken as a sign that I think my own style is, at length, more or less formed'. Parody in its avowed and narrow sense is an occasional satiric technique or an act of homage. But so much of Beerbohm's parody is unavowed that it appears, far from marginal or occasional, the central motive of his long career. It is an amusing but also a potentially disturbing fact to contemplate.

Discussions of parody often defy experience by claiming that it is

[42] Letter 'For the editor of *The Century*' with MS of *The Mirror of the Past*, in the Taylor Collection, Princeton University.

[43] David Bromwich, 'Parody, Pastiche, and Allusion', in *Lyric- Poetry: Beyond New Criticism*, ed. Chaviva Hosek and Patricia Parker (Ithaca, NY: Cornell Univ. Press, 1985), 330.

necessary to love what one mocks. It is true that the successful parodist hears, and the caricaturist sees, with an intensity of discrimination rare in any social intercourse. But the loving aspect of that attentiveness needn't obscure the obvious fact that parody is also an aggressive, often hostile, voodoo art. I stress this because the success of Beerbohm's pose as harmless trifler may keep us from seeing his strangeness and strength. But for the moment what interests me about Beerbohm's parody is that we cannot always say precisely what it is a parody *of*. It is a parody of writing: writing as parody. And if it has a precise object, the object may be itself: it is a tautology which leaves us wondering where the parodied self came from. Beerbohm's insistent elusiveness—the quality of being always present to the reader yet comically ungraspable—is a stylistic strategy of habitual self-parody. I will discuss other aspects of Beerbohm's parody in their proper places; here I want to demonstrate how he achieves the effect of personality by means of self-parody, and how parody makes that personality as inviolable, undefinable, and unconstrainable as the text in which it has its being.

The essay 'Pretending' (1898, *More*, pp. 55–61) is typical. It begins: 'So far as I can, I avoid that channel of all that is unloveliest in London, the Strand. Some folk profess a charm in it. Me it has repelled always.' The pose of fastidiousness, present in the initial aloofness from the 'rather too abstruse' charm of the Strand's busy scene, is embodied stylistically in the characteristic inversions, 'Me it has repelled always'. Immediately we know we are in the presence of Max. And Max, happening to be in the Strand as the theatres are letting out at five o'clock on a Saturday, sees loitering at a stage-door 'the solitary, melancholy figure of a young man':

The figure had been dressed with pathetic care. A crooked stick hung from one arm, and an eyeglass was screwed into the face. The hat, which was worn at a raffish angle, had evidently been medicated with some oily nostrum. The scarf-pin had been bought from a hosier. The boots had that blue and blotchy surface which means varnish on common leather.

This awful apparition is 'some poor City clerk' ' "seeing life" ' and ' "making believe" '. He is pretending 'that his was a career of brilliant profligacy'. Max watches as two girls 'did a contemptuous titter which caused him to walk quickly away, crimson with humiliation'. And the discomposing of 'the tragic ass' is the occasion for essayistic reflections on the prevalence of social pretence: 'How much better for that young man, had he been content to be, without masquerade, simply himself; content to take the humble pleasures of his own class, without pretending to those pleasures which are meant for men of "luckier birth"!'

The trite moral—that one should be 'without masquerade, simply himself'—is momentarily redeemed by an ironic reflection about the uselessness of socialism for the eradication of snobbery. But the essay continues with unexceptionable illustrations of the general proposition, 'All of us pretend'. No one has sufficient philosophy 'to enjoy, simply, the things that are ours': 'What we have not, we simulate; and of what we have, we are heartily ashamed.' The histories of Cicero and Congreve and Gustave Doré are adduced in support of the general proposition. Finally, in what has become a litany of stylistically impeccable moral clichés, 'Pretending' concludes: 'Philosophers make ghastly efforts to be frivolous, and—but I will leave the reader of this essay to complete my antithesis.'

Only at the point of the ellipsis do we realize that we have been reading a parody, so successfully has Max pretended to be the generic essayist, so fully captured the reflective method derived by Addison from Montaigne by way of Bacon. The serious moral point about the universal futility of pretending has allowed him to enact his own pretence. The serious proposition that a person ought to be himself has been made by a 'frivolous' writer in a ghastly effort to be philosophical. And if the proposition that one ought to be oneself comes, in fact, from a frivolous writer, then the essay may seriously suggest the alternative proposition that one ought not to be oneself. In fact, however, it is impossible to say what the essay seriously proposes, since its every serious proposition is undermined by the revelation that the essay has been, all along, both itself and a parody of itself. What the essay does—and it is typical of Beerbohm's writing—is make us attend carefully to the voice of Max Beerbohm simultaneously creating and parodying itself. And the personality in the essay is the sum of all the essay's twistings and turnings of appropriated thoughts and styles, its use and mockery of the conventions of writing—including the convention that in the personal essay a writer can be himself without pretence.

Self-consciousness about writing turns the writing into parody and makes a conundrum of the self that ostensibly does the parodying. Max is vividly present in the essays as the voice that is (to borrow

Virginia Woolf's phase) never itself and yet always. The reader who is
left to complete the antithesis at the end of 'Pretending' helps to
create the authorial personality, both by believing and by being
disabused of the belief that the author is what he seems to be. Let me
demonstrate with another early essay. In 'Groups of Myrmidons'
(1898, *More*, pp. 47–53) Max reflects in an elegiac tone on 'the custom
of the little clubs at Oxford to be photographed in every Summer
Term'. Surrounded in the club-room by these 'records of forgotten
faces and modes discarded', he grows philosophical about time passing
and to come: 'Where are they, these leaves which the unsparing wind
has scattered? Where are they, the outcast citizens of this gay and tiny
commonwealth, these old "Myrmidons"?' The essay holds a marvellous poise between sincere nostalgia and the awareness that nostalgia
is inherently a fictionalizing mood. The Myrmidons' memorialist was
barely four years out of Oxford at the time of writing. Sincerity in
such a case will tend anyway to self-parody, either unconscious or, as
in Beerbohm's essay, perfectly conscious.

'Groups of Myrmidons' concludes with reflections about the career
of the only old Myrmidon 'who has achieved great fame. The "group"
in which he appeared (prepare, reader, to be disappointed—I could
not afford the cheap jest you are expecting) is dated 1870 . . .' This
characteristic moment sums up much of what I have been saying by
way of introduction to Beerbohm's art. The direct address calls upon
our awareness of the impudent Max who might play such a 'cheap
jest', and of the fastidious Beerbohm who keeps that impudence as
only one in an array of techniques. Each possibility parodies the other,
creating an author who is not quite either. The fact that the famous
Myrmidon goes unnamed (he is Lord Randolph Churchill) engages
the reader's complicity; we are flattered to participate in the author's
creation. The end of his reflections on Churchill is also characteristic.
He compares Churchill's life with the lives of his less-distinguished
contemporaries:

Would one rather be, as, I take it, they who were here portrayed with him still
are, sane, healthy, happy, stupid, obscure, or have led, like that young tribune,
a short, swift life of triumph and tragedy? Which of these two lots would one
rather draw? Which is the luckier? I do not know.

The refusal to draw a conclusion is further ironized by the parody of
a high, Paterian style. The essay itself is simultaneously sincere
reflection and self-conscious act, a playing with the possibility of

sincerity in writing. Its explicit question about mortality, fame, and obscurity is related to the question implicitly posed by its self-parodic strategy: how, in whatever picture we appear, do we manifest ourselves? How in seeming do we come to be ourselves?

The ironist frees himself from the trap of sincerity but exposes himself to other dangers. 'One is taught', Beerbohm writes (ironically) in *Zuleika Dobson*, 'to refrain from irony, because mankind does tend to take it literally. In the hearing of the gods, who hear all, it is conversely unsafe to make a simple and direct statement. So what is one to do? The dilemma needs a whole volume to itself' (*Zuleika Dobson*, p. 289). Of the ironist's occupational hazards, sentimentality is the one to which Beerbohm is most prone. Sentimentality is the unintentional self-parody that undoes the intentional. 'William and Mary' (1920), one of his most famous story-essays, seems to me a sentimental failure. 'Something Defeasible' (1919) compares the miners' leader and labour party politician Robert Smillie to a little boy who has built a sand castle only to exult in its destruction by the sea:

He leapt, he waved his spade, he invited the waves with wild gestures and gleeful cries. His face had flushed bright, and now, as the garden walls crumbled, and the paths and lawns were mingled by the waters' influence and confluence, and the walls of the cottage itself began to totter, and the gables sank, and all, all was swallowed, his leaps were so high in air, that they recalled to my memory those of a strange religious sect which had once visited London; and the glare of his eyes was less indicative of a dreamer than of a triumphant fiend. (*And Even Now*, pp. 228–9)

As an analysis of a moment in Labour Party history this is crude, at best. (Beerbohm usually treats political subjects more successfully in caricature than in writing.) It is always risky to decide that this or that essay of Beerbohm's is meant to be taken straight: who's to say? But in 'Something Defeasible' a failure of irony seems to me to produce a merely sentimental conservatism.

Sentimentality, nostalgia: these are the obvious dangers for a backward-looking ironist. But one of his most openly nostalgic essays, 'The Golden Drugget' (1918, *And Even Now*, pp. 117–24), keeps a perfect balance. It is poised between wholehearted affirmation and a distanced, even aloof attitude; and that poise comes partly from its subtle recognition of itself as a fiction in a world of fictions. It acknowledges the artist's unavoidable exile from the object of his representation; its nostalgia derives as much from its mediated status as art as from its specific occasion, the First World War. It begins by asserting that 'Primitive and essential things have great power to touch the heart of the beholder'. But those things—'a man ploughing a field, or sowing or reaping; a girl filling a pitcher from a spring; a young mother with her child; a fisherman mending his nets; a light from a lonely hut on a dark night'—belong to a genre of painting or poetry as much as they belong to the life nostalgically indicated: they are pictures of pictures. Max knows this: 'Nature is interesting only because of *us*'. But he purposefully obscures the Wildean proposition by trying to have the artworks independently of the artist: 'the best symbols of us are . . . sights that in all countries always were and never will not be'.

The essay contrasts these 'best symbols' with such ephemeral modern works as 'Brown's Ode to the Steam Plough, Jones' Sonnet Sequence on the Automatic Reaping Machine, and Robinson's Epic of the Piscicidal Dynamo'; unlike 'the primitive and essential things', these others 'leave unstirred the deeper depths of emotion in us'. But of course it is Max's parody of industrial-age titles, rather than anything intrinsic, that makes the unwritten poems ridiculous. In the following contrast it is again language that is ridiculous, rather than the ostensible object: 'I yield to no one in admiration of Smithkins' "Facade of the Waldorf Hotel by Night, in Peace Time". But a single light from a lonely hut would have been a finer theme.' The contrasts (Waldorf Hotel/lonely hut, night/single light) set up expectations for other contrasts between Smithkins's picture and the 'finer' one Beerbohm is creating; in that creation, 'peace time' will be answered by the as-yet-unspoken war time, but 'facade' will just as interestingly *not* be answered by interior. The superiority of Max's 'greatly romantic' picture is secured by a technique borrowed from Matthew Arnold, who made the name 'Wragg' condemn a whole society:

I should like to show Smithkins the thing that I call The Golden Drugget. Or rather, as this thing is greatly romantic to me, and that painter is so unfortunate in his surname, I should like Smithkins to find it for himself.

The Germanic name 'Beerbohm', eloquent in its absence, makes yet another comparison in this supposed set of contrasts.

Max is writing in England in war time, in 'the nostalgic present [tense], as grammarians might call it'. Present tense and absent place therefore create a picture of something that exists only in its own representation. The object itself, 'the lonely wayside inn' on 'the high dark coast-road between Rapallo and Zoagli' literally disappears: 'It is nothing by daylight, that inn.' It is re-created by association with other objects of memory and language. I call this a parodic creation because, as with any parody, its meaning is its relation to the linguistic things it distances itself from by imitation. Max's inn, for instance, is not Cervantes's inn, and Max is no Don Quixote: 'Don Quixote would have paused here and done something. Not so do I.' When Max first saw the strip of light from the inn door 'it seemed to me conceivably sinister. It brought Stevenson to my mind: the chink of doubloons and the clash of cutlasses.' Thus 'The Golden Drugget' is created in relation to *Don Quixote* and *Treasure Island*, as well as Brown's ode, Jones's sonnet sequence, Robinson's epic, and Smithkins's picture.

The golden drugget is the light shed across the dark road from the doorway of the little inn. In Beerbohm's world of parody and caricature all things can speak. This golden carpet of light speaks differently from other carpets.

A drugget of crimson cloth across a London pavement is rather resented by the casual passer-by, as saying to him 'Step across me, stranger, but not along me, not in!' and for answer he spurns it with his heel. 'Stranger, come in!' is the clear message of the Golden Drugget. 'This is but a humble and earthly hostel, yet you will find here a radiant company of angels and archangels.'

But the 'clear message' is strictly unbelievable except as a successful exercise in literary sentimentality. It invites emotional indulgence but it also allows intellectual distance; the dissonance between those possible effects is a token of exclusion from the objects that language creates and keeps inviolable. Beerbohm enacts that exclusion in the essay's ending: 'I do not go in at that open door. But lingering, but reluctant, is my tread as I pass by it; and I pause to bathe in the light that is as the span of our human life, granted between one great darkness and another.' Writing in London, where there is no golden drugget, Max pauses to bathe in the absent light. The most affecting images are of absent things—the never-visited interior, the unreal radiant company, the time of peace when (as the essay earlier has it) the 'narrow door will again stand open, giving out for wayfarers its old span of brightness into darkness'.

Max stands in the light of a doorway through which he has never gone and will never go. He will not experience either the squalor or the radiance of the interior. That exclusion is the price exacted by his irony. The essay is sombre but its attitude is otherwise typical. Its present tense is 'nostalgic' because it creates a moment that is never truly occupied. Its image of light surrounded by darkness is one of the 'primitive and essential things' the essay prizes but it also suggests some more particular images associated with Beerbohm's career. It suggests his place in a dark theatre confronting a brilliant stage he never mounts. It suggests his exile—from England when he is in Italy, from Italy when he is in England; yet always seemingly at ease because exile is native to him. It suggests the way a child stands at the door of a room where adults smoke and drink and talk, an unseen observer of a scene he will always comprehend as caricature. It suggests the very page he writes and draws on, where black lines and white spaces define one another, creating the illuminated place for imagination to play.

In the next chapter I return to the beginnings of Beerbohm's career. Much of what I have to say there and in successive chapters involves his relations with other artists and art-forms; his personality as an artist was created in those relations, just as he created 'The Golden Drugget' in relation to Cervantes, Stevenson, several fictive artists, and the language of sentimental popular religion. As parodist and caricaturist, his self-creative act can be literally antagonistic, even destructive. In endless ways he commits 'The Crime' he confesses in the essay of that title: he submits the books of his rivals to the flame of his competing creativity. In 'The Crime' (1920, *And Even Now*, pp. 245–53) he tries to burn a book by a woman author who has been praised by reviewers for her 'Immense vitality'. But his fire cannot entirely consume her book: 'It was a book that would live—do what one might.' Traces of her sentences remain in the ashes; on the charred page he can still make out the letters 'lways loathed you, bu' and 'ning. Tolstoi was right'. As the essay ends, Max remembers the words of another old author who 'wrote long ago, that the lamp of the wicked shall be put out, and the way of transgressors is hard'. Original artists transgress on prior originals; even the 'vital' author whose book Max tries to burn goes on smokily invoking the name of Tolstoi. Beerbohm is the comedian of this criminal condition, an incendiarist charmed by the creativity of the flames.

2.

Forging a Classic

THE title of his first book, *The Works of Max Beerbohm*, published in 1896 when he was twenty-four, winks at the idea of a literary canon. Long labour, authorial anxiety, the judgement of marketplace and critical forum all vanish at youth's bidding. The title claims to have won what by the same token it mocks, a literary reputation. This is lower-school disguising in which the boy dressed in his father's clothing is that much more the child for tripping on the tails of his outsized coat. But by the end of the little book the idea of precocious old age has also managed to maintain itself erect, in the suggestion that the author is indeed an instantly 'outmoded' 'classic' of literature. On both counts, as parodic satire and as careerist ploy, *The Works* was a success. It was published at the Bodley Head by John Lane, source of the *Yellow Book* and much else that gave 'the Beardsley period' its dubious fame. Lane's imprint perfectly crowns Beerbohm's joke. It allows him to satirize the movement from an insider's point of view. The imprint is earned by the contents, yet like the title it is also part of the book's masquerade.

The Works came equipped with scholarly apparatus including a bibliography (ostensibly supplied by Lane) that traces its author's small labour from cradle to college. With its references to drawings and articles published in the *Pall Mall Budget*, *Pick-Me-Up*, and *Vanity*, the bibliography shows Beerbohm alchemizing journalism into literature, ephemera into art. The cultural upgrading performed at The Bodley Head makes Beerbohm's position in the literary world elusive from the moment of his inception. He is a brash young man-on-the-make in the volatile world of popular art, the world brokered by Frank Harris at the *Saturday Review* and Alfred Harmsworth at the *Daily Mail*; yet he is also the new aesthete, chief claimant to the throne of high art, and even purer in devotion to his art than the litigious Whistler or the feckless Wilde. We watch him from the start, that is,

being Max Beerbohm by parodying the idea of Max Beerbohm, along
with the literary history that contributes to that idea.

It is a bravura performance, threatening at times to be too clever,
too self-delighted. At its worst it is strictly college humour. 'A Good
Prince'—*good* because he is still an infant—is the first of many
Beerbohm satires on royalty, but it is a one-idea joke that might have
been more successful as a caricature. ('Though short, even insignificant, in stature and with an obvious tendency to be obese, he had that
unruffled, Olympian air, which is so sure a sign of the Blood Royal'
[*Works*, p. 33].) Throughout the book, all is indirect, nothing quite
what it seems to be. 'Poor Romeo!', for instance, is apparently the
story of a Regency madman whose lunacy took the form of a pretence
of dandyism. The eponymous 'Romeo' Coates, wealthiest rake in
Regency Bath, is commanded by a lady to make a fool of himself.
Given the opportunity to act the part of Romeo on the stage, he
perverts (or perfects: the indeterminacy is to the point) the histrionic
basis of his own dandyism; he plays Romeo as a ludicrous parody of
himself. The story is told in mock-scholarly fashion (parts of it pretend
to be pieced together from fragments of an old letter), creating a
fictional biography of a real person: There *was* a 'Romeo' Coates, and
some of Beerbohm's facts are indeed facts.[1] The mock-biography
evokes the idea of fashionable Bath, where the wealthy acted out their
fantasies of love; that idea in turn evokes ideas about acting and
romance on and off stage: 'Whether we think of him in his relation to
history or psychology, dandiacal or dramatic art, he is a salient,
pathetic figure' (*Works*, p. 145).

The dandiacal biographer is as important to the essay as the lunatic
dandy himself. Only months before John Lane published *The Works*
he had published Will Rothenstein's portraits of *Oxford Characters*; the
first words of the biographical copy accompanying Beerbohm's portrait
declare him 'A dandy'. And the first essay in *The Works* is called
'Dandies and Dandies'. The history of 'Romeo' Coates, one supposes,
will reveal something about his young avatar, Max Beerbohm; but
Beerbohm's figure, for all its delight in self-display, remains inacces-

---

[1] For information about Coates, as well as Brummell and others, Beerbohm drew on
*The Reminiscences and Recollections of Captain Gronow, Being Anecdotes of the Camp, Court,
Clubs, and Society 1810–1860*. Late editions of these volumes contain Joseph Grego's
engravings from contemporary sources; cf. the inaccurate opening of 'Dandies and
Dandies': 'How very delightful Grego's drawings are!'

sible behind the dandiacal pose. His research shows that Coates 'took himself quite seriously. Only the insane take themselves quite seriously' (p. 145).

The Works opens with an epigraph to introduce its art of indirection. It is a supposed quotation from an unnamed authority, set on the page in the form of an inverted pyramid, its weight poised on the concluding word:

> *'Amid all he has here already achieved, full, we may*
> *think, of the quiet assurance of what is to come,*
> *his attitude is still that of the scholar; he*
> *seems still to be saying, before all*
> *things, from first to last, "I*
> *am utterly purposed*
> *that I will not*
> *offend."'*

The periodic sentence, phrase piled on phrase and quotation within quotation, enacts (not only typographically) a descent or diminuendo. It moves from assurance to ambiguity. The encomiast's opening review of a career full of achievement and 'the quiet assurance of what is to come' is only slightly troubled by our knowledge that this is a young man's first slim volume. 'His attitude is still that of a scholar': but what sort of attitude is that? Isn't the laborious pursuit of truth quite different from what magazine readers already knew about Beerbohm's attitude? (In the essay '1880' he admits, 'To give an accurate and exhaustive account of the period would need a far less brilliant pen than mine' [*Works*, p. 55].) The encomiast himself, it appears, is on shakier ground than we supposed, for like any reader he can only try to interpret what his author '*seems* still to be saying, before all things, from first to last'.

And what his author seems so firmly to be saying dissolves in ambiguity: 'I will not offend.' Offend how or whom? Not to offend the reader might indeed be a scholar's aim. But a young man who writes for the *Yellow Book*, makes fun of his elders, sounds like Oscar Wilde, and belongs 'to the Beardsley period' needs must offend. Or does the author mean he will not offend in some other sense—not offend, for instance, against his art, his own standards? If the latter, then the one promise (not to offend against his own standards) may entail breaking the other (not to offend the reader). Refusing to let us know what it purposes, the epigraph undermines our security as competent readers. We cannot know whether it is offered in sincerity or sarcasm. It may not mean what it says, nor its opposite; and it may mean various shades in between.

Like the title and the bibliography, the epigraph is parody in the service of masquerade. But it is not merely oppositional to the thing parodied. We do not uncover the reality about *The Works* by asserting that it is *not* scholarly or that it *is* offensive. The parody's relation to the thing parodied—in this case, to the critical language that confers high cultural status—becomes more various the more closely it is read. And an effect of this, which is typical of *The Works* as a whole, is that the reader tries to engage the author himself precisely because the words that constitute the author are unreliable. What does Max Beerbohm think of what Max Beerbohm creates? The pervasive irony, which makes us uncertain of ourselves as readers, leaves us more dependent on the absent author. Irony makes Max inaccessible but desirable; absence gives him an identity and a personality.

His promise not to offend is most grossly ironic because the offence has already been given. In their original appearances, especially in the *Yellow Book*, the essays had achieved just the notoriety Beerbohm intended. 'A Defence of Cosmetics' (revised in *The Works* as 'The Pervasion of Rouge') was published in April 1894 in the first volume of the *Yellow Book*; the fuss it created justified Beerbohm in neglecting his studies at Merton, where he was still nominally an undergraduate. David Cecil quotes *The Times*'s description of that first *Yellow Book* as 'A combination of English rowdiness with French lubricity' and *The Westminster Gazette*'s call for 'an act of parliament to make this kind of thing illegal'.[2] Beerbohm's essay came in for special abuse, which under the circumstances meant special success. In *Punch*, where he was known as 'Max Meerboom', it was given the dubious honour of a parody—a much less subtle parody than the original. Barry Pain, writing in *Black and White*, called 'A Defence of Cosmetics' 'the very rankest and most nauseous thing in literature that I have ever read'.[3] The *Spectator* said it was 'not merely indecent and indecorous, it is also inartistic and untrue to Nature, and offends the moral sense'.[4]

    [2] Cecil, *Max* (London: Constable, 1964), 98.
    [3] Quoted in Max Beerbohm, *Letters to Reggie Turner*, ed. Rupert Hart-Davis (London: Hart-Davis, 1964), 135 n.
    [4] Quoted by John O. Kirkpatrick, *Max on View* (Austin: Univ. Of Texas Humanities Research Center, 1978), 9, item 15.

The anger may seem out of proportion to the occasion. Beerbohm made one source of the anger more apparent when he retitled the essay 'The Pervasion of Rouge', where the word 'perversion' can almost be heard. Critics may have been genuinely upset to be told that 'Artifice must queen it once more in the town'; they were surely more upset to be told it by a dubiously gendered youngster whose purpose in saying it may (or may not) have been to make them angry. The essay, subversive enough of Victorian values on its surface, might have a more perverse subtext; at least, it might seem that way to a reader who recognized its derivation from Oscar Wilde. The critic who thought he spied a perverted basis for Beerbohm's paradoxes was in the annoying position of not being able to say out loud what it was that so annoyed him. And there was always the chance that the critic was wrong.

Beerbohm answered his critics in a letter published in the July *Yellow Book*. He teased them for not understanding that the essay was a satire on modern writing, but he also blamed them for failing to appreciate such writing. David Cecil points out that the defence is contradictory.[5] But then the essay itself is contradictory: the divided defence continues the essay's strategy of unsettling the reader by constituting itself in parody. In 1894 the paradoxical claim for the superiority of artifice to nature was old hat; 'A Defence of Cosmetics' could not exist without its lineage of prior defences. Thirty years earlier, Baudelaire had attacked nature in *Le Peintre de la vie moderne*: crime and ugliness are natural, but beauty and virtue, being products of art and reason, are artificial: therefore Baudelaire is 'led to consider personal adornment as one of the signs of the primeval nobility of the human soul', and fashion 'a symptom of the taste for the ideal which surmounts everything coarse, earthly and foul'. Writing in praise of make-up, then, Baudelaire claims that face powder, rouge, and eye-liner elevate the wearer above nature toward the statuesque realm of the 'superior and divine being'. The proper use of make-up is not to make the old look young, because that would be a mere imitation of nature. Cosmetics is not an ancillary art: 'Make-up does not need to hide itself, to avoid being noticed; on the contrary, it can display itself, if not ostentatiously, at least with a kind of ingenuousness.'[6]

---

[5] Cecil, *Max*, pp. 100–1.

[6] *Baudelaire as a Literary Critic*, ed. and trans. Lois Boe Hyslop and Francis E. Hyslop, Jr. (University Park: Pennsylvania State Univ. Press, 1964), 297–300. Baudelaire's essay was written in 1859–60 and published in *Le Figaro* 1863.

This was the aesthetic message Oscar Wilde carried to England and America in the 1880s, making it in transit entertainingly disingenuous and, as he moved toward the debacle of 1895, increasingly self-parodic.[7] The first maxim in the Preface to *The Picture of Dorian Gray* (1890) declared that 'The artist is the creator of beautiful things'; four years later, in 'Phrases and Philosophies for the Use of the Young', it had become a wisecrack: 'The first duty of life is to be as artificial as possible. What the second duty is no one has as yet discovered.' In Beerbohm's essay the praise of artifice is ventriloquized as undergraduate humour. Wilde had written that 'If one tells the truth, one is sure, sooner or later, to be found out.' What truth did Beerbohm's essay tell? Some readers may have thought that Beerbohm meant what he said; most would have seen that he was making fun—but of whom or what?

The essay proposes a cyclical theory of history, in which eras of artifice and eras of naturalness succeed one another: 'The Victorian era comes to its end and the day of sancta simplicitas is quite ended.' He compares the present *fin de siècle* to Rome 'in the keenest time of her degringolade'. Now the wheel has come full circle and again it is 'a time of jolliness and glad indulgence'.

For the era of rouge is upon us, and as only in an elaborate era can man, by the tangled accrescency of his own pleasures and emotions, reach that refinement which is his highest excellence, and by making himself, so to say, independent of Nature, come nearest to God, so only in an elaborate era is woman perfect. (*Works*, p. 103)

The elaborateness of the sentence and its apparently universal claims conflict with the smallness of its context, which is a comic treatment of a 'nineties commonplace, the supposedly alarming rate at which differences between the sexes are disappearing—a theme that seems to have been treated by everyone from Beardsley to Shaw (in his portraits of 'New Women' like Vivie Warren) and Wells (in the epicene Eloi of *The Time Machine*). Max's evidence for his cyclical vision of history includes the current prevalence of women who ride

---

[7] See Patricia Clements, *Baudelaire and the English Tradition* (Princeton, NJ: Princeton Univ. Press, 1986), for an excellent analysis of Baudelaire's influence on, among others, Swinburne, Pater, and Wilde. Cf. Richard Ellmann, *Oscar Wilde* (New York: Knopf, 1988), 90: 'Oxford aestheticism, as developed by Wilde, proved to be of a peculiarly knowing kind. Self-parody was coeval with advocacy.'

bicycles and play tennis. On one level, then, aestheticism is being pressed into the service of a local satire on late Victorian styles. And to that extent, at least, the aestheticism is endorsed. But the aestheticism is itself undermined because it is simultaneously a parody of aestheticism—and that is apparent partly because it sounds *almost* like what Oscar Wilde had been writing in the brilliant few years immediately previous.

Beerbohm echoes the Wildean keyword 'surface'—as in 'All art is at once surface and symbol' (Preface to *Dorian Gray*); for instance:

And, truly, of all the good things that will happen with the full revival of cosmetics, one of the best is that surface will finally be severed from soul. That damnable confusion will be solved by the extinguishing of a prejudice which, as I suggest, itself created. Too long has the face been degraded from its rank as a thing of beauty to a mere vulgar index of character or emotion. (*Works*, pp. 107–8)

The imitation is nearly perfect. One has to notice little touches—the stridency of 'damnable', the clichéd borrowing in 'thing of beauty', the excess of 'a mere vulgar index'—to notice that Wilde is as much subject as source. Wilde's elevation of the critic, in 'The Critic as Artist', with its intent to free both art and criticism from the fetters of imitation, is parodied in Beerbohm's claims for the creative independence of the cosmetician: 'At the touch of a true artist, the plainest face turns comely. As subject-matter the face is no more than suggestive, as ground, merely a loom round which the beatus artifex may spin the threads of any golden fabric' (p. 111).[8] The sentence slyly reminds us, not only that 'the beatus artifex' may be a homely woman, but also that the weaver of the sentence is aping the manner of a fat Irishman, who in turn had plagiarized a misogynistic Frenchman.

In April 1893 Beerbohm had written his friend Reggie Turner one in a series of letters recounting Wildean *bon mots*:

Speaking of plagiarism the other day, Oscar said: 'Of course I plagiarise. It is the privilege of the appreciative man. I never read Flaubert's *Tentation de St*

---

[8] Cf. Wilde: 'Criticism is no more to be judged by any low standard of imitation or resemblance than is the work of poet or sculptor. The critic occupies the same relation to the work of art that he criticises as the artist does to the visible world of form and colour, or the unseen world of passion and thought. He does not even require for the perfection of his art the finest materials. Anything will serve his purpose.' ('The Critic as Artist', in *The Complete Works of Oscar Wilde* [London: Collins, 1948], 1026.)

Antoine without signing my name at the end of it. *Que voulez-vous?* All the Best Hundred Books bear my signature in this manner.[9]

I will discuss elsewhere Beerbohm's debt to Wilde. Here I only want to suggest a difference between Wilde's plagiarism and Beerbohm's parody: you could get caught at the one but not the other. I am not referring to any moral flaw in Wilde, or even superior cunning in Beerbohm, but to different attitudes toward the business of meaning. Wilde's defences of artificiality are no closer to Baudelaire's than Beerbohm's are to Wilde's; but Wilde's defences are serious while Beerbohm's are playful. Wilde's plagiarisms are a part of his pose, but his pose is himself and he means what he says.

By contrast, the aestheticism of 'The Pervasion of Rouge' is source material out of which Beerbohm creates something quite different. Throughout his career, the postures (literally) of the aesthetic movement—of Rossetti, Swinburne, Pater, Whistler, Wilde—exist for him to caricature, parody, satirize. They go into the creating of his artistic presence; their caricature is his self-portrait. And not only them. The author of *The Works* takes shape in relation to Beau Brummell ('Dandies and Dandies') and the dandy's *doppelgänger*, 'Romeo' Coates; to Disraeli, Gladstone, and the other men of '1880'; most surprisingly, perhaps, to King George IV and his antagonistic biographer, Thackeray.

The essay 'King George the Fourth' is an especially good example of Beerbohm's parodistic self-creation. Posing as a 'student of royalty', Max begins by explaining the need for a revisionist history: 'How strange it must be to be a king! How delicate and difficult a task it is to judge him! So far as I know, no attempt has been made to judge King George the Fourth fairly' (*Works*, p. 60). One rival in the field is easily dismissed: 'Mr Percy Fitzgerald has published a history of George's reign, in which he has so artistically subordinated his personality to his subject, that I can scarcely find, from beginning to end of the two bulky volumes, a single opinion expressed, a single idea, a single deduction from the admirably-ordered facts.'[10] Thackeray's *The Four Georges* is harder to get around:

[9] 15 April 1893, *Letters to Reggie Turner*, p. 36.
[10] The reference is to *The Life of George the Fourth, including his Letters and Opinions, with a View of the Men, Manners, and Politics of his Reign* (London: Tinsley Brothers, 1881). Percy Fitzgerald (1834–1925) was a prolific literary scholar and biographer.

All that most of us know of George is from Thackeray's brilliant denunciation. Now, I yield to few in my admiration for Thackeray's powers. He had a charming style . . . But truth after all is eternal, and style transient, and now that Thackeray's style is becoming, if I may say so, a trifle 1860, it may not be amiss that we should inquire whether his estimate of George is in substance and fact worth anything at all. (*Works*, p. 61)

Beerbohm attributes to Thackeray just the faults that could be charged against himself: 'a charming style' rather than a strict regard for 'substance and fact', and (further along) a tendency to create 'types' or caricatures: 'Thackeray made no attempt at psychology.' Beerbohm finds in Thackeray a partial image of himself; he revises in the direction of fuller self-portraiture.

At Oxford, according to Will Rothenstein, Beerbohm claimed to have read only three books: Lear's *Book of Nonsense*, Wilde's *Intentions*, and Thackeray's *The Four Georges*.[11] He acknowledges the last two by incorporating their voices in his own first book. It is an equivocal act of displacement—aggressive, but also, because it is self-constitutive, honorific. Like much of Beerbohm's work in all the genres, it is parasitic, but it raises the question whether originality can be achieved through any less opportunistic means. The scholarly Percy Fitzgerald subordinates 'his own personality to his subject', with results that are honest and dull. Beerbohm creates his own personality through his subject, which in this case is Thackeray's prior self-creation through the subject of George IV.

Like Beerbohm, Thackeray was a comic illustrator was well as an author; like Beerbohm he was a satirist; and like Beerbohm he turned an ephemeral popular form into art: *The Four Georges* was originally delivered as a series of lectures, then published in *The Cornhill Magazine* (1860) before being published as a book (1861). Thackeray's attack on the fourth George was iconoclastic but also quintessentially Victorian in its fierce indignation at the King's drinking, gambling, wenching, and mistreatment of Queen Caroline: 'Swaddled in feather-beds all his life, lazy, obese, perpetually eating and drinking . . . I can't fancy a behavior more unmanly, imbecile, pitiable. This a defender of the faith! This a chief in the crisis of a great nation! This an inheritor

---

[11] Rothenstein, *Men and Memories 1872–1900* (London: Faber and Faber, 1931), 146.

of the courage of the Georges!'[12] Beerbohm revises Thackeray by submitting his high Victorianism ('a trifle 1860') to a cool aestheticism—with the effect of parodying both modes. Thus the object of the essay is perfectly unclear: overtly it is about King George; less overtly it is about Thackeray; and less overtly still, about aestheticism.

Beerbohm pretends to instruct us in the proper way to take the essay. He begins with a disclaimer of any paradoxical intention:

> I feel that my essay may be scouted as a paradox; but I hope that many may recognise that I am not, out of mere boredom, endeavouring to stop my ears against popular platitude, but rather, in a spirit of real earnestness, to point out to the mob how it has been cruel to George. I do not despair of success. I think I shall make converts. The mob is really very fickle and sometimes cheers the truth. (*Works*, p. 62)

The statements are dizzyingly self-subverting. Against 'popular platitude' he opposes his own 'real earnestness'—more a dilemma than an alternative, since we cannot believe that he intends to be either earnest or platitudinous. His success in the essay will be measured by the cheers of the fickle mob, from among whom he will have made converts. Does the reader want to be a member of that mob? If not, the alternative is not to believe Beerbohm.

The latter seems, for a moment, a possible choice, as Max indulges in some unsubtle satire on the decadent effeminacy of modern young men and the unladylikeness of young women. At other points, too, the ostensibly objective tone is allowed to drop and a joke bobs up, with bad results for the surface of the whole. (About the Duke of Wellington: 'I am not sure the old soldier was at Waterloo himself. In a room full of people he once referred to the battle as having been won upon the playing-fields of Eton. This was certainly a most unfortunate slip, seeing that all historians are agreed that it was fought on a certain field situate a few miles from Brussels' [*Works*, p. 85].) The essay is not consistent in its satire or in the point of its joking. But for the most part, the tone is measured, informative, and apparently modest: 'Merely is it my wish at present to examine some of the principal accusations that have been brought against him, and to point out in what ways he has been harshly and hastily judged' (p. 73).

---

[12] Thackeray, *The Four Georges: The English Humorists: Sketches and Travels in London* (Boston and New York: Houghton, Mifflin, 1889), pp. 99, 100.

Thackeray's essay, which Beerbohm's intends to supplant, had as its overt motive to deplore the immorality of George IV. But it also intended to be the occasion for good writing. Beerbohm makes that covert motive primary. His George is an aesthetic phenomenon, whether he is seen 'falling into hysterics' over Mrs Fitzherbert or 'perpetually driving, for wagers, to Brighton and back (he had already acquired the taste for Brighton which was one of his most loveable qualities)' or 'laughing or sobbing over the memories' that lay in the folds of his extensive collection of old clothes. The clothes had been the occasion for Thackeray's famous anatomy of the empty king:

> I try and take him to pieces, and find silk stockings, padding, stays, a coat with frogs and a fur collar, a star and blue ribbon, a pocket-handkerchief prodigiously scented, one of Truefitt's best nutty brown wigs reeking with oil, a set of teeth and a huge black stock, under-waistcoats, more under-waistcoats, and then nothing.[13]

Beerbohm's observation of the King George phenomenon owes its specificity directly to Thackeray, and its ironic admiration indirectly:

> I like to think of the King, at Windsor, lying a-bed all the morning in his darkened room, with all the sporting papers scattered over his quilt and a little decanter of the favourite cherry-brandy within easy reach. I like to think of him sitting by his fire in the afternoon and hearing his ministers ask for him at the door and piling another log upon the fire, as he heard them sent away by his servant. It was not, I acknowledge, a life to kindle popular enthusiasm. (p. 88)

That final wry comment undercuts both George and the enthusiastically indignant Thackeray.

As the ageing George becomes more monstrous he becomes more mysterious, and Max imagines others trying to catch sight of his reclusive image. He tells of four gentlemen who hid at Windsor after a night of drinking:

> The conspirators in the tree held their breath, till they caught the distant sound of wheels. Nearer and louder came the sound, and soon they saw a white, postillioned pony, a chaise and, yes, girth immensurate among the cushions, a weary monarch, whose face, crimson above the dark accumulation of his stock, was like some ominous sunset. . . . He had passed them and they had seen him, monstrous and moribund among the cushions. He had been

---

[13] Ibid. p. 81

borne past them like a wounded Bacchanal. The King! The Regent! . . . They
shuddered in the frosty branches. The night was gathering and they climbed
silently to the ground, with an awful, indispellible image before their eyes.
(pp. 89–90)

It is a great comic image, both as the apotheosis of a carnival spirit
and as the satiric bloating of one bad man; it functions equally well in
either direction.

Max claims that the king's 'life was a poem, a poem in praise of
Pleasure'. This is Beerbohm playing with aestheticism. It is comically
akin to Wilde's appreciation of Salomé or the poisoner Thomas
Griffiths Wainewright (in 'Pen, Pencil and Poison'). Max's aesthetic
appreciation of the monstrous George is like his professed fondness
for destructive fires: a fire is beautiful, hence in a later essay, 'An
Infamous Brigade', the men who extinguish them are 'hired ruffians'
engaged in 'vandalism'. The fire brigade has no sense of drama. At
'the most tragic moment of your life', as the exciting flames rise to
engulf you, 'The sash of the window is thrown up. In jumps a perfect
stranger in fancy dress and proceeds to play snap-dragon with you
and your wife and children. An anti-climax! The whole scene is
ruined' (More, p. 70).

In 'An Infamous Brigade' Wildean paradox suffers the deformation
of burlesque. The joke is crude, compared to the subtlety (at its best)
of the Wildean originals. It is Max as a very talented wiseguy. In 'King
George the Fourth', despite some missteps, the comic mechanisms
are more firmly controlled.

Shortly after 'King George the Fourth' was published in the *Yellow
Book*, Beerbohm was interviewed for the magazine *The Sketch*. It was
part of what we might now call the media campaign for Max's
launching; it ran from Rothenstein's up-market *Oxford Characters* to
this comparative low.[14] For all his Wildean posing, Beerbohm gave

[14] Beerbohm caused himself to be interviewed only as long as the interviewers could
accomplish something that he could not do for himself. When he succeeded as his own
image-maker, he refused the interviews. Behrman's *Portrait of Max* is the great
exception, but at the beginning of their association Beerbohm wrote to Behrman:
'*Interviewed* I cannot be. I have for thirty years and more refused to be so by any one,
and have offered my word of honour to every successive applicant that I wouldn't be
interviewed by any other. In the days when I was interviewed from time to time the
result was always disastrously dull' (Rapallo, 13 July [?1952], at the Humanities
Research Center, Austin, Texas.)

the interviewer an accurate description of the essay's artful refusal to be either serious or joking, history or satire, or to be about anything so much as it is about Beerbohm writing:

I meant all I said about George, but I did not choose to express myself quite seriously. To treat history as a means of showing one's own cleverness may be rather rough on history, but it has been done by the best historians, from Herodotus to Froude and myself. Some of my 'George' was false, and much was flippant; but why should a writer sit down to be systematically serious, or else conscientiously comic.[15]

He sums the matter up with a characteristic coinage: 'Style should be oscillant.'

The interviewer was Ada Leverson. Wilde called her 'Sphinx'; he said to her that Max 'plays with words as one plays with what one loves', and asked her 'When you are alone with him, Sphinx, does he take off his face and reveal his mask?'[16] She knew more about the essay's composition than she let on in the interview. She had visited the seaside with Beerbohm and his sister Con. When she returned to London he wrote her:

I am quite wretched—Broadstairs since you left is like a local branch of Hell. I made a *wretched* tea and a *wretched* dinner and am writing a wretched monograph on George the Phorth or was he the Phiphth? This evening Con and I have been out on the parade. The Band was playing its loudest selection so that people might not hear the sea which was moaning piteously for you. My monograph on George a dead failure.[17]

The moment of dramatized self-doubt is unusual, even among his personal letters. His signature itself is surprisingly uncertain: the 'Max' in 'Yours, Max Beerbohm' is scratched out, and a private nickname, 'Baby', is written in its place. In the letter, then in the essay, then in the interview, Ada Leverson could see and even help Beerbohm take off his face and reveal the mask that became Max.

The metaphor of the mask belongs to the ideology of the dandy,

---

[15] Quoted by Cecil, *Max*, p. 104.   [16] See Chapter 1 n. 38.

[17] In the Taylor Collection, Princeton University: n.d. Beerbohm was in New York touring with Tree and company when Leverson's interview appeared in the *Sketch*. He wrote to her: 'It was so nice of you to write it. It will set the coping-stone to the already tottering edifice of my reputation.' His letter goes on to comment on 'the sad news about O[scar] and Q[ueensberry]' ([? March 1895], at the Humanities Research Center, Austin, Texas).

with its notion that the expressive self is an aesthetic achievement. *The Works* opens with the essay 'Dandies and Dandies': along with the early self-caricatures, and with the help of friends like Rothenstein and Leverson, this essay enrolled Beerbohm himself among the dandies. But it is the essay's parodic indirection, more than its ostensible dandyism, that makes it the appropriate prologue to Beerbohm's works. Dandyism rests upon a fantastic inversion: proclaiming disinterestedness as the basis of art, it nonetheless centres all things in the self—so that the disinterestedness of art becomes the most intense interest in the self. Conversely, it makes the self a product of its art, especially the art of costume. Beerbohm was a dandy, if everyone said he was; but he was also a parodist of the dandiacal idea. The authentic dandy, like Brummell, caricatures the manners of his society; he is an inherently satirical figure. Beerbohm, as an inauthentic dandy, is able to do the dandy's caricatural work while also satirizing the dandy-satirist. The result of this formal complexity is to place Max closer to Matthew Arnold than to the Count D'Orsay.[18]

The whole history of dandyism is one of satires and satires-upon-satires. With fierce irony Carlyle in *Sartor Resartus* (1833–4) declared in the voice of Teufelsdrock that 'A dandy is a clothes-wearing man, a man whose trade, office, and existence consists in the wearing of clothes'. In 'Dandies and Dandies' Beerbohm satirizes Carlyle's satirical phrase by quoting it approvingly: 'Those are true words. They are, perhaps, the only true words in *Sartor Resartus*' (p. 10). His essay skips the next important inversion that marked the dandy's history: in *Le Peintre de la vie moderne* (published 1863) Baudelaire wrote that 'the word *dandy* implies a perfect character and a subtle understanding of the whole moral mechanism of this world . . . the dandy aspires to insensibility'. The artificiality Carlyle attacked Baudelaire sublimed and diabolized as 'une espèce de culte de soi-meme'.[19]

Baudelaire's priestly devotion to perversity became more amusingly self-indulgent when it was practised in England by Whistler or Swinburne. As Poe in Baudelaire's French seems a darker figure than

---

[18] Robert Viscusi ingeniously analyses the psychology of the dandy in *Max Beerbohm: The Dandy Dante* (Baltimore: Johns Hopkins Univ. Press, 1986). I scant the subject partly to avoid duplicating effort but partly because elaboration risks emphasizing the wrong thing. See also the good historical account by Ellen Moers, *The Dandy: Brummell to Beerbohm* (London: Secker & Warburg, 1960).

[19] Quoted in Clements, *Baudelaire and the English Tradition* (Princeton, NJ: Princeton Univ. Press, 1986), 295, 155.

his American original, so Baudelaire imitated in Chelsea seems lighter and more ironic: a butterfly with a sting in his tail. In the literature of the early 1880s, as satiric inversion followed inversion, this 'perfect character', the thoroughly artificial dandy, could appear either pettily awful or merely ridiculous. Once, in Henry James's *The Portrait of a Lady* (1881), the dandy was made recognizably human and, by the same token, authentically frightening. The cold-blooded Gilbert Osmond is the dandy demystified, a man pathologically devoted to appearances because terrified of being found out. His devious partner Madame Merle shocks Isabel Archer with the literalness of her statement of dandiacal philosophy, 'One's self—for other people—is one's expression of one's self; and one's house, one's clothes, the books one reads, the company one keeps—these things are all expressive' (Chapter 19).[20] But the year of James's novel is also the year of Gilbert and Sullivan's *Patience*, when the aesthetic Bunthorne walked down Piccadilly with a poppy and a lily in his medieval hand. At about the same time, George Du Maurier's series in *Punch*, called *Nincompoopiana*, had identified the dandy-artist with 'the least attractive physical and psychological characteristics of Oscar Wilde'.[21]

Wilde's supremacy among the dandies made the job of satire more delicate than ever. In 1894, Beerbohm's friend Robert Hichens published *The Green Carnation*. It is not a bad country-house novel but a poor thing in its attempt to satirize Wilde (called Esmé Amarinth) and Lord Alfred Douglas. The satire is tripped up by Hichens's obvious fascination, even admiration, for his subject. Hichens knows what really goes on behind closed country-house doors, and the reader knows that he's dying to tell. In *The Importance of Being Earnest* Lady Bracknell calls it 'a book about the culture of exotics': 'It seems', she says, 'a morbid and middle-class affair'. Hichens can only crudely copy the subtler self-parody of the original. Wilde himself had to provide the next twist to the now literally decadent history of the dandy, through the satire of the play and the tragedy of the courtroom. That was in 1895. In 1893 Beerbohm published 'The Incomparable Beauty of Modern Dress' in Lord Alfred Douglas's Oxford magazine *Spirit Lamp*; this he revised and combined with several other pieces to

[20] Cf. Beerbohm in 'Dandies and Dandies': 'Yes! costume, dandiacal or not, is in the highest degree expressive, nor is there any type it may not express.' *The Works of Max Beerbohm* (London: John Lane, Bodley Head, 1921), 22.

[21] Ellen Moers, *The Dandy*, p. 296.

make 'Dandies and Dandies' for *The Works* in 1896—the year after the dandy had been sentenced to hard labour.

Beerbohm's essay harks back to the dandy's younger and happier days, the days of Brummell, before the philosophical intensities of either Carlyle or Baudelaire. Max poses as a back-to-basics man among the more decadent dandies. The 'first aim of modern dandyism [is] the production of the supreme effect through means the least extravagant' (*Works*, pp. 4–5); hence the gold rings and chains affected by D'Orsay and Disraeli are 'vulgar' compared to the severe purity of their precursor, 'Mr Brummell'. The dandy and the aesthete tend, throughout their twinned later history, to merge. But Max holds on to the original, pure idea, accidentally articulated by Carlyle, that dandyism is about nothing else but wearing clothes. Attention to anything but clothes-wearing is a falling off from the ideal: 'There have been dandies, like D'Orsay, who were nearly painters; painters, like Mr Whistler, who wished to be dandies; dandies, like Disraeli, who afterwards followed some less arduous calling' (p. 5). Brummell alone, from cradle to grave, devoted himself purely to getting dressed.

Max's historical survey implicitly acknowledges the darker tendency of dandyism, but his treatment is closer to Gilbert and Sullivan's than to either Baudelaire's or James's. The style is 'oscillant' in more than its local excesses. The extravagance of his position—praising Brummell, for instance, for his undivigating nullity—makes him a satirist of dandies. But by pretending to take Carlyle's satire of dandies as praise, he satirizes the dour satirist. He seems to be on both sides simultaneously. In fact the whole business of dandyism is merely the occasion for a series of loops and whirls around the subject of costume and, of course, the wearers of them. Brummell and D'Orsay will do, but once the dandiacal idea has been purged of its excesses and returned to its primitive ideal of clothes-wearing, so will anyone else:

Yes! costume, dandiacal or not, is in the highest degree expressive, nor is there any type it may not express. . . . The bowler of Mr Jerome K. Jerome is a perfect preface to all his works. The silk hat of Mr Whistler is a real *nocturne*, his linen a symphony *en blanc majeur*. To have seen Mr Hall Caine is to have read his soul. His flowing, formless cloak is as one of his own novels, twenty-five editions latent in the folds of it. Melodrama crouches upon the brim of his *sombrero*. (pp. 22–3).

The movement in the essay from Carlyle to Hall Caine epitomizes the elusive position of *The Works* as a whole, perched somewhere between topical satire and an ideal of timeless art.

'King George the Fourth' and 'Dandies and Dandies' are comic variations on aestheticism. The essay '1880' is literally about the aesthetic period, 'when first society was inducted into the mysteries of art and, not losing yet its old and elegant *tenue*, babbled of blue china and white lilies, of the painter Rossetti and the poet Swinburne' (*Works*, p. 41). In 1880 Beerbohm was eight years old; and in the essay '1880' he consigns the adults of that year to near-oblivion. Here Max is the archaeologist uncovering traces of a vanished civilization, the scholar providing learned footnotes on the etymology of the word 'masher' or the identity of Lily Langtry. He was twenty-three when the essay was published—not, in fact, young enough to be a certifiable prodigy. He therefore forges his certification by making his veritable maturity seem like a comic pose.[22]

But it is the concluding essay, 'Diminuendo', that most ingeniously manipulates the extremes of age gathered in the compound Max. Like the volume's epigraph, the contents of *The Works* come to rest on the diminishing point of the slipperiest utterance. It caps the joke of the volume's title and form: this is the essay in which Max makes his bid for fame by proclaiming its achievement—and having won the goal, retires:

I shall write no more. Already I feel myself to be a trifle outmoded. I belong to the Beardsley period. Younger men, with months of activity before them, with fresher schemes and notions, with fewer enthusiasms, have pressed forward since then. *Cedo junioribus.* Indeed, I stand aside with no regret. For to be outmoded is to be a classic, if one has written well. I have acceded to the hierarchy of good scribes and rather like my niche. (p. 160)

The immediate point of the joke is the contrast between Max's cosy apotheosis in 'a pleasant little villa in ——ham', where 'Those of the inhabitants who do anything go away each morning and do it elsewhere' (p. 157), and his reader's knowledge that the retiree is one of the most upwardly mobile of literary controversialists. In light of Beerbohm's subsequent life in the Villino Chiaro, however, the absurd

[22] This time *Punch* was more on target with a parody called '1894' by Max Meerboom (2 February 1895).

image reads as an uncannily accurate prediction. Its most bizarre aspect is its truth; as such it is not the end but the prelude to The Works of Max Beerbohm.

It begins 'In the year of grace 1890', the 'more decadent days of [Max's] childhood' (p. 149)—five years, that is, before its original publication in *The Pageant*, where it was called 'Be it Cosiness'. It is a mini-*Bildungsroman*, a mock tale of the artist's disillusionment and recovery. Successively, the young author encounters Oxford and London. Each is a trap he must learn to avoid. Each place has its tutelary genius, and those geniuses must also be avoided. Avoidance is the essay's goal, but parody is its tactic. What is avoided is therefore also engaged, indeed virtually engorged. The essay's busy if covert aggressiveness justifies the image of satiation with which it concludes.

In 'King George the Fourth' Thackeray was a merely literary figure—only a style—to be displaced by Beerbohm's revisionism. But in 'Diminuendo' Max literally encounters one of the major figures of aestheticism. Walter Pater's *Studies in the History of the Renaissance* was published within a year of Beerbohm's birth; it therefore belongs to precisely the period which, he later wrote, 'lays a really strong hold on one's heart'.[23] He begins the essay by remembering how his tutor laughed (implausibly enough) when he said he wanted to attend Pater's lectures:

Also I remember how, one morning soon after, I went into Ryman's to order some foolish engraving for my room, and there saw, peering into a portfolio, a small, thick, rock-faced man, whose top-hat and gloves of *bright* dog-skin struck one of the many discords in that little city of learning or laughter. The serried bristles of his moustachio made for him a false-military air. I think I nearly went down when they told me that this was Pater. (p. 149)

(A caricature drawn in 1926 [Plate 4], with the caption 'Oxford, 1891. Mr Walter Pater taking his walk through the Meadows', depicts Pater very much as Max had described him some thirty years earlier in 'Diminuendo'.)

Having distanced himself by verbal caricature from the incongruous Pater, Max goes on to deny any literary affinity: 'Not even in those more decadent days of my childhood did I admire the man as a stylist.' The denial modulates into the more complex distancing of parody:

[23] Letter to Holbrook Jackson, 30 October 1913, in the Taylor Collection, Princeton University.

1. 'Me as I more or less am nowadays. Certainly an older and possibly a wiser man'
1946

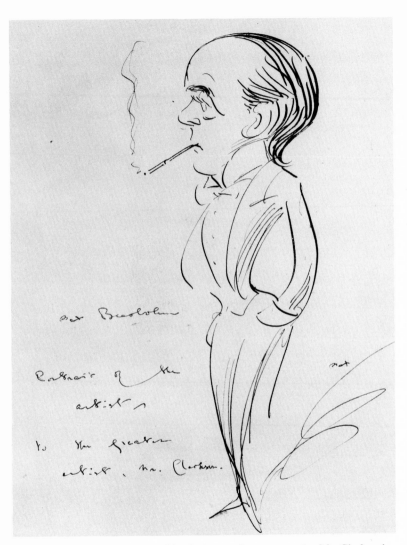

2. 'Max Beerbohm. Portrait of the Artist—to the greater artist, Mr. Clarkson'
[n.d.] (Willie Clarkson [1865–1934] was a well-known theatrical wig-maker and
costume designer)

3. 'Genus Beerbohmiense. Species Herbertica Arborealis, Species Maximiliana'
[n.d.]

Oxford, 1891.

Mr Walter Pater taking his walk through the Meadows.

4. 'Oxford, 1891. Mr. Walter Pater taking his walk through the Meadows' 1926

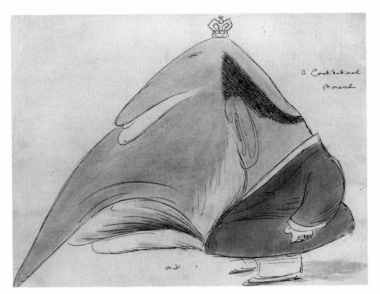

5*a*. 'A Constitutional Monarch' [n.d.]

5*b*. 'The Happy Prince by the Master' (Prince of Wales, drawn in a copy of Wilde's *The Happy Prince* [signed with monogram, n.d.])

6. 'At the First Night, 1892' (Wilde, drawn in a copy of *Lady Windermere's Fan*)
1895

7. 'Oscar Wilde and John Toole - Garrick Club - '93' 1898

8a. Wilde, drawn in a copy of *The Happy Prince*

8b. Profile of Wilde, drawn in a copy of *Lady Windermere's Fan*

Even then I was angry that he should treat English as a dead language, bored by that sedulous ritual wherewith he laid out every sentence as in a shroud—hanging, like a widower, long over its marmoreal beauty or ever he could lay it at length in his book, its sepulchre. From that laden air, the so cadaverous murmur of that sanctuary, I would hook it at the beck of any jade. (p. 150)

The descent from 'marmoreal beauty' to 'the beck of any jade' belongs to the same deflationary tactic that recalls *Marius the Epicurean* as 'a tale of adventure, quite as fascinating as *Midshipman Easy*, and far less hard to understand, because there were no nautical terms in it' (p. 150).

Max is bored with Pater's style (which he apes) and amused by Pater's appearance (which he caricatures). But style and appearance do not exhaust Pater's usefulness in 'Diminuendo'. In the famous Conclusion to *The Renaissance* Pater asks his reader to think about 'our physical life', to 'Fix upon it in one of its more exquisite intervals'. The Conclusion was omitted from the second edition because 'it might possibly mislead some of those young men into whose hands it might fall'.[24] Max is among the misled. He takes Pater's advice literally and pretends that the exhausting excitement of the physical is what Pater is all about. The military-moustachioed aesthete becomes the proponent of gross physicality. But the physical world, figured for Max by Oxford, is at best disappointing: '*On aurait dit* a bit of Manchester through which Apollo had once passed' (p. 152). He finds himself assaulted by a loud, fast, modern world: 'here, among the hideous trams and the brand-new bricks—here, glared at by the electric lights that hung from poles, screamed at by boys with the *Echo* and the *Star*—here, in a riot of vulgarity, were remnants of beauty, as I discerned. There were only remnants' (p. 152). Thus assaulted, the question becomes how best to avoid what Pater called a 'variegated dramatic life'.

Oxford is all vulgar modernity and Pater's aestheticism is a risky athleticism:

That abandonment of one's self to life, that merging of one's soul in bright waters, so often suggested in Pater's writing, were a counsel impossible for to-day. . . . I must approach the Benign Mother with great caution. And so,

[24] Pater's footnote appears in the Conclusion in subsequent editions of *The Renaissance: Studies in Art and Poetry*; in *Walter Pater: Three Major Texts*, ed. William E. Buckler, (New York and London: New York Univ. Press, 1986), 217.

while most of the freshmen were doing her honour with wine and song and wreaths of smoke, I stood aside, pondered.' (p. 153)

In Max's parodic portrait of the artist, his period of testing is appropriately compressed: 'At the end of term I came to London' (p. 154). There too he is assaulted by the tumult of a too exciting world: 'Around me seethed swirls, eddies, torrents, violent cross-currents of human activity. What uproar! Surely I could have no part in modern life' (p. 154). In London, as in Oxford, he is an observer. He observes the Prince of Wales, Pater's (supposed) disciple in physical pleasure, the coarse sensualist who knows better than anyone else how 'to burn always with this hard, gem-like flame, to maintain this ecstasy'.

The incongruous association of Pater and the Prince of Wales extends the essay's long list of opposites satirically dissolved in sameness. Aestheticism becomes crude physical indulgence. The railroad makes ancient Oxford and modern London suburbs for one another. 'The townspeople now looked just like undergraduates and the dons just like townspeople' (p. 152). And the dissolute Prince of Wales, from whom no 'experience has been withheld' (p. 154), is the centre of Paterian gravity: 'He has been "present always at the focus where the greatest number of forces unite in their purest energy," for it is his presence that makes those forces unite' (p. 155). The essay goes from Pater 'peering into a portfolio' in Ryman's to the Prince of Wales 'hunt[ing] elephants through the jungles of India, boar through the forests of Austria, pigs over the plains of Massachusetts' (p. 154). Edward's pursuit of rough beasts gives new meaning to Pater's 'desperate effort to see and touch'. Who, in Pater's phrase, is less likely than Edward, 'On this short day of frost and sun, to sleep before evening'? Who has less time than he 'to make theories about the things we see and touch'?[25]

The Prince of Wales, later Edward VII, was always a favourite subject for Max to caricature (Plate 5*a*). 'Was ever so supernal a type, as he, of mere Pleasure?' (p. 154), he asks in 'Diminuendo'. As prince and as king, Max's Edward is a squat, unsmiling, stupid figure. He looks hard and hateful. In the series of nine drawings called *The Edwardyssey* (drawn 1903, exhibited 1945; Hart-Davis, *Catalogue*, nos. 486–94) Max uses a pictorial variation of the satirical technique in

[25] Pater's phrases are from the Conclusion to *The Renaissance*, ibid. p. 219.

'Diminuendo': the (morally) low is made ridiculous by assimilation to the (culturally) high. Edwardysseus passes through the dangers and temptations of his ceremonial visits; the series concludes at Windsor Great Park with 'The Happy Ending: "Whosoever shall smoke the cigar of Edwardysseus, him will I wed"', says the kneeling Queen to the King with his enormous cigar. In a drawing 'Illustrating the force of ancient habit' (c.1903, no. 495), the King mistakes a convent for a brothel; a row of young nuns faces him, and the balding, check-suited visitor says to their Mother Superior, *'Enfin, Madame: faites monter la premiere à gauche'*. In 'The rare, the rather awful visits of Albert Edward, Prince of Wales, to Windsor Castle' (1921, no. 1503) the middle-aged man stands like a chastened schoolboy with his face to the corner of the wall; his mother, sitting in the middle of the enormous room, is not amused. Edward provokes Max to the exuberant tastelessness of eighteenth-century cartooning. In 'The Prince and his Friends' (n.d., no. 474), the friends are Jewish financiers, and Edward also has a caricatured Jewish nose. A series of drawings done in 1921 trace HRH from the 'forties when he is a child, through his decades of womanizing, to the 'teens when he is 'Angel Edward', still heavy with flesh but playing a harp in heaven. Their exhibition in 1923 caused a small uproar ('Teutonically brutal'—*The Times*; 'a scarifying exhibition'—the *Daily Telegraph*).[26] Beerbohm had the drawings removed, acknowledging (in his Note to *Things Old and New*) that they were 'likely to be misunderstood by the general public and to worry it'.

He was still drawing 'The Old Familiar Figure' in 1953 (no. 522). But he had begun at least sixty years earlier, while he was an undergraduate and signed his drawings with the monogram he used before he adopted the signature 'MAX'. One such drawing is a mock-title page for 'The · Happy · Prince · by · the · Master'—that is, Oscar Wilde (Plate 5*b*). *This* happy prince, heavy-eyed and unsmiling in his pleasure, holds aloft a champagne glass while he dances in a vastly larger glass. He is crowned with his triple plumes and he wears his garter, but the regal symbols look as though they might have been snatched from a chorus girl. He needs a shave—and his happiness is not at all like that of Wilde's prince. The association of Wilde's fairy tale with the all-too-historical Albert Edward predicts the tactic of *The*

[26] Cecil, *Max*, p. 398.

Happy Hypocrite, which I will discuss in the next chapter; and it is similar to the coarsening, literalizing tactic he uses in 'Diminuendo' to parody Pater's aestheticism.

At the end of that essay the cautionary examples of the scholar and the ruler, of Oxford and London, force Max to retreat. For the sake of a life of thought he must avoid a life of pleasure:

> It was, for me, merely a problem how I could best avoid 'sensations', 'pulsations', and 'exquisite moments' that were not purely intellectual. I would not attempt to combine both kinds, as Pater seemed to fancy a man might. I would make myself master of some small area of physical life, a life of quiet, monotonous simplicity, exempt from all outer disturbance. I would shield my body from the world that my mind might range over it, not hurt nor fettered. As yet, however, I was in my first year at Oxford. (*Works*, p. 157)

Incongruity is the most immediate source of humour as he imagines himself in retirement, 'among books that charm, and give wings to the mind' (p. 160). But much of the incongruity is imported by the reader from his own knowledge of the author; and the extent to which Beerbohm can count on that knowledge measures the success with which he has already constructed his personality, as well as the continuing success of that construction in 'Diminuendo'.

He reminds us that 'Once, in the delusion that Art, loving the recluse, would make his life happy, I wrote a little for a yellow quarterly and had that *succès de fiasco* which is always given to a young writer of talent' (p. 160). Each phrase of the sentence empties itself to make way for the ironic knowledge the sophisticated reader is flattered to supply—and then fills itself up again to displace the reader's irony with a counter-truth. The aesthetic ideal of Art (with, as he puts it, 'a capital H') has been caricatured throughout *The Works*; this sentence continues the satire on the pretensions of high art, yet it is part of a volume intended to elevate the author beyond Art's alternative, the world of popular journalism. The 'recluse' of the sentence is the much-interviewed and often-painted Max, who has recently returned from touring America with his brother Herbert Tree and is currently to be seen in the domino room of the Café Royal. His *Caricatures of Twenty-Five Gentleman* is to be published within the year. The joke is apparently one of mere reversal (the recluse is the least reclusive person in London), except that Max does in fact remain elusive, if not reclusive, with each self-revelation. This sentence itself exemplifies his way of publicizing himself by staying aloof.

The reader knows all about that 'yellow quarterly', and knows how eagerley Max welcomed his *succès de fiasco*. The prosperity of the jest depends on the cosy relationship Max establishes with his reader. But the cosiness is threatened by further ironies which subvert the ironies the reader comfortably supplies. The most subversive such counter-irony is the possibility that the author actually means what he says. His estimate of himself as 'a young writer of talent' is disconcerting because it is accurate; in this context, a statement of unexaggerated fact is suspect. As we read the sentence—as we read the essay—we draw on our knowledge of the disparity between the writer and his pose, and then are caught in the realization that the disparity may be (ironically) less than we supposed.

As Max retires Pater reappears, assimilated now into the styles of Beerbohm's pastiche: 'In summer cool syrups will come for me from the grocer's shop. Autumn will make the boughs of my mountain-ash scarlet, and, later, the asbestos in my grate will put forth its blossoms of flame' (p. 158). The grocer and the grate domesticate 'that laden air, the so cadaverous murmur' of the Paterian sentence's 'marmoreal beauty' (p. 150). Max's retirement also echoes that of a rougher essayistic forebear: Hazlitt's 'Farewell to Essay-Writing' begins with a quotation from *Cymbeline*, 'This life is best, if quiet life is best', and continues: 'Food, warmth, sleep, and a book; these are all I at present ask—the *ultima thule* of my wandering desires'.[27] But Hazlitt's 'farewell' quickly becomes a characteristically pugnacious statement of his unwavering revolutionary commitment and an answer to Leigh Hunt's disparagement of his histrionic mannerisms: 'Why should everything be construed into air and affectation?' Hazlitt asks; 'With Hamlet, I may say, "I know not *seems*"'.[28] Max may say it too, but in this context the echo of an echo is doubly ludicrous. Beerbohm displaces his influential elders through covert parody; he makes himself seem, in the process, instantly old and, by the same token, innocent of aggression.

Fifteen years would in fact pass before Beerbohm's move to Rapallo made good his claim in 'Diminuendo'. In 1896 he was not safe from the waters of journalism he saw threatening him in the self-parody 'A

[27] William Hazlitt, 'A Farewell to Essay-Writing', in *The Complete Works*, ed. P. P. Howe (London and Toronto: J. M. Dent, 1933), xvii 313.   [28] Ibid. 318.

Vain Child'. For four months in 1897 he had a column of 'Commentary' in the *Daily Mail*. *The Happy Hypocrite* first appeared in the same 'yellow quarterly' as his earliest *succès de fiasco*. Then there would be a dozen years at the *Saturday Review*. *The Works of Max Beerbohm* was remarkable as a début, but his next collections of essays, *More* (1899) and *Yet Again* (1909), marked time, just as their titles imply. It was not until the publication of *Zuleika Dobson* (1911), followed by *A Christmas Garland*, *Seven Men*, and *And Even Now*, that the claims he made for himself in *The Works* would seem funnier for being simply true.

It was a risky way to start, not only because it left open, with a vengeance, the question of an encore. Every young author, in the process of showing himself off, inevitably shows off the authors he has read. Originality comes not by being uninfluenced but by turning influence to advantage. In that sense, Beerbohm was only doing what comes naturally in his appropriations of Thackeray, Barbey D'Aurevilly, Carlyle, Pater, and the others whose works he turned into *The Works*. But for Beerbohm parody is not a stage to get beyond or a comic diversion from serious business. With him, as with his poor Romeo Coates, parody is the essence. Thus he is anything *but* 'incomparable': the constant invitation to comparison is one of the things that makes *The Works* so risky.[29] The problem is less one of comparative greatness—is Max the parodist a bigger or a smaller writer than Pater the parodee?—than of originality and personality. How in imitating others to be oneself?

The most important model for Max's original creation is barely mentioned in *The Works*. That model was Oscar Wilde. Unlike Pater, who was already safely in the past and didn't need Beerbohm to make a relic of him, Wilde was the present. He was the most prominent 'aesthetic' figure in Oxford and London. When they first met, Beerbohm was not, as a writer, himself. In the act of admiring Wilde, then in imitating, parodying, and satirizing him, assimilating what he needed and expelling what he feared, he became himself. Part of their

[29] Cf. J. G. Riewald, *Sir Max Beerbohm Man and Writer* ('s-Gravenhage: Martinus Nijhoff, 1953), 'The "incomparable" Max is most incomparable when, in his work, he consciously or unconsciously invites comparison with that of others. It is only in this sense that Shaw's equivocal appellation can contribute to a better understanding to Beerbohm's art' (p. 146); and Beerbohm's letter to Bohun Lynch, in Lynch's *Max Beerbohm in Perspective* (London: Heinemann, 1921), 'Years ago, G.B.S., in a light-hearted moment, called me "the incomparable". Note that I am *not* incomparable. Compare me' (p. ix).

confrontation took place more or less privately, in letters, unpublished drawings, and one unpublished satire. Another part included Beerbohm's first published (but anonymous) article and his second book, *The Happy Hypocrite*. It is material for a chapter of its own.

3.

The Mimetic Marvel

'PERSONALITY' is a Beerbohm keyword, as in 'In every art personality is the paramount thing, and without it artistry goes for little.'[1] It is a term of praise though the thing it praises may also be ridiculous or stupid. For instance, Clement Scott, the drama critic for the *Daily Telegraph*, 'is a personality, a definite and unmistakable personality; and in all kinds of writing it is this which is of most account. I care little whether the personality be admirable or otherwise; my demand is that it be genuine and distinct.' Yet for several years Scott was one of the people, like Edward VII and Jerome K. Jerome, Beerbohm treated with unvarying contempt. Scott's writing is full 'of nonsense and bad taste':

Never since I learned to read, and used that accomplishment on his copious output, has he written about drama one sentence which seemed to me fraught with the sense of understanding what is not stupid, or with the taste for appreciating what is not common in dramatic art.[2]

But because Clement Scott is a personality, his stupid criticism is 'worth more than the work of most of his colleagues rolled together'.

George Bernard Shaw was 'the most distinct personality in current literature', Beerbohm wrote in 1903 *(Around Theatres*, p. 272). In my next chapter I will show how he tried to efface or rearrange that distinctiveness. The relative fierceness with which he redrew the Shavian image is in proportion to the distinctiveness of the Shavian personality, which challenged the caricaturist on his own ground. A personality is 'definite' and 'distinct', it resists mutation, it may or may

---

[1] Obituary of the music-hall comedian Dan Leno, 5 November 1904, in *Around Theatres* (New York: Simon and Schuster, 1954), 349.

[2] 'Ought Theatres to be Rased?' 23 November 1901, in *More Theatres 1898–1903* (London: Hart-Davis, 1969), 419–20. Cf. 'A Vanished Hand', 9 December 1899: 'Mr Scott has a personality, and therefore I delight in him. It is not, perhaps, a very fine personality, and it is, in many respects, a very absurd personality; and as such, it always claims some of my attention' *(Around Theatres*, p. 46).

not be 'admirable', and it presents itself to Beerbohm as a standing temptation either for caricature or parody.

The distinct personalities, in all their variety, exist as a class in relation to the 'dim'. Enoch Soames, in Beerbohm's story, is the very personification of the dim type, insofar as a non-entity can personify anything. To Will Rothenstein, Soames 'doesn't exist'; the story is about Soames's doomed efforts to write a personality for himself. Sometimes the dim achieve distinction by parasitic relation with the personalities. The dim Hall Caine (in *Rossetti and his Circle* and *The Mirror of the Past*) clings to the massive personality of Rossetti, and makes himself a personality, however absurd, in the process. Theodore Watts-Dunton is dim, but his relationship with Swinburne at No. 2 The Pines gives him form. The dim risk extinction, except that they may be redeemed by contact with the personalities; and the personalities risk the absurdity of their distinctiveness. But sometimes the dim accomplish their own personalities. George Moore would have drifted into indistinction except that his dimness simply refused to acknowledge itself; his 'vague formless obscene face' (as Oscar Wilde described one of Max's caricatures of Moore)[3] bespeaks both essential dimness and triumphant egotism.

Max himself, as a figure in his own work, challenges the line between personality and dim indistinction. He negotiates the small distance between self-effacement and self-creation. He is perfectly self-expressed yet always the onlooker. He is sufficiently dim to take on, as a parodist, the colouring of the more aggressive personalities; and he is sufficiently a personality to preserve his distinction. In 1896, when he first met Enoch Soames, he was already what he would always be, 'a—slight but definite—"personality"' (*Seven Men*, p. 27).

And then there was Oscar Wilde. He was absolutely the largest artistic personality in England at the time that Max began his own act of self-creation. 'Oscar Wilde was immutable . . . a character so strong

[3] Letter from Wilde to Reginald Turner, 3 February 1899, in *Letters of Oscar Wilde*, ed. Rupert Hart-Davis, (New York: Harcourt, Brace & World, 1962), p. 778. The caricature Wilde refers to was published in the *Daily Chronicle*, 30 January 1899. It is no. 24 in Hart-Davis's *Catalogue of the Caricatures of Max Beerbohm* (Cambridge, Mass.: Harvard Univ. Press, 1972): 'Illustrating a long letter by W. B. Yeats on "Mr Moore, Mr Archer and the Literary Theatre". It shows George Moore as a tipsy Irish peasant with a shillelagh in one hand and a trailed coat in the other. W[illiam] A[rcher], dressed in kilt and glengarry, has one foot on Moore's coat, at which he is pointing in an admonitory way.'

that no force of circumstance could change it, or even modify it.'[4] Wilde had already achieved things Beerbohm sought: he was interviewed and quoted, instantly recognizable by face and name, the master of a variety of artistic forms and simultaneously the parodist of each. But Wilde was set on a self-destructive course, both personally and professionally. And while Beerbohm might flirt with the power of self-effacement, survival was his goal. Wilde was for Beerbohm, then, both model and warning.[5]

They were antitheses—little and big, contained and overflowing, survivor and doomed—distant originals of the paired characters Beerbohm was to create in Hilary Maltby and Stephen Braxton, Walter Ledgett and Felix Argallo, Sylvester Herringham and Dante Gabriel Rossetti.[6] Such opposites are also doubles, secret sharers or sappers of one another's lives. Part of Beerbohm's effort, even as he was learning from Wilde how to be a personality, was to set artistic distance between them. Five years after Wilde's death, upon the publication of De Profundis, Beerbohm wrote an appreciation that reads almost like a self-criticism, but so unacknowledged and apparently impercipient that it can be seen as a last stage in the effort to separate himself from Wilde. He raises the question of sincerity: 'The right way of depreciating Oscar Wilde would have been to say that, beautiful and profound though his ideas were, he never was a real person in contact with realities. He created his poetry, created his philosophy: neither sprang from his own soul or his own experience.' And with it comes the question of originality: 'Herein, too, I find the key to an old mystery: why Oscar Wilde, so saliently original a man, was so much influenced by the work of other writers; and why he, than who none was more fertile in invention, did sometimes stoop to plagiarism' (Peep into the Past, p. 38). Beerbohm criticizes Wilde for

[4] 'A Lord of Language', first published Vanity Fair, 2 March 1905; in A Peep into the Past and Other Prose Pieces, ed. Rupert Hart-Davis (Brattleboro, Vt.: Stephen Greene Press, 1972), 40.

[5] Beerbohm's parodic relationship with Wilde has been traced by J. G. Riewald, Sir Max Beerbohm Man and Writer ('s-Gravenhage: Martinus Nijhoff, 1953) 129–41, and analyzed by John Felstiner, The Lies of Art: Max Beerbohm's Parody and Caricature: (New York: Knopf, 1972): 'His first sense of himself as "Max" entailed getting free of Wilde, whose presence evoked the whole progression of Beerbohm's comic responses, from adulation to hoax and parody. Most of what makes his later writing distinctive stems from his passage with Wilde . . .' (p. 54).

[6] In, respectively, Seven Men, 'Not That I Would Boast' (A Variety of Things), The Mirror of the Past.

attempting, like himself, to convert influence into originality, for inscribing his own artistic signature on the images of others. But unlike Oscar, Max chose never to stoop; he deflected influence into caricature and legitimized plagiarism as parody.

The Picture of Dorian Gray and *Intentions* were published during his freshman year, 1890–1. They were major unofficial parts of his curriculum. In what he designated as 'Hedony term '94'—the term in which he was in the process of not completing his degree at Oxford— he wrote a mock examination paper on the subject of *Dorian Gray*. (He described it later as 'a *very* pale imitation' of 'the archetypal examination paper set by Calverley on "Pickwick"'.) The candidate is allowed forty-eight hours and advised not to attempt more than two of the fourteen questions. They include the detailed—'Is anyone, besides Dorian, credited with a *moue?*'—and the general—'Define the proper limits of paradox'.[7] The examination paper itself barely gestures toward the limits of paradox; in *The Happy Hypocrite*, his revised version of *Dorian Gray*, he would go further.

The Works of Max Beerbohm is literally inconceivable without the model of the essays in *Intentions*. It is there in the details: Wilde's 'To give an accurate description of what has never occurred is not merely the proper occupation of the historian, but the inalienable privilege of any man of parts and culture',[8] becomes Beerbohm's 'To give an accurate and exhaustive account of that period would need a far less brilliant pen than mine' (*Works*, p. 55). And it is there in the paradox that original artistic identities can be created, as well as mocked, by parodic imitation.

Privately, Beerbohm refers to *Intentions* simply as 'The Book'[9]: it is an unholy gospel to be subtly revised by the disciple who created (in *Zuleika Dobson*) a college called Judas. His copy of 'The Book' is elaborately 'improved' with pen-and-ink drawings. Even these graffiti paid homage to Wilde's teaching; Wilde told him that 'All the Best

[7] Holograph 'Dorian Gray. An examination paper by Max Beerbohm. [dated] Broadstairs. Hedony term '94' in the Taylor Collection, Princeton University; Beerbohm's later description is in a letter to C. S. Millard, 4 February 1911, forbidding publication of the parody (also in the Taylor Collection).

[8] 'The Critic as Artist', in *The Complete Works of Oscar Wilde* (London: Collins, 1948), 1015.

[9] Beerbohm, *Letters to Reggie Turner*, ed. Rupert Hart-Davis (London: Hart-Davis, 1964), 24 August 1893, p. 57.

Hundred Books bear my signature'.[10] The witticism puts the same case Wilde made in 'The Critic as Artist': 'Criticism is no more to be judged by any low standard of imitation or resemblance than is the work of poet or sculptor. The critic occupies the same relation to the work of art that he criticises as the artist does to the visible world of form and colour, or the unseen world of passion and thought.'[11] Wilde's argument for pure *poesis*, which makes the artistic product everything and the object nil, can also be used to justify creative plagiarism, or parody. Facing the first printed page of 'The Critic as Artist' Max drew a jolly cartoon of a Grecian setting where a figure labelled 'creator' slaves with shovel while an insouciant figure labelled 'critic' lazily smokes a waterpipe.[12]

In the life as in the work, Wilde was his master in the arts of parody and self-parody. They first met in 1889, at dinner with Herbert, his brother. It was only a glimpse. Their closer acquaintance came in 1892–3, and its progress can be traced in Beerbohm's letters to Reggie Turner. At first Max is only a small boy seeing giants—to use the title of a much later essay: 'Oscar is writing a play which my brother will *probably* have, but this is a secret' (September 1892, *Letters to Reggie Turner*, p. 25); '. . . the play has been finally accepted by my brother. Please thank Mrs Lawson for her kind letter and for *The Happy Prince*. Have you quite persuaded her that you did not annotate the Giant story?' (? 14 October 1892).[13]

Turner's gift to him of the French edition of *Salomé* provokes a first tentative parody:

The book that they have bound in Parma violets and across whose page is the silver voice of the Master made visible—how could it not be lovely? I am enamoured of it. It has charmed my eyes from their sockets and through the voids has sent incense to my brain: my tongue is loosed in its praise. Have you read it? In construction it is very like a Greek play, I think: yet in conception so modern that its publication in this century would seem premature. It is a marvellous play. If Oscar would re-write *all* the Bible, there would be no sceptics. (25 February 1893).

[10] Ibid. 15 April 1893, p. 36.   [11] Wilde, *Complete Works of Oscar Wilde*, p. 1026.
[12] Copy in the Clark Library, University of California, Los Angeles.
[13] The annotations in this copy of *The Happy Prince*, now at Merton College, Oxford, are signed 'R.T.' Turner did not have Beerbohm's talent for marginalia. They are of the 'How obvious' and 'Stuff and nonsense' and 'Pooh!' variety.

He was seeing Wilde more frequently now, not only through Herbert's mediation but as part of the circle around Lord Alfred Douglas in Oxford and London. Like his *Salomé*, Oscar himself is a gift to the young artist.

The letters to Turner are full of Oscar-anecdotes in which Max tries to capture the Wildean manner and voice. Hero-worship alternates with a more objective criticism: the parodic focus is not yet clear. Thus, in a letter of 12 April 1893 there is first a display of Oscar in his glory: 'Oscar was speaking the other day of old Irving's *Lear* and was furious that all the "wretched little donkeys of critics" had dared to attack him. "Surely," he said, "a gentleman has a right to fail if he chooses".' And immediately after the display of his wit comes an alternative vision:

I am sorry to say that Oscar drinks far more than he ought: indeed the first time I saw him, after all that long period of distant adoration and reverence, he was in a hopeless state of intoxication. He has deteriorated very much in appearance: his cheeks being quite dark purple and fat to a fault. I think he will die of apoplexy on the first night of the play. What a lot I have written about him!

From the first, then, Beerbohm is attracted by the wittily paradoxical self-creativity of the Wildean personality, and repelled by the descent into mere self, figured in the Wildean fleshiness and appetite.

In the letters to Turner, Wilde becomes the model (in several senses) for Beerbohm's own narrative art:

Did I tell you about Oscar at the Restaurant in my last note to you? I think not. During the rehearsal, he went to a place with my brother to have some lunch. He ordered a watercress sandwich: which in due course was brought to him: not a thin, diaphanous green thing such as he had meant but a very stout, satisfying article of food. This he ate with assumed disgust (but evident relish) and when he paid the waiter, he said 'Tell the cook of this restaurant with the compliments of Mr Oscar Wilde that these are the very worst sandwiches in the whole world and that, when I ask for a watercress sandwich, I do not mean a loaf with a field in the middle of it.' (15 April 1893)

Again the anecdote is followed by a distancing criticism: 'It seems that he speaks French with a shocking accent, which is rather a disillusionment, and that when he visits the *Décadents* he has to repeat once or twice everything he says to them, and sometimes even to write it down for them.' Max has not yet integrated criticism and admiration into a perfect caricature, but he is conscientiously working at it. A few months later, when Wilde apparently objected to an actual drawing of him, Max would write that Oscar 'is simply an unpaid model of mine and as such he should behave' (2 October 1893).

A Woman of No Importance opened 19 April 1893: 'When little Oscar came on to make his bow there was a slight mingling of hoots and hisses, though he looked very sweet in a new white waistcoat and a large bunch of little lilies in his coat' (21 April 1893). He combines satiric observation of Wilde with imitation of the Wildean manner: 'The notices are better than I had expected: the piece is sure of a long, of a very long run, despite all that the critics may say in its favour.' Along with the paradoxes he gives Turner the anecdotes:

A little journalist who had several times attacked him vulgarly came up to him in the street the other day and cordially accosted him. Oscar stared at him and said after a moment or two 'You will pardon me: I remember your name perfectly but I can't recall your face.'

But this time he follows with an anecdote in which he is himself the central figure. He does the Wildean manner without Wilde: 'After supper I walked as far as Hyde Park Corner when I saw a glare in the sky like some false dawn. A cabman told me it was a fire and drove me to it—right away past Westminster. It was quite lovely, though there was no life lost I am afraid.' The false note of 'there was no life lost I am afraid' is neither good Wilde nor good Beerbohm. His parodic work was not yet done, but it was going well.

'Oscar thinks my article (which he has read in proof and which will appear today) "incomparably brilliant", though he is rather hurt at my reference to *Dorian Gray* . . .' (25 March 1893); 'Also my O.W. article has appeared and I send you a copy of it. Oscar himself (of whom I have seen a great deal this vac) liked it very much and said he thought it "incomparably clever" which was nice of him, wasn't it? I still admire him immensely . . .' (12 April 1893); 'Oscar talked a great deal about my article—said that he knew no other undergraduate who could have written it, that I had a marvellous intuition and sense of the phrase, that I must take to literature alone, and that my style was like a silver dagger. I am becoming vainer than ever' (21 April 1893).

The article was titled 'Oscar Wilde by an American', his first publication. It appeared without other attribution in the *Anglo-American Times* ('a very good paper of recent birth', according to Beerbohm) on 25 March 1893: 'It is very brilliant', he wrote to Turner, 'and consists of fulsome praise of the Master and filthy abuse of his disciples: of whom I say that "sitting eternally at the feet of Gamaliel, they learn nothing but the taste of boot-polish". You must read it. Behold, high and sheer into the air rise the walls of the Temple of Fame: against them is a ladder placed and on the first rung of it rests my foot' (3 March 1893).

In fact, 'Oscar Wilde by an American' is not very brilliant. Like the letters from this period, it uneasily combines a satirist's intentions with a disciple's awe. But shortly after this he wrote another article on Wilde called 'A Peep into the Past'. Its provenance is not certain. On the title-page of the manuscript he wrote 'For the first No. of the "Yellow Book"'—which appeared without it in April 1894. Later, after a pirated American printing, he denied that he had intended to publish it at all: 'It was just a squib to amuse a few people'.[14] 'A Peep into the Past' has been called 'a delicate, good-natured satire', 'gently satirical', 'light-hearted'.[15] Beerbohm's own estimate of its aggressiveness is implied by his refusal to publish it, and seems to me more accurate. A comparison between the earlier 'Oscar Wilde by an American' and 'A Peep into the Past' shows several things. It shows how quickly Beerbohm learned his craft; it shows what Beerbohm found both of utility and threat in the figure of Oscar Wilde, and by the same token it shows what aspects of himself Beerbohm would repress in future perfections of Max; and it shows how Beerbohm contemplated, through the case of Wilde, the relations between derivativeness and parody, imitation and originality.

'Oscar Wilde by an American' begins in a typically retrospective manner: One evening last winter, its American author writes, he saw a man 'wrapped from head to foot in a fur coat of great size' entering 'the most charming of all Paris restaurants, the Maison Dorée'.[16]

[14] Letter to A. J. A. Symons, 1 March 1926, in the Taylor Collection, Princeton University. The same disclaimer is made in the prefatory Note to the American edition of *A Variety of Things* (New York: Knopf, 1928) where he disclaims responsibility for 'the publication . . . of some gibes against a distinguished writer whose life was to end in disaster' (p. ix).

[15] Riewald, *Sir Max Beerbohm*, p. 273; *Letters of Oscar Wilde*, p. 355 n.; David Cecil, *Max* (London: Constable, 1964), 97.

[16] Printed as Appendix A in *Letters to Reggie Turner*, pp. 285–92.

Vaguely he recalls having seen him, possibly 'during a visit which I had paid to Europe many years ago'. He asks his host for assistance. ' "The fat man?" he replied. "Oh, don't you know? It's Oscar Wilde" ' (*Letters to Reggie Turner*, pp. 285–6).

Oscar Wilde! And all at once I remembered that years ago, in the rooms of an Oxford undergraduate, I had been introduced to a young man who was called Wilde and whose curious grey eyes had impressed me at the time; then I had forgotten all about him, had never associated his name with that of the man of whom I afterwards read, in the American papers, that his manners and his theories of art had struck a fresh note in English Society. (p. 286).

Just as the enormous figure of Oscar Wilde enters the author's life he begins to recede harmlessly into the historical past. This technique of relegation will be developed further in 'A Peep into the Past'. But 'Oscar Wilde by an American' is remarkably laudatory; it still shows, in the persona of the uncritical American, the young Englishman's actual excitement at being included in the Master's circle.

'A Peep into the Past' is not laudatory.[17] Its knowing references to Wilde's homosexuality are only part of what makes it so damning. (The dim journalist, who purportedly writes the essay as part of his research 'for an article . . . upon the life of the Early Victorian Era', mentions 'the constant succession of page-boys, which so startles the neighbourhood' [*A Peep into the Past*, p. 4]; as he enters Wilde's study he hears 'the quickly receding *frou-frou* of tweed trousers' and finds Wilde 'a little dishevelled', reclining on a sofa and adjusting his wig [pp. 6–7].) More basic is its promotion of Wilde, then at the peak of his fame and power, to the status of 'old gentleman'. In 'Oscar Wilde by an American', the name brought a rush of recollection; 'A Peep into the Past' begins with that name but the result is different: 'Oscar Wilde! I wonder to how many of my readers the jingle of this name suggests anything at all? Yet, at one time, it was familiar to many . . .' (p. 3).

The American persona of the earlier essay is an unintersting ruse; in 'A Peep into the Past' the relation of the writer to his text is a more complicated pretence. And the encomiastic language of the earlier essay is deformed by irony in the later. For instance, both essays acknowledge Wilde's supposed indolence. In the earlier essay, it is

---

[17] In *A Peep into the Past and Other Prose Pieces*, ed. Rupert Hart-Davis (Brattleboro, Vt.: Stephen Greene Press, 1972).

defended: '... he has a most fastidious literary taste and so has produced nothing which is not in its way perfect' (*Letters to Reggie Turner*, p. 289). In 'A Peep into the Past' Beerbohm's journalist describes the 'old gentleman's' domestic evening which ends with '... a glass of grog and bed-time':

But not always rest! Often, his good lady tells me, has she woken at three or four in the morning to find her husband still sitting up in bed or pacing up and down the bedroom in parturition of that same joke of which he sketched for her the outline as they were retiring to rest. Yes, it is in this indomitable perseverance, this infinite capacity for taking pains, this 'grit,' as they call it in the North, that lies Mr Wilde's secret. (*A Peep into the Past*, p. 5)

The product of this 'grit' is differently assessed in the two essays. In the earlier, Wilde 'has passed through as many phases as Proteus, yet never surrendered one tittle of his personality':

He is a writer of poetry, and he is a writer of plays; a critic of books, and of painting, a philosopher, an essayist and a teller of fairy tales; two or three of the few well-written short stories in this language are by him; he has introduced a new form of novel, has lectured upon art and has even touched politics with a light hand. (*Letters to Reggie Turner*, p. 289)

The effective cruelty of the revised version comes partly from its superfluity of detail. But the most interesting change is that the claim for Wilde's originality becomes, with just a slight shift in emphasis, a charge of derivativeness or plagiarism:

True that the whole body of his signed work is very small—a book of parodies upon Rossetti, a few fairy-tales in the manner of Hans Andersen, an experimental novel in the style of Poe, a volume of essays, which Mr Pater is often obliged blushingly to repudiate, a French play written in collaboration with Mr Louys and one or two English ones in collaboration with Mr G. R. Sims. But surely we must judge an artist, not so much by his achievement as by his method of procedure, and though such a story as *The Theory of Mr W. S.* (I came across a copy of it lately at an old bookstall in Vigo Street) occupied only the extreme middle of no more than forty pages, the author has given me his word that it took him six months' hard unremitting labour to complete. (*A Peep into the Past*, p. 5)

The American of the earlier piece repeats the commonplace praise of Wilde as a conversationalist, and adds that Wilde 'is as charming a listener as he is a talker' (*Letters to Reggie Turner*, p. 287). In 'A Peep into the Past' this is deformed into the charge of tediousness and, again, plagiarism. The journalist recalls a scene between Wilde and Whistler. 'Mr Whistler, then quite a young boy, perpetrated some daring epigram'; Wilde's response, 'How I wish I had said that', is interpreted by the journalist as encouragement for Whistler; and when 'Young impudence' cries 'You will, Sir, you will' the old gentleman replies 'quick as thought', 'No, I won't'.

Since then, the old journalist [Wilde] has contracted a strange habit of chuckling to himself inordinately at whatever he says and to such a degree has this habit grown upon him that at the last dinner-party he ever attended it was decided he had a rare faculty of keeping a whole table perfectly serious, whilst he himself was convulsed with laughter. (*A Peep into the Past*, p. 7)

The scene between Wilde and Whistler recalls a famous polemical episode conducted first in the newspapers and preserved in the poisonous amber of Whistler's *The Gentle Art of Making Enemies*. Beerbohm makes farce out of what was originally mock-heroic. The actual paper-battle began with Wilde's review (21 February 1885) of Whistler's 'Ten O'Clock' lecture, and the question of whether the poet or the painter is 'the supreme Artist'.[18] But it quickly became a question of plagiarism. Wilde got off one especially good shot in the letters column of *The World* ('With our James vulgarity begins at home, and should be allowed to stay there'), which Whistler back-handedly complimented: '"A poor thing" Oscar!—"but," for once, I suppose, "your own"' (*Gentle Art*, p. 165). That was in 1886; in 1890 they were still at it, with Whistler calling Wilde the 'arch-imposter and pest of the period—the all-pervading plagiarist!' (*Gentle Art*, p. 236).

The question was not merely who had first defined a disciple as 'one who has the courage of the opinions of his master' (*Gentle Art*, p. 239). Whistler was applying to Wildean paradox the blunt instrument of his ferocious common sense. He flattened the playful reversals of 'The Decay of Lying' into the old antinomies—a thing is either true or false, original or plagiarized. And he thereby re-polemicized issues that are at the heart of Wilde's project as, in a different way, they are of Beerbohm's too. For the proposition that art imitates life, Wilde had performed the aesthetic switch, life imitates art. Beer-

---

[18] *The Gentle Art of Making Enemies*, (1892; rpt. New York: Dover, 1967), 161.

bohm's parody of aestheticism goes a step further, or back; now art imitates art. That proposition—which Whistler in effect labels plagiarism—has been relatively unproblematic in various art historical contexts: in neo-classical art, for instance, 'imitation' meant literally the following of artistic models; and again in post-modernism, the previously constructed is the unavoidable material for an art founded on the premise of parody. Whistler's attack on Wilde is a belated version of romanticism; it assumes the possibility of unmediated originality. By contrast, Wilde's boast that 'All the Best Hundred Books bear [his] signature' is avant-garde. The nearness of parody to plagiarism has often been noticed, by critics as well as lawyers: Linda Hutcheon, for instance, quotes Dr Johnson's definition of parody—'a kind of writing, in which the words of an author or his thoughts are taken, and by a slight change adapted to some new purpose'—and adds that it 'defines plagiarism as well'.[19] Beerbohm as parodist, then, carries on Wilde's work; he moves (as Hutcheon says that much modernist art does) 'away from the tendency, within a Romantic ideology, to mask any sources by cunning cannibalization, and towards a. frank acknowledgement (by incorporation) that permits ironic commentary'.[20]

Where does the imitation leave off and originality begin? Where is the ground of a representation? Wilde's 'The Portrait of Mr W.H.' (which the narrator of 'A Peep into the Past' calls *The Theory of Mr W.S.)* is a parable about the difficulty of such questions. Wilde creates a narrator who tells the story of his friend Erskine; Erskine in turn tells the story of Cyril Graham who invented a character, the Elizabethan boy-actor Willie Hughes, and had a portrait forged to prove Hughes's existence. Erskine warns the narrator against pursuing Graham's theory ('There is nothing in the idea of Willie Hughes. No such person ever existed'[21]), but the narrator becomes convinced that it was indeed Willie Hughes who inspired Shakespeare to write the sonnets and create the part of Rosalind for him to play. The layers of representation stretch from the boy playing Rosalind to Wilde creating the story of the forged portrait—which was created to explain the story of Shakespeare's sonnets, which may or may not tell the story of Shakespeare's homosexual infatuation. The search for an 'onlie

---

[19] Hutcheon, *A Theory of Parody* (New York and London: Methuen, 1985), 36.
[20] Ibid. p. 8.   [21] *Complete Works of Oscar Wilde*, p. 1161.

begetter', whose identity could anchor fiction in supposed reality, only makes more problematic the status of the writer (Wilde) whose own authorial identity is precariously derived from his representations of what never existed.

The parodist, making the basis of his art the art of another, threads his way through a similar maze of mimesis. As 'The Portrait of Mr W.H' suggests, and as Beerbohm demonstrates in *Seven Men*, the art that art imitates need not have an actual prior existence: Cyril Graham's forged portrait of the non-existent Willie Hughes belongs to the class of fictitious representations Beerbohm parodies in 'Savonarola' Brown's verse tragedy or the unwritten letters in 'How Shall I Word It'. To the nexus 'originality-parody-plagiarism', then, Beerbohm adds the word 'hoax'. And he does this partly in imitation of Wilde, and partly to set distance between himself and Wilde. For, as I have already said, a main difference between Wildean plagiarism and Beerbohmian parody is that you can get caught at the one and not at the other. One of the things to notice in Beerbohm's relationship with Wilde is how Beerbohm learned the art of not getting caught—how, that is to say, he learned to keep the paradoxes of representation alive, without allowing them to collapse into the bathos of Wilde's life and work.

The fictitious American author of Beerbohm's earliest essay has only praise for Oscar Wilde the dramatist. In 'A Peep into the Past' there is nothing of dispraise, but an amazed regard that is all the more damning, for 'that Oscar Wilde should have written a four-act play and got it produced by a London manager, fairly beat all records of senile enterprise' (*A Peep into the Past*, p. 6). The play is *Lady Windermere's Fan*, and Wilde's impertinence on its opening night is described in verbal caricature. Here is one version of the scene, represented a lifetime after the event by Wilde's son Vyvyan Holland:

There were loud cries of 'Author!' at the end of the play and Wilde came on to the stage with a cigarette in his gloved hand and said: 'Ladies and Gentleman. I have enjoyed this evening immensely. The actors have given us a charming rendering of a delightful play, and your appreciation has been most intelligent. I congratulate you on the great success of your performance, which persuades me that you think almost as highly of the play as I do.'[22]

22 Ibid. p. 12.

This may be taken as the official portrait or authorized version of Wilde's staging of himself. In Beerbohm's version, Wilde appears before the curtain 'bowing with old-fashioned grace to the Public whom he had served so faithfully':

Those of us who had known him in the old days, observed that he seemed for the moment dazed and noted with feelings of pity that in his great excitement he had forgotten to extinguish his cigarette, an oversight that the Public was quick to pardon in the old gentleman. (*A Peep into the Past*, p. 6)

The preemptive ageing of Wilde, which allows mock-sympathy to displace admiration, epitomizes the specific satiric technique of the essay. More generally, the technique is verbal caricature that takes Wilde's self-preservation as the text for ironic representation, varying not just the features of a verbal style but of personality in the broadest sense. It extends the idea of parody. The texts that can be imitated, parodied, caricatured—in Whistler's reductive term, plagiarized, in another term, made Beerbohm originals—need not be written texts at all.

At the front of his own copy of *Lady Windermere's Fan* Beerbohm drew an actual caricature of Wilde 'at the first night—1892' (Plate 6). It is in striking contrast to an earlier caricature he had drawn in his copy of *The Happy Prince* (Plate 8a).[23] The contrast is similar to the contrast between 'Oscar Wilde by an American' and 'A Peep into the Past'. In the *Happy Prince* drawing, a serious, winged Wilde floats through a dark sky of stars and crescent moon, his right hand held somewhere near his heart, his left flung out in a gesture of oratory or benediction. The mouth is full, sensuous, even sad; the eyes peep out beneath wavy, elegant hair. There is humour here, as there is in the description of Wilde 'by an American', but nothing of the damning visual satire of the drawing in *Lady Windermere's Fan*. There, Wilde, cigarette held in a puffy hand, is heavily chinned, fat in the waist; the leanly pious fabulist of *The Happy Prince* drawing is dissolved in pinky-flesh tones and fleshy folds. The copy of *Lady Windermere's Fan* has another caricature at the back of the book (Plate 8b). This one is a drawing of Wilde in profile and it further emphasizes the awful flesh colour and the grotesquely doubled chin. In this profile drawing, Wilde wears a

[23] Both volumes are at Merton College, Oxford. Neither is dated. *The Happy Prince* volume is the same one Reggie Turner irreverently annotated (see above, n. 13).

carnation and a jewelled solitaire in his shirt front—or (it is hard to say which) he exposes a hugely nippled female breast.

Looking at these caricatures or reading a verbal caricature like 'A Peep into the Past', it is difficult not to feel that Beerbohm is disingenuous in his description of 'The Spirit of Caricature' (1901): 'true caricature', he writes, is 'the delicious art of exaggerating, without fear or favour, the peculiarities of this or that human body, for the mere sake of exaggeration' (*Variety of Things*, p. 119). For the elongated body of Arthur Balfour or the heaviness of Sir William Harcourt it may conceivably be true that caricature implies 'no moral judgment of its subject' (p. 124). But in his treatment of Oscar Wilde it is impossible not to find 'moral judgment', as well as other motives beside the 'merely aesthetic' (p. 125).

Max drew (or preserved) surprisingly few caricatures of Wilde— fewer, for instance, than of George Moore or Shaw and (of course) many fewer than of himself. There are three fairly distinct incono- graphies. First is that represented by a page of sketches done when Max was an undergraduate and Oscar a distant object for amused admiration (Hart-Davis, *Catalogue*, no. 1778): they are self-consciously childlike in execution, emphasizing (like the verbal portrait in 'Oscar Wilde by an American') Oscar's admirable versatility. This Oscar is the champion in his own mock-heroic campaign of self-publicity, physically distinguished only by a slight corpulence and long hair. Much later, after Wilde's death, Max did a different sort of Oscar. The most famous of these appears in *Rossetti and his Circle* (no. 1784, drawn 1916). A svelte long-haired Oscar, in breeches, holding a lily, lectures to a stern-faced American audience (on the wall is a portrait of Abraham Lincoln, not amused). The caption reads: 'The name of Dante Gabriel Rossetti is heard for the first time in the western states of America. Time: 1882. Lecturer: Mr Oscar Wilde'. The figure is distanced in the most literal chronological and geographical senses. As with the undergraduate sketches, the humour of the caricature is in the situation, not in the bland portrait of Wilde himself.

Between these two types of drawing came the sort found in his copy of *Lady Windermere's Fan*. The most notorious, and one of the best of his early caricatures, appeared in the magazine *Pick-Me-Up*, 22 September 1894 (no. 1779).[24] These caricatures overwhelm Wilde in

---

[24] Reprinted in *The Poets' Corner* (1943), *Max's Nineties* (1958), and *Caricatures by*

flesh—soft, pink, shapeless, sensual, engrossing. The mouth and lips are enormous. Face and figure are intimidatingly androgynous: this Oscar, an 'enormous dowager',[25] could play his own Lady Bracknell. Such drawings express the antithetical and frightening aspect of Wilde's otherwise sympathetic genius: his self-destructive hedonism, his mental and physical grossness, his propensity for getting caught in some dreadfully embarrassing position.

There seem to have been no caricatures of this sort after Wilde's death, but from 1898—after the trial—there is one of 'Oscar Wilde and John Toole - Garrick Club - '93' (Plate 7). The comedian Toole, a small, furious-looking, starchy man, makes Oscar even more enormous by contrast.[26] There is humour in the situation: the funny-man Toole as sober as can be, the artist Oscar idiotically grinning. And there is also personal, physical caricature of the sort Beerbohm describes in the one section of his essay on 'The Spirit of Caricature' that is not obviously disingenuous:

The whole man must be melted down, as in a crucible, and then, as from the solution, be fashioned anew. He must emerge with not one particle of himself lost, yet with not a particle of himself as it was before. And not only must every line and curve of him have been tampered with: the fashion of his clothes must have been re-cut to fit them perfectly. His complexion, too, and the colour of his hair must have been changed, scientifically, for the worse. And he will stand there wholly transformed, the joy of his creator, the joy of those who are privy to the art of caricature. (*Variety of Things*, p. 128)

Max (1958). In 1911, Stuart Mason [Christopher Millard], the author of *Bibliography of Oscar Wilde* (1914), asked for permission to reprint the *Pick-Me-Up* caricature. Beerbohm sent instead another drawing, from the later iconography; it shows a stately gentleman with walking-stick and elegant clothes and even a rather finely cut chin and nose. He wrote: 'It gives a much more *essential* view of Oscar. The other one showed only the worse side of his nature. At the time when I did that other one, and even when it was first published, I hardly realised what a cruel thing it was: I only realised that after Oscar's tragedy and downfall.' Quoted in Hart-Davis, *Catalogue*, p. 158, no. 1783.

[25] From a holograph notebook in the Berg Collection, New York Public Library.

[26] Beerbohm wrote an obituary of Toole in the *Saturday Review*, 4 August 1906 (*Around Theatres*, pp. 439–42); it can bear comparison with Lamb's essay 'On Some of the Old Actors'. The description of him as 'the volatile low-comedian—the little man with the elastic face and the eyeglass, the odd gambols and catch-words, the ridiculous high spirits . . . full of the rough-and-ready give-and-take of friendship and acquaintance' (p. 440) gives added point to the caricature of the serious Toole with the comic Wilde.

Elsewhere in the essay, Beerbohm makes caricature seem the most harmless of arts, the product of a disinterested quest for beauty. Here, however, the scientific vocabulary makes the caricaturist a Dr Frankenstein among artists. In the caricatures of Oscar done in Max's intermediate iconography, between the high spirits of first acquaintance and the revisionary softening of post-mortem hindsight, we feel the caricaturist's full power over his subject: the power to 'melt down' and 'fashion anew', to 'tamper' with identity, to 'transform', to make the subject not his own person but 'the joy of his creator'.

Wilde's homosexuality seems not to have bothered Beerbohm so much as the flamboyance of the sexuality itself; not, that is to say, the object of Wilde's lust but the fact that he visibly lusted. The fleshiness of these caricatures suggests something beyond the obvious matter of sex. The Wildean flesh—chins, fat hands, dowager breasts—suggests a fatal limitation in Wilde's entire self-creation. He was indeed (in the Marquis of Queensberry's misspelled but insanely precise phrase) 'posing as a somdomite'; his carefully staged naughtiness paid Victorian social convention its due in a way that Beerbohm's punctiliousness never did. The entire Wildean panoply was created with an earnestness that was impeccably Victorian; the trials would prove how fully Wilde believed in himself. In Max's version, Oscar's heavy, tinted flesh suggests the immutability of his personality—not just its ridiculous but its tragic immutability. His pose says that you can't escape yourself.

The time of Beerbohm's fascination with Wilde is also that of his distantly adoring romance with the teenage music hall performer Cissie Loftus—'The Mimetic Marvel' (as she was billed), famous for her virginal appeal (Plate 9a).[27] In the same letters to Reggie Turner that create the story of Max and Oscar, 'we get' (as Frank Kermode describes it) '. . . the whole strange story of Max watching Max being enamoured of Cissie Loftus'.[28] The two stories wove themselves together in Beerbohm's second book, *The Happy Hypocrite*, published by John Lane in 1897 after its original publication in the *Yellow Book*.

Beerbohm met Cissie—the only time they met more than in

---

[27] Hart-Davis (*Letters to Reggie Turner*) gives her date of birth as 1876, which would make her seventeen at the time of Max's infatuation—though he seems to have thought she was only fifteen.

[28] Kermode, 'Whom the Gods Loathe', *Encounter*, 24 (March 1965), 74.

passing—when he interviewed her for the *Pall Mall Gazette*. The unsolicited article was rejected. But throughout the summer of 1893 his letters to Reggie are full of fantastic effusions about the white girl, Mistress Mere, Lady Cecilia, the Blessed Damozel, the small saint— as he experimentally called her in what became (like the anecdotes about Oscar) both a writing-workshop and a rehearsal for life. The language throughout is Wildean: excessive, self-delighting, paradoxical. 'Oh God—how I wish myself wholly free and able to lay vast riches at her feet and live with her unhappily ever after' (10 August 1893, *Letters to Reggie Turner*, p. 45). Alternatively, how blissful to have been married for a year, and then to have her die in childbirth (13 August 1893). Lovelorn, Max wanders the streets of Cissie's native Herne Hill. Furious, he observes her at the theatre surrounded by lecherous men. He suggests that Reggie save the epistolary record of this great affair, which will make him famous to posterity as 'the friend of Henry Beerbohm' (15 August 1893). Finally, when Cissie reveals her true colours by piling 'a Pelion of rouge upon an Ossa of powder' (29 September 1893), Max falls abruptly out of love—the pervasion of rouge, in this special case, disastrously calling to mind the reality of flesh. In the interim, however, Cissie has provided him with an entirely undemanding romantic interest, given him something to write about, and by her supposed claims on his affections protected him from the actual importunities of the flesh, of whatever sex.

Beerbohm's infatuation with Cissie Loftus is an odd instance of the otherwise normal narcissism of adolescence. She was pure absence, and therefore the ideal object for his idealizing. Like Max, she was a 'mimetic marvel'; her distinct dramatic personality was enacted pastiche. Like him, she was at once infantile and aged. She emphasized the childlike part of the compound, as he did, by aping the manners of her elders. But Cissie, unlike Max, mimicked performers of both sexes, making androgyny part of her appeal. Max's mature art of parody and caricature—the art that turns all the world into The Works of Max Beerbohm—is a triumph of socially acceptable narcissism. Like Cissie's act, it coyly entices the audience with a personality that is vividly *there* but unreachable, inviolable. And in these letters to Reggie Turner, Beerbohm indulges his infatuation with Cissie while performing for Reggie the art of enticing with evasions.

If Cissie was the ideal object to write about, Reggie Turner was the ideal audience (Plate 9*b*). During that summer of Max's supposed adoration, Reggie kept up his part in the fiction-making process; he pretended that he was interested in the progress of Max's affair with Cissie rather than in Max himself. To complete the fiction, Max feigned interest in Reggie's own feigned infatuation with an otherwise-unidentified Miss Cumberlidge—an affair even less likely of consummation than Max's affair with Cissie. Cissie gave Max the occasion for showing off to Reggie. He could try out his whole repertory of stylistic tricks, many of them currently being learned through observation of Oscar Wilde. And Cissie and Miss Cumberlidge together assured that Max could fascinate but still stay relatively distanced from Reggie. The whole business, as revealed in the letters, is amusingly, typically adolescent, with both young men finding safe ground on which to try out a variety of poses and emotional possibilities: Max as adorer of Cissie and seducer of Reggie, Reggie as long-suffering lover of Miss Cumberlidge and Max.

During this period of his imitation of Oscar and his acquaintance with the Douglas circle at Oxford, Beerbohm stood close enough to feel both attracted and threatened by what he later called 'the Sodomitic cesspool ... that was opened in 1895' by Wilde and Queensberry.[29] A letter to Reggie on 19 December 1893 contains news about 'very great and intimate scandals and almost, if not quite, warrants'. The scandals involved Bosie and Bobbie Ross and 'the schoolboy Helen' 'stolen from Bobbie by Bosie and kept at the Albemarle Hotel'. In the same letter he writes, 'Dear Lady Cecilia, how I do wish I were still in love with her: for I never was so happy before nor have been since the time.' Chaste love for Cissie is prophylactic against more dangerous love. A similar conjunction appears in a letter written earlier that year, describing a 'fatuous' Oscar at the Haymarket Theatre, waving 'his cigarette round and round his head': 'Of course', Max tells Reggie, 'I would rather see Oscar free than sober, but still, suddenly meeting him after my simple and lovely little ways of life since the Lady Cecilia first looked out of her convent window, I felt quite repelled' (19 August 1893).

In the early months of 1895, Herbert's company toured America and Max went along as Herbert's secretary. He therefore missed the opening of *The Importance of Being Earnest* on 14 February, and the opening of the Queensberry affair on 1 March. From Chicago he wrote to Ada Leverson:

---

[29] Letter to John Middleton Murry, 7 August 1920, in the Taylor Collection, Princeton University.

I read this morning the sad news about O and Q—O will not be able to remain in England I fear. I wish I were on the spot. What a lurid life Oscar does lead—so full of extraordinary incidents. What a chance for the memoir writers of the next century—the Thackerays and the Max Beerbohms of the future.[30]

But he returned from America in time to attend proceedings at the Old Bailey. On the spot, and writing to Reggie (who was in France because England was not safe for him), his tone was less flip:

Oscar has been quite superb. His speech about the Love that dares not tell his name was simply wonderful, and carried the whole court right away, quite a tremendous burst of applause. Here was this man, who had been for a month in prison and loaded with insults and crushed and buffeted, perfectly self-possessed, dominating the Old Bailey with his fine presence and musical voice. (3 May 1895)

'Hoscar is thinner and consequently finer to look at', Max tells Reggie—adding (later in the letter) news about 'Dear Miss Conover', the actress in Herbert's company who became Cissie Loftus's replacement in Max's love-life.

In *The Happy Hypocrite* Beerbohm united those objects of his intense regard, the posing 'somdomite' and the virgin actress. It is an odd and only partly successful performance. It uses Wilde to parody Wilde: the style of the wry, sentimental-sophisticated fairy tales of *The Happy Prince* undercuts the matter of *Dorian Gray*. But in the process it loses much of Max. On the one hand it is not strict parody; and on the other hand it lacks his distinct first-person authorial presence—the unmistakable presence of the essays from 'Diminuendo' through the BBC talks printed in *Mainly on the Air*.[31]

It is the story of the wicked Regency rake Lord George Hell, who falls in love with the innocent little actress Jenny Mere. Because Jenny

---

[30] March 1895 [?], at the Humanities Research Center, Austin, Texas.

[31] Riewald, *Sir Max Beerbohm*, calls it 'a curious blend between a Wildean fairy-tale and a parody of *Dorian Gray*' (p. 132), and enumerates specific parallels between *Dorian* and *The Happy Hypocrite* (pp. 134–6). He claims that *The Happy Hypocrite* 'transcend[s] the limits of parody. The mimicry in this story is so completely integrated into the harmless-looking fairy-tale frame that, on the face of it, the piece seems to have lost its critical character ... Its strength lies in the almost imperceptible exaggeration of his mimetic pose, and its operation is so subtle that it largely depends on the response of the reader whether it assumes the character of mockery, or not' (p. 145).

can only give her love to 'That man, whose face is wonderful as are the faces of the saints', while his 'is even as a mirror long tarnished by the reflection of this world's vanity' (*Happy Hypocrite*, p. 15), Lord George has himself fitted with a saintly mask and under that mask he woos and wins Jenny Mere. He takes her from the stage and they live blissfully in a country cottage until a jealous former mistress invades their paradise, snatches the mask from his face—and 'lo! his face was even as his mask had been. Line for line, feature for feature, it was the same. 'Twas a saint's face' (p. 51). Artifice transforms evil to saintliness; the mask becomes the man. Lord George (happier in this regard than Dorian Gray) is redeemed by a good woman's love.

Wilde said that *Dorian Gray* had a 'terrible moral . . . a moral which the prurient will not be able to find in it, but which will be revealed to all whose minds are healthy'. He said it was 'the only error in the book'.[32] The moral in *The Happy Hypocrite* is easier to find; and Beerbohm's witty reversal—making overt the sentimental morality that Wilde made covert in *Dorian Gray*—does not keep his parody entirely uncloying. According to Wilde, the moral of *Dorian Gray* is that 'All excess, as well as all renunciation, brings its own punishment'. Wilde obscures the moral cosiness of his story with his gestures toward unspeakable acts and sins too awful for describing; Beerbohm foregrounds it, partly by addressing his tale to an audience of infantile sophisticates:

None, it is said, of all who revelled with the Regent, was half so wicked as Lord George Hell. I will not trouble my little readers with a long recital of his great naughtiness. But it were well they should know that he was greedy, destructive, and disobedient. I am afraid there is no doubt that he often sat up at Carlton House until long after bed-time, and that he generally ate and drank far more than was good for him. His fondness for fine clothes was such, that he used to dress on week-days quite as gorgeously as good people dress on Sundays. He was thirty-five years old and a great grief to his parents. (p. 3)

Wilde himself had done this sort of thing better in *The Importance of Being Earnest*. Take, for instance, the matter of buns. Beerbohm's Jenny sees them heaped in the window of 'Herbert's' pastry shop in Kensington (an in-joke, since Kensington was the site of the Beerbohm family home); her childish hunger ('Jenny was only a child, after

<hr>

[32] To the Editor of the *St James Gazette*, 21 June 1890, in *Letters of Oscar Wilde*, p. 259.

all') awakens latent memories in Lord George: 'Which are buns, Jenny? I should like to have one, too' (p. 39). They eat, and 'He seemed to rise, from the consumption of his bun, a better man.' Later, in their pastoral retreat, they celebrate the 'mensiversary' of their wedding with 'no less than twelve of the wholesome delicacies'. 'They dallied in childish anticipation', and Jenny builds a pagoda of buns:

She laughed so loudly (for, though she was only sixteen years old, she had a great sense of humour), that the table shook, and alas! the pagoda tottered and fell to the lawn. Swift as a kitten, Jenny chased the buns, as they rolled hither and thither, over the grass, catching them deftly with her hand. Then she came back, flushed and merry under her tumbled hair, with her arm full of buns. (p. 46)

Jenny's 'great sense of humour' is a good joke, but her chasing buns 'swift as a kitten' is too much even in a parodic context. The whole story, like the bun-episode, is in danger of becoming the sentimental thing it parodies. Wilde himself was more in control of the material in *The Importance of Being Earnest*, where he reduced wickedness to childishness and the sins of his characters to the lust of buns. Cecily and Gwendolyn are products of sharp authorial detachment; by comparison, Jenny Mere is a narcissistic indulgence, treated with the only half-mocked adoration Max had lavished on Cissie Loftus. Jack and Algernon are farcical monsters of selfish sentimentality; but Lord George hides under his Wildean *embonpoint* the slender good looks of a devoted Victorian husband. His redemption is partly parody, but partly (one suspects) idealized self-portrait.

Wilde recognized his role in Beerbohm's cautionary tale. *The Happy Hypocrite* was one of the books (the other was *The Works*) that Beerbohm contributed to Wilde on his release from prison. Writing to Reggie Turner, Wilde paid it a backhanded compliment by approving its indebtedness: 'I have just read Max's *Happy Hypocrite*, beginning at the end, as one should always do. It is quite wonderful, and to one who was once the author of *Dorian Gray*, full of no vulgar surprises of style or incident.'[33] And to Beerbohm himself: 'The implied and accepted recognition of *Dorian Gray* in the story cheers me. I had always been disappointed that my story had suggested no other work of art in others.'[34] Both comments show Wilde at his most magnificent,

---

[33] 27 May 1897, *Letters of Oscar Wilde*, p. 575.
[34] *ca.*28 May 1897, *Letters of Oscar Wilde*, p. 576.

the 'immutable' Wilde described by Beerbohm as 'a character so strong that no force of circumstance could change it, or even modify it', still 'with the same artistry in words, still with the same detachment from life . . . the spectator of his own tragedy'.[35]

But precisely because Wilde's comments on *The Happy Hypocrite* are in character they have an edge to their expressions of pleasure. There are some things about Beerbohm's version of a Wildean story that Wilde cannot approve, partly, I think, because he cannot understand them:

> *The Happy Hypocrite* is a wonderful and beautiful story, though I do not like the cynical directness of the name. . . . I don't like you wilfully taking the name given by the common spectators, though I know what a joy there is in picking up a brickbat and wearing it as a buttonhole. . . . But in years to come, when you are a very young man, you will remember what I have said, and recognise its truth, and, in the final edition of your work, leave the title unchanged.[36]

For Wilde, the label 'hypocrite' could only be an insult or, as he interpreted Beerbohm's use, a defiant irony. He could not understand that Max was actually happy to be a hypocrite: that is, an actor, one who plays a role. Beerbohm said that Wilde 'never was a real person in contact with realities'. But in reality, as Beerbohm knew, the most distinct personality is a 'mimetic marvel', acting in order to be himself. That is the moral of *The Happy Hypocrite*, but in the sentimentality of the story, possibly because he was provoked by the example of Wilde, he seems to have wanted more.

Two other stories from this period (1897), 'The Story of the Small Boy and the Barley-Sugar' and 'Yai and the Moon',[37] are also pastiches of the Wildean fairy tale. They too combine sentimentality with arch knowingness. 'The Story of the Small Boy and the Barley-Sugar' begins, 'There was only one shop in the village, and it was kept by Miss Good, and everybody was very proud of it' (*Variety of Things*, p. 199). Like *Dorian Gray* it includes a moral about the punishment inevitably inflicted on the over-indulgent. (Miss Good eats too many of her own sweets and can't keep shop the next day; the Queen of

---

[35] 'A Lord of Language', in *Peep into the Past*, p. 40.

[36] *Letters of Oscar Wilde*, p. 576.

[37] The first appeared originally in *The Parade. An Illustrated Gift Book for Boys and Girls*, the second in *The Pageant*. Both are reprinted in *A Variety of Things* (1928).

Fairies sends a fairy assistant 'On the condition that you never again exceed' [p. 203]). It also has what Wilde might have called a more 'terrible moral'. The fairy shop-assistant gives poor little Tommy Tune a stick of magic barley sugar. With each bite he will be granted one wish. Tommy loves the heartless Jill Trellis. Jill has had an awful day in school (she misspelled 'cow' and 'kite' and 'box') and has to stay after school wearing a dunce's cap. Tommy's first wish is to have Jill free and by his side. It is granted; but the magically transported Jill immediately grabs Tommy's barley-sugar stick and eats the whole thing. Her only wish was that Tommy 'hadn't eaten that first bit' (p. 209).

In the essay 'Hosts and Guests', written in 1918, Max remembers how, when he was a school-boy, he ate the contents of a gift hamper without sharing it with his messmates. He explains that sharing his twelve sausage rolls would have made him a leader among boys—a fate he wanted to avoid because 'Leading abashed me. I was happiest in the comity of a crowd.' He is a born guest, not a host, and humility 'is a virtue innate in guests' (*And Even Now*, p. 138). Eating the sausage rolls was a sign of humility. 'Hosts and Guests' is typical of Beerbohm's best essays. In it, as in the earlier Wildean fairy tale, he is still recalling the child in the man; but in the early story he was out to shock—a *little*—with a mild sexual innuendo and a cynical comment-ary on female rapaciousness; while in 'Hosts and Guests' he wears his habitual pose of a friendly if fastidious talker, the most ordinary of people—if ordinary people could write so well. The paradoxes he plays with in 'Hosts and Guests' are, in fact, more complicated than the pseudo-paradoxes of *The Happy Hypocrite* and 'The Small Boy and the Barley-Sugar'. He sounds sincere, because he sounds like himself; yet the whole essay is a series of sophistries. Justifying himself as a natural-born getter rather than giver, reasonably making the lesser cause into the better, he plays an essayistic game that was played by Erasmus (on folly), Donne (on suicide), Swift (on colonialism), DeQuincey (on murder as a fine art), and of course Wilde (on the critic as artist, among other things). The ostensible triviality of his subject stamps it as his own; but to sound both sincere and original in the ancient game of writing is in fact no trivial achievement.

4.

Illudings

WITH his first book Beerbohm had 'acceded to the hierarchy of good scribes'. He would write no more, for he had written well and become a classic. The presumption that 'Art with a capital H' exempts her henchmen from the slog of long life and economic necessity made *The Works* a slightly bitter joke. Beerbohm would have to keep on refashioning himself as a 'classic', and each effort at immutability paid its tribute to time. In his series of caricatures called 'The Old and the Young Self' (in *Observations* 1925), eighteen famous men are imagined confronting themselves across the length of their own lives. *The Works* and *The Happy Hypocrite* were the first in Beerbohm's own series of comic efforts to close the gap between first setting out and arriving.

But from 1898 to 1910 he lived by journalism, a way of marking time. He wrote almost 500 weekly essays as drama critic for the *Saturday Review*. 'On and on I went, doggedly, from the age of twenty-five to the age of thirty-seven. It seems incredible; but it is a fact.'[1] It seems incredible, of course, only because Beerbohm was simultaneously creating the pose of 'leisurely perfectionist who ever since his earliest years . . . avoided all uncongenial work'.[2] In the grind of weekly reviewing Beerbohm learned how to make it look easy—a necessary trick in his act of writing. In his last regular *Saturday Review* column he confessed the secret:

Writing has always been uphill work to me, mainly because I am cursed with an acute literary conscience. To seem to write with ease and delight is one of the duties which a writer owes to his readers, to his art. And to contrive that effect involves very great skill and care: it is a matter of technique, a matter of construction partly, and partly of choice of words and cadences. There may

[1] 'Epistle Dedicatory to Edward Gordon Craig', 1924, in *Around Theatres* (New York: Simon and Schuster, 1954), p. vii.
[2] John Rothenstein, 'Introduction to *The Poets' Corner*', rpt. In *The Surprise of Excellence: Modern Essays on Max Beerbohm*, ed. J. G. Riewald (Hamden, Conn.: Archon Books, 1974), 1.

be—I have never met one—writers who enjoy the act of writing; but without that technique their enjoyment will not be manifest (16 April 1910, *Around Theatres*, p. 578).

This is demonstration as well as declaration. The late Victorian author of *The Works* could not have written anything as direct or convincing. Regular reviewing can be bad for a writer in the development of his craft, but it helped Beerbohm add the voice of sincerity to his authorial repertoire. In 1898 his style was that of a first-class wiseguy; by 1910 it could, when occasion required, actually be wise.

He owed his job to his immediate predecessor at the post, George Bernard Shaw. Being tied to the oar of weekly reviewing was an ambiguous benefit; being indebted to Shaw did not make it easier. Nor did his relationship to one of the leading actor-managers of the day. As Herbert Tree's little brother, Max was a natural for the reviewer's job, but by the same token he had to fight harder to become his own man.

Enter fighting: had it been a drama on the order of 'Savonarola', that would be the opening stage-direction. Since 1896 he had been contributing brash articles to the *Saturday Review* in which he had taken on such middle-brow icons as 'Doctor Conan Doyle' and Clement Scott. The first such article was a mock-panegyric on Scott, 'the poet of the Seaside', as love-lorn laureate of Bexhill-on-Sea. The review was unsigned, and it provoked Scott's indignant protest that he had 'been bitten by a Rat who dared not show his face'. 'Here I am', Beerbohm replied on cue, 'a real, live Rat; young, it may be, but quite calm; rejoicing in a Christian name and a surname (both printed below), and a fairly keen sense of humour; delighted to emerge from my miserable hole in the office of the "Saturday Review" and put my back to the wainscot. In a word, here I am.'[3] Thus self-identified he was ready to take on rougher opponents, including the *Saturday Review*'s regular drama reviewer—and already the most controversial figure in the English-speaking theatre—George Bernard Shaw.

On 14 and 21 May 1898 he contributed a two-part critique called 'Mr Shaw's Profession': Shaw (he said) knew nothing of flesh and blood; burdened with a 'moral purpose' he could create only puppets; his philosophy rested 'on a profound ignorance of human nature'. What Shaw did possess, Beerbohm allowed, was a sense of humour:

[3] 'Hold, Furious Scot!', *Saturday Review*, 10 October 1896, p. 395.

He may try, and try again, to be serious, but his nationality will always prevent him from succeeding in the attempt. When he writes seriously, he is always Paddy *malgré lui*. He should be himself simply. I hope that in future Mr Shaw will be Paddy, and leave the rest to chance. If he will do that, he has a great future in English drama.

That was on page 679. On page 682 appeared the regular column signed G.B.S., irregularly titled 'Valedictory'. This time it was Shaw's turn to say *cedo junioribus*. One week later 'Max Beerbohm' appeared where 'G.B.S.' had been.

The whole thing had, in fact, been stage-managed. As early as 8 April 1898 Shaw had written to Frank Harris, the magazine's editor, 'to say that I must hand over the Saturday to Max Beerbohm at the end of the season'.[4] The schedule for Shaw's departure had to be moved up when he developed a painful infection in his foot. His column for 14 May, when the first part of Beerbohm's critique of him appeared, was called 'G.B.S. Vivisected', an account of the operation on his foot. Behind the scenes, Shaw suggested that Beerbohm make his debut by reviewing 'young George Bancroft's maiden effort "Teresa" at the Metropole in Camberwell'.[5] Beerbohm replied that 'George Bancroft's play would be a rather dreary occasion for my debut'. He reminded Shaw that the second part of his G.B.S. critique would appear that week, and suggested that Shaw 'ought to have some kind of farewell to your readers in the next issue'.[6] Paddy was down but not out. In his valediction he borrowed a line from Ibsen, casting himself in the role of the ageing Master Builder and leaving for Max the role of a sweetly destructive Hilde Wangel: 'The younger generation is knocking at the door; and as I open it there steps spritely in the incomparable Max.'

Shaw's 'incomparable' saddled him forever with *le prénom just*. 'Spritely' was an odder choice. Beerbohm entered with his characteristic combination of aggressiveness and self-effacement: the daring

---

[4] Letter to Charlotte Payne-Townsend, in George Bernard Shaw, *Collected Letters of Bernard Shaw 1898–1910*, ed. Dan H. Laurence (London: Max Reinhardt, 1972), 28.

[5] 17 May 1898, Shaw, *Letters*, p. 43. Sometime earlier, Beerbohm had written to the publisher Grant Richards: 'I hear that GBS's plays are just appearing. I should like to write about them somewhere, and will do so—if you care to send me the book—for the Saturday or the Daily Mail.' Undated MS at the Humanities Research Center, Austin, Texas.

[6] Quoted in *Max and Will*, ed. Mary M. Lago and Karl Beckson (London: John Murray, 1975), 7.

young man now stood in Shaw's place under the heading 'Why I Ought Not to Have Become a Dramatic Critic' (28 May 1898, *Around Theatres*, pp. 1–4). Some of the objections he advances to himself serve mainly to recreate the image of Max: Herbert's flamboyant tenancy at Her Majesty's Theatre did not, as he claimed, disable his younger brother as a critic; and the fact that 'Most of the elder actors have patted me on the head and given me sixpence when I was "only *so* high"', while 'Many of the younger actors were at school with me', was no bar to criticism, any more than friendship was a bar to parody. As he undertakes a grown-up's job, Max re-makes himself as the precocious younger brother and perpetual schoolboy, a pose he will use (sometimes by playing against our expectation for it) in several of his early reviews. His confession 'that I have never regarded any theatre as much more than the conclusion to a dinner or the prelude to a supper' can be dismissed as a late echoing of Wildean wit. But he also announces that 'in drama I take, unfortunately, neither emotional nor intellectual pleasure. I am innocent of any theories on the subject. I shall have to vamp up my first principles as I go along, and they shall probably be all wrong and all dull.' Here the irony is more complex because parts of it are simple truth.

Beerbohm was not 'a born playgoer', and that, as he wrote in 1904, 'is, in some respects, of course, bad for a dramatic critic in the exercise of his craft' (*Last Theatres*, p. 85). For twelve years, with each weekly outing, Beerbohm had to act in his writing as though he took his subject seriously. Insofar as that subject was the current English theatre, the cause was often hopeless. He salvaged it by allowing the ironic possibility that the caring was a comic act with an ulterior motive, serious but playfully achieved. Many of his reviews, that is, like most of his essays, set their ostensible purpose against their playful subversions. Parody is a chief means. There are strict parodies, for instance of the literary styles of Pinero and Shaw or of his fellow-reviewers A. B. Walkley and William Archer. There are frequent verbal caricatures. And repeatedly there are self-parodies of Max Beerbohm in the act of writing like a critic who cares about plays. Beerbohm's collected drama reviews have an independent interest as a record of the English stage during an important transitional period. They have the additional interest of adding the word 'criticism' to the paradoxical grouping originality-parody-plagiarism-hoax.[7]

---

[7] Cf. Stanley Wells, 'Shakespeare in Max Beerbohm's Theatre Criticism', *Shakespeare*

The reviewer who is not 'a born playgoer', he says in his 1904 column 'is apt to be unduly harsh, condemning plays for obedience to conventions which are really inevitable. On the other hand, he has this virtue, denied to the critic who is a born playgoer: he is merciless to the false conventions which the born playgoer either imagines to be inevitable, or imagines not to be conventions at all' (*Last Theatres*, p. 85). Many of the reviews actually achieve that independence of judgment. Others, however, rely on the current avant-garde version of theatrical history and dramatic theory. Beerbohm began at the *Saturday Review* when the days of negligible melodrama and Englished versions of French farce were slowly drawing to an end. The elaborate spectacles presented by Henry Irving at the Lyceum and by Tree earlier at the Haymarket and now at Her Majesty's were staples of the rearguard. A New Drama was dawning; its herald was the critic William Archer. Archer believed in Progress: out of the pit of Elizabethan extravagance and the night of Restoration rhetoric, English drama was emerging into a rational day when playwrights would present a faithful depiction of the externals of Real Life. Archer's line of progress ran from Eugène Scribe (whose 'well-made' plays taught the tightness of structure necessary for the New Drama), through T. W. Robertson (who had introduced 'real' subject matter to the English stage), to Ibsen (who invested the realistic well-made play with Ideas), and home again to Sir Arthur Wing Pinero. With Pinero's *The Thunderbolt* (1908) and *Mid-Channel* (1909)—or as Beerbohm called it, *Mid-Gutter*—English drama had, according to Archer, entered its destined maturity.

Beerbohm would never kiss Ibsen's foot, as the caricatured Archer does in *The Poets' Corner*. But his reviews often echo Archer's views: 'Our drama is not yet very much to boast of', he writes in 1900; 'but it is better than nothing, and its superiority to nothing is being annually increased. Our playwrights are pressing nearer and nearer to life, and are, moreover, becoming less and less coy of ideas. In a word, they are progressing' (*More Theatres*, p. 304). Like a playgoer born to the New

---

Survey, 29 (1976), 132–45, on a mock-quotation in an 1898 review of *Macbeth*: 'Here Max is the total ironist, employing his gifts as a parodist in a completely straight-faced manner which may easily go undetected . . . Max was indulging here the strange impulse that led him to spend so many hours in his later years decorating his books with incongruous but totally convincing additions . . .' (p. 136).

Drama, Beerbohm asserts that the modern illusionistic stage is better than anything the technically impoverished Elizabethans had to contend with; that soliloquies, or 'talking to oneself', whatever other advantages they may have, are 'one of the early symptoms of insanity'; that Shakespeare's 'crude farces and melodramas, native or exotic, used by him as vessels for his genius, are not good enough for this sophisticated age'. He finds William Poel's experiments with Elizabethan staging boring or silly. And because 'modern realism is the only direction in which our drama can really progress' (1900, *More Theatres*, p. 278) he finds Gordon Craig's abstract stage designs interesting, pretty, worthy of support, but limited in their usefulness: 'The three-sided rooms inhabited by the dramatis personae' are one of modern drama's 'necessary' conventions. (Beerbohm dedicated *Around Theatres* [1924] to Craig, who was a neighbour in Rapallo; and Craig, for his part, seems not to have resented the implied slight in Beerbohm's hewing to the Archer line of progress. In *Index to the Story of my Days*, Craig lists his formative influences. There are only four writers: 'Oscar Wilde, Max Beerbohm, Shakespeare, Montaigne'.[8])

The drama is progressing by getting nearer and nearer to real life: why then, throughout his critical career, Beerbohm's scorn for 'Pinerorobertsoniana'? Part of his objection to Archer's pantheon is merely revisionist. Without questioning the doctrine of realism he simply finds Pinero (to say nothing of Tom Robertson) unconvincing. His review of *Mid-Channel* is a model of understatement: 'That a middle-aged man of sober habit must suddenly become a drunkard when he separates from his wife and takes a mistress, is a proposition which one's experience of actual life does not support' (1909, *Last Theatres*, p. 482). Writing of *The Thunderbolt*, he notes that Pinero, 'good man, has an inveterate weakness for "the cloth" as a means to a happy ending; and when the Rev George Trist appears in the second act of this play it is not for no apparent reason—to pinerologists: it is in order that in the fourth act the heroine may fall back on him.' But, 'Barring the customary clerical bathos', Beerbohm takes 'exception to nothing in the play', because 'One doesn't (as soon as one's criticism of it has been written) remember such a play as *The Thunderbolt*' (1908, *Last Theatres*, pp. 368–9). (To see how gentle this is, compare

[8] Edward Gordon Craig, *Index to the Story of my Days* (New York: Viking, 1957), 213.

it to Beerbohm on 'Mr Jerome Klapka Jerome. This tenth-rate writer has been, for many years, prolific of his tenth-rate stuff. But I do not recall, in such stuff of his as I have happened to sample, anything quite so vilely stupid as *The Passing of the Tenth Floor Back*' [1908, *Around Theatres*, p. 516].) Max, who frequently caricatured Pinero as all nose and magnificent eyebrows (Plate 10), parodied the pomposity of Pinero's pseudo-literary style,[9] but his basic objection was that Pinero was not coming closer and closer to life. He could not. He was trapped by those conventions which the born playgoer 'imagines not to be conventions at all'.

Only once, in fact, had the whole bundle of modern conventions come importantly to life, but that was in the frankly fantastic *The Importance of Being Earnest*.[10] Wilde sent up the conventions in the very act of perfecting them; he exploded the basis of his own dramatic fiction much as Algernon explodes the unfortunate Bunbury. And at its best, Beerbohm's reviewing treats the realist party-line with a similarly anarchic impulse. He repeatedly subverts the doctrines on which his reviewing ostensibly rests; and each defection serves the cause of his comic self-creation. 'I try hard to be an Optimist', he writes in 1902:

Sometimes I almost persuade myself, through assuring you, that the stage is in rather a good way, that steady progress is being made, that the auguries for the future are very propitious. And then, up, invariably, crops some grotesque and appalling fact to hit the poor little pretence on the head. (*More Theatres*, p. 456)

The professorial tone is typical, as is the pratfall that mocks the pedantic pose. Week after week, Beerbohm lays down his rules for

[9] 'The previous instalment of my hedbomadal adventures into the variegated realm of things theatrical involved me in a consideration of that recent contribution to national dramatic art which is known by the homely but euphonious diminutive as Laetitia, and which is at the moment on public view at the playhouse whose cognomen is derived from a whilom namesake of the august deceased personage who similarly supplies a certain well-known culumnal structure situate not a hundred miles from that rendezvous of the eminent, the Athenaeum Club.' And so on ('Mr Pinero's Literary Style', 1903, in *Around Theatres*, p. 286).

[10] 'Of a play representing actual life there can be, I think, no test more severe than its revival after seven or eight years of abeyance. . . . Last week, at the St James', was revived "The Importance of Being Earnest," after an abeyance of exactly seven years—those seven years which, according to scientists, change every molecule in the human body, leaving nothing of what was there before. And yet to me the play came out fresh and exquisite as ever . . .' ('The Importance of Being Earnest', 18 January 1902, in *Around Theatres*, p. 188).

modern drama, only to acknowledge that the main purpose of critical rules is to get reviews written. A critic must have theories, but Theory is a banana peel: pedestrians slip on it, while performers exploit its entertainment value.

The comedy of Max as theatregoer sometimes has a sad, even a desperate, subtext. The subtext is most explicit in the return-from-vacation piece he writes most Septembers. The very first of these, called 'A Startled Faun' (3 Sept. 1898, *More Theatres*, pp. 46–7), sets the theme, though the treatment became less coy as the years went on. He describes this first-night as a 'vague, familiar nightmare'. There at the Globe Theatre was the audience, 'all of them nodding to one another like mandarins and beaming through spectacles or pince-nez', while 'From an upper-box a programme fluttered down, as usual, and fell on somebody's head, making somebody very cross'. And there on stage 'was the usual garden, with a young lady (dressed up to the nines) in it, saying, "So, sir, that decides me! From this day forth we shall be as strangers!" And there were men tapping one another on the chest and saying "Look here! You don't split on me: I don't split on you!"' Everything was as it should have been, the audience roared with laughter, but 'I alone was unable to enjoy myself; my heart was far away, on the coast. My ears were as two shells, where the murmur of the waves is yet lingering—how could I hear well?' He asks the reader to forgive his reticence about the play (*Tommy Bell*, which he has in fact just reviewed by way of an incidental parody), because he is 'simply the young man up from the country', a startled faun.

It is not only the stupidity of most plays that makes the return-from-vacation such a trial. Nor is it only the 'hebdomadal' drudgery of reviewing. He wilts at the confrontation with artistic illusion itself. On holiday he becomes 'more and more enamoured of the-world-at-first-hand, until I positively sicken at the mention of anything connected with the art of the theatre' (1904, *Last Theatres*, p. 84):

After tasting life itself, after knocking up against nature and mankind and so forth, it is a bitter thing to be forced back on that familiar, but for a while forgotten, imitation of life and nature and mankind and so forth which constitutes theatrical art. The whole thing seems so unnecessary, so unsuccessful. In the course of eleven months, compulsory playgoing dims one's ken of men and women as they are: one accepts the stage's simulacra of them, quite amenably, as being an excellent imitation of the real thing—nay! as being the real thing itself. But after a rest, how brief soever, one *sees* and, seeing, sighs. (1902, *More Theatres*, pp. 488–9)

Thus the unself-conscious 'born playgoer' has the advantage over a critic like Max Beerbohm: the former prefers the theatre's 'neatly cooked slices of life' to life 'diffuse and raw'; while Beerbohm, though his business is to live in artistic illusion, longs to be 'quit of theatrical art' (1904, *Last Theatres*, p. 84).

The nostalgic longing for things-in-themselves is incurable. Realism is an anodyne that only makes the disease worse; the more the theatre progresses in the art of approaching life, the more starkly it draws the line between represented being and some imaginable state of pure being. Henry Arthur Jones, for instance, is 'of all successful playwrights the most nearly in touch with actual life—a man of the theatre, assuredly, but a man with only one foot planted in it, with only one eye on it: a man who tries to bring life into the theatre, rather than to clap the theatre down on life'. So it is a relief, returning to the theatre one September, to be spared Sydney Grundy and granted, instead, the realistic Jones. His new play, *Chance the Idol*, is one 'by which you will be much excited'. Yet look at that stage: 'Men and women? They? Let us not insult humanity by listening to so preposterous a notion. Voice, face, port, gesture, all betray them as quite inhuman' (1902, *More Theatres*, p. 489). At his best, even Henry Arthur Jones, straddling that line between art and life, only makes the line more apparent.

As, of course, does Max Beerbohm. His own efforts to implicate life in art drive the wedge deeper. His portraits of real people are caricatures that mock the pretences of realism. His fictional characters mingle with the ostensibly real but evanesce at the point of embrace. The ghost of art haunts his every approach to reality. The spriteliness with which he seems to accept his exile from the real is only occasionally dampened, as it is, for instance, in the return-from-vacation pieces. Drama is the most depressingly fictive of art forms precisely because its appurtenances of life—those bodies and voices on stage—increase the nostalgia for the real. Writing criticism about theatre makes the situation doubly hard. It requires, in response to the theatre's own blatant pretences, cunning pretences on the part of the writer lest the lure of reality silence him entirely. Writing from Paris about the English theatre, for instance, he wonders why he is writing at all, then checks himself:

But I must not let the holiday-mood instil into me a sense of proportion. Though here, far from the foggy four-mile radius, I am peculiarly susceptible to that paralysing poison, I can at least inoculate myself with an injection of commercialism—*aur: sac: fam:* as it is called in the prescriptions. Though I cannot persuade myself that there is any true justification for my hebdomadal excursus, I can at least write it, write it in time for the post. (1901, *Around Theatres*, p. 139)

Unreality is the problem: the briefest holiday is dangerous for the critic because, returning from it, 'All art will strike him as mere artifice, as a fuss about nothing' (1901, *More Theatres*, p. 402). But more artifice is the only recourse. Max must write to re-create the reality of himself as writer; and for that purpose, theatre criticism will do as well as another form.

Beerbohm calls actors and actresses, without distinction of gender, 'mimes'. The aim of a mime is to 'illude'. Both noun and verb are keywords in his dramatic criticism. *Illude* as the verb of illusion is unknown to the *Oxford English Dictionary*. Transitively, *illude* has or had the obsolete meaning 'to mock, make sport of, deride'. It means 'to trick, impose upon, deceive with false hopes'—nearer to Beerbohm's usage, but not quite there. It means (or meant) 'to cheat out of (something)', and it means 'to evade, elude'—ideas that are neatly tucked into Beerbohm's portmanteau. *Webster's Third International* adds a nearer definition, 'to subject to an illusion', on the authority of James Agate, who probably learned the word from Beerbohm: 'at the cinema [writes Agate] I am ... completely *illuded*'. Etymologically, illude (like illusion) derives from *ludere*, to play. So the word contains the idea of play as well as the idea of illusion: to be successfully illuded, one must play at believing an illusion, become a participant in a hoax, a happy hypocrite. Transitively, to illude is to deceive with art's false hopes, eluding the claims of reality.

So Dr Johnson, we might say, was not illuded when he saw in the theatre neither Alexandria nor Rome but only the actors reciting 'a certain number of lines ... with just gesture and elegant modulation'. And Charles Lamb was not illuded at a performance of *King Lear* when he saw only an old man tottering on a stick, not the titanic image his mind had conceived in the reading.[11] Johnson and Lamb were

[11] Johnson, 'Preface to Shakespeare' [1765], in *Samuel Johnson on Shakespeare*, ed, W. K. Wimsatt, Jr. (New York: Hill and Wang, 1960), 38; and Lamb, 'On the Tragedies of Shakespeare', in *The Works of Charles and Mary Lamb*, ed. E. V. Lucas (London: Methuen, 1903–5), i. 107.

hard cases: their resistance to being illuded was in proportion to their need, for each was painfully conscious of the lure of imagination. Lamb, especially, was a great but not a *born* playgoer. He wore the shackles of reality (he says in his essay on 'artificial comedy') more contentedly for having respired the breath of an imaginary freedom; but he knew the painful difference between a law-court and a dream-while.[12] The born playgoer, however, is unconcerned at the difference and is easily illuded.

Beerbohm claims that the modern realistic theatre has made great strides in its ability to illude. It has, for instance, banished soliloquies because 'they are unnatural, they spoil illusion' (1900, *More Theatres*, p. 311). Modern playwriting is a precise art or science; if the exposition is not sufficiently concise, 'it does not illude us' (1901, *More Theatres*, p. 361); and though 'We can be intellectually interested in figures that do not illude us as real . . . we cannot feel for such figures' (1902, *Around Theatres*, p. 193). Shakespeare, who 'wrote real plays', aimed 'to produce in the spectators an absolute illusion of reality' (1899, *More Theatres*, p. 222), and Beerbohm for his part concedes that he 'was illuded at first sight of [Elsinore], but that was long before I came to years of discretion' (1902, *More Theatres*, p. 485). Technology could have helped Shakespeare:

He would be the first to admit that the modern method of production is a great convenience, and to welcome everything which contributes to illusion— all the imitations of distance, of sunlight or moonlight, of trees, palaces, cottages—everything, in fact, which saves one the trouble of imagining the accessories and so allows one to be illuded by the essentials. (1899, *More Theatres*, p. 222)

Sometimes, however, reality defeats all desire to be illuded. Of Sarah Bernhardt as 'Hamlet, Princess of Denmark', 'the only compliment one can conscientiously pay her is that her Hamlet was, from first to last, *très grande dame*' (1912, *Around Theatres*, p. 37). The problem of theatrical illusion raises for him the theoretical issue, 'how far is it artistically possible to introduce into a play the figures of men or women who are known to exist or to have existed in real life?' The spectacle of a player-Queen Victoria leaves him unmoved, despite the facts (as he claims them to be) that he is 'an emotional loyalist' and 'as illudible in theatres as anyone else' (1900, *Around Theatres*, p. 55).

[12] 'On the Artificial Comedy of the Last Century', Lucas ii. 142.

The word 'mime', he claims, is used 'with no derogatory intent, and simply because, as a noun of common gender, it saves the time and space which would be wasted by "actors and actresses"' (1905, *More Theatres*, p. 182). In fact, the relation of a mime to its role is different from that of an actor or actress to his or her role. The mime (I would say) puts on a role and never confuses it with his or her personality, unlike the actor or actress whose personality, including gender, is deeply involved in the act. Mimes declare themselves as simulacra. Actors and actresses declare themselves as people. If so, why does Beerbohm think mimes are better at illuding us? Actors and actresses cannot give the illusion of life because they *are* life. Only artifice can illude.[13]

As dramatic theory, this whole business is no great intellectual shakes. It is the doctrine of realism pressed into the service of aestheticism—Mrs Tanqueray playing the Countess Cathleen. But Beerbohm is using it less as dramatic theory than as dramatic licence. The doctrine of realism is part of his own act. It is what he does to illude us. A non-theatrical essay called 'The Ragged Regiment' (1904, *Yet Again*, pp. 227–35) nicely works out some of the paradoxes. Max is in Westminster Abbey 'to see certain old waxen effigies that are here'. In eery present tense, he makes his way up a winding wooden staircase 'into a tiny paven chamber'. He becomes dimly aware that someone is watching him. 'Like sentinels in sentry-boxes, they fix me with their eyes, seeming as though they would challenge me. . . . Immobile and dark, very gaunt and withered, these personages peer out at me with a malign dignity, through the ages which separate me from them, through the twilight in which I am so near to them. Their eyes . . .'

And he breaks off, cheering himself up with some sober art-theory:

Come, sir, their eyes are made of glass. It is quite absurd to take wax-works seriously. Wax-works are not a serious form of art. The aim of art is so to imitate life as to produce in the spectator an illusion of life. Wax-works, at best, can produce no such illusion. Don't pretend to be illuded. For its power to illude, an art depends on its limitations. Art can never be life, but it can seem to be so if it do but keep far enough away from life.

[13] See Roy Huss, 'The Aesthete as Realist', in Riewald, *Surprise of Excellence*, p. 113–22.

The lifelikeness of a work of art in any medium derives from its obedience to the conventions of that medium, not to its aping the conditions of life itself. 'A painting is a thing in two dimensions, whereas man is in three', he patiently explains:

> If a painter swelled his canvas out and in according to the convexities and concavities of his model, or if a sculptor overlaid his material with authentic flesh-tints, then you would demand that the painted or sculptured figure should blink, or stroke its chin, or kick its foot in the air. That it could do none of these things would rob it of all power to illude you.

The tone is convincingly academic, and the argument sufficiently cogent. Only it doesn't serve his purpose. He has proved that waxworks, 'being so near to life', 'give you the illusion of death'; and with that he breaks off once again:

> . . . You see, I have failed to cheer myself up. Having taken up a strong academic line, and set bravely out to prove to myself the absurdity of wax-works, I find myself at the point where I started, irrefutably arguing to myself that I have good reason to be frightened, here in the Chapel of Abbot Islip, in the midst of these, the Abbot's glowering and ghastly tenants. Catalepsy! death! that is the atmosphere I am breathing.

Max has been illuding us in two successive roles, as frightened tourist and as sensible theorist. Now he takes illusion one step further by calling attention to the conditions of his acting:

> If I were writing in the past tense, I might pause here to consider whether this emotion were a genuine one or a mere figment for literary effect. As I am writing in the present tense, such a pause would be inartistic, and shall not be made. I must seem not to be writing, but to be actually on the spot, suffering.

The ostensibly unperformed change to past tense cues his recollection of a visit to Madame Tussaud's and some general reflections on mortality and art. He admits that in fact the 'ragged regiment' of effigies in the Abbey fills him 'with a kind of wondering pity': 'My academic theory about wax-works has broken down utterly. These figures of kings, princes, duchesses, queens—all are real to me now, and all are pathetic, in the dignity of their fallen and forgotten greatness.'

We are back in present tense to Max in the Islip Chapel, viewing with him now 'the battered and disjected remains of the earlier effigies—the primitive wooden ones'. There is no question of being illuded by these fragments of unrealistic statuary. Yet they provoke emotion in the writer and his reader. The writer?

I feel that I ought to be more deeply moved than I am by this sad state of things. But—well, I seem to have exhausted my capacity for sentiment, and cannot rise to the level of my opportunity. Would that I were Thackeray! Dear gentleman, how promptly and copiously he would have wept and moralised here, in his grandest manner, with that perfect technical mastery which makes even now his tritest and shallowest sermons sound remarkable, his hollowest sentiments ring true!

And the essay ends with Max making his way down the stairs, trying to imagine how Thackeray would have ended the essay, as the verger's voice takes over from both: 'was interred with great pomp on St Simon's and St Jude's Day October 28th 1307 in 1774 the tomb was opened when——'

The essay does something that early twentieth-century realistic theatre seldom does: it plays across the conventional divide between life and art. It calls into question the distinction between genuine emotion and literary effect, precisely by seeming to affirm it. It illudes us into taking the fiction for the emotional reality, then makes that fiction effectually real—an actually moving reflection on mortality and on the pathetic effort of art to preserve us. Incidentally, it suggests why the best playgoer is not the 'born playgoer' for whom dramatic convention is transparent. Because 'a life spent in and around the theatre is bound to sap the instinct for reality' (1905, *Last Theatres*, p. 182), it also saps the instinct for being creatively illuded by reality's alternatives.

In the Epistle Dedictory to the 1924 *Around Theatres* Beerbohm told Gordon Craig, 'If ever you do dip into the books, I advise you to start at about the year 1901. So as not to offend my earlier self by leaving it unrepresented, I have begun at the year 1898. But I do think I improved as I went on.' His earliest reviews are full of the sort of advice he had given to Shaw. He tells Pinero and Jones and Mrs Craigie that they too should leave ideas alone and concentrate on being amusing. This is not Beerbohm at his best. It is true that what was passing for serious thought on the stage would not have passed for thought elsewhere. The demand for 'ideas' in realistic drama gave currency to a pseudo-seriousness that justifies Beerbohm's preference for technically excellent frivolity. Modern dramaturgy, according to

Beerbohm, is so highly specialized a skill, like juggling, that the adept
has little energy left over for thinking. Therefore, 'Of our good
playwrights (by which phrase I mean those who can be trusted to write
technically good plays) not more than two (I give the highest estimate)
could, in point of brain-power or sense of beauty or knowledge of life
or any other good quality, stand comparison with a novelist of (I give
again the highest estimate) fourth rank' (1903, *More Theatres*, p. 555).
But Beerbohm's early reviews are limited not only by their raw
materials. He seems unable to deal with 'ideas' in drama unless they
come wrapped in a veil of mystery like Maeterlinck's.

After 1901 a new attitude begins to dominate. One of the drawings
in the 1901 *Cartoons: The Second Childhood of John Bull* is called 'De
Arte Theatrali'. The smug John Bull, as master of his house, has
called his two housemaids, the Muses of Tragedy and of Comedy, on
the carpet:

Melpomene, you're dismissed [he says]. I aint so young as I was, and that
gloomy face of yours is more than I can stand about the 'ouse. Thalia, you
can stay on. Not as 'ow I've been puffectly satisfied with you either, o' late.
Don't let me 'ave to make any more complaints about you trying to get *Ideas*
into your 'ead. You keep to your station; or, I cautions you, *you'll* 'ave to go
too my girl.

And by 1909 Beerbohm himself, no John Bull, is taking Somerset
Maugham to task for saying that 'ideas' are out of place in the theatre
and that as a playwright he aims only to entertain.[14] It is not that
Beerbohm became more serious—whatever that might entail; but he
did achieve a finer adjustment of the potentially conflicting demands
of irony and criticism. The best irony means what it says, however
complexly; cheap irony lets the meaning take care of itself. In 1898
William Archer in effect accused Beerbohm of using cheap irony.
'[Archer] complains publicly of me that I am in the habit of "fabricating authorities" and "fabricating opinions". This', Beerbohm protests,

[14] In this review Beerbohm says that 'what is really needed for the drama's future is
a permanently endowed little Experimental Theatre'; and he repeats his doubts about
the sort of National Theatre then being promulgated by Granville Barker and William
Archer: 'A National Theatre, however elastic the intentions of its pious founder, would
inevitably, sooner or later—and, I think, sooner—sink into majestic academicism, and
be nothing but a great rich paddock for the war-horses of the past.' (A Parenthesis',
9 January 1909, in *Last Theatres 1904–1910*, introd. Rupert Hart-Davis [New York:
Taplinger, 1970], 419–22).

'is not quite just': 'As to my "opinions," I assure Mr Archer that they are all quite genuine, natural and sincere. I may often exaggerate things. I may often invent things. But that does not mean that my general opinions are not honestly held by me' (*More Theatres*, p. 62). It is a perfect statement of the ironic method that a serious writer like Archer will find hard to understand. But in 1898 Beerbohm's command of the method was not always at the level of his definition of it.

The theory of dramatic realism helped make the difference. For one thing, it gave him a running joke. The idea that the modern playwright's aim is to approach as nearly as possible the conditions of actual life allows him to turn the plots of Jones and Pinero into paradoxes they were never meant to be. His tone is commonsensical, patient, and worldly-wise as he points out the utterly conventional bases of plays that lay claim to mimetic realism. But mimetic realism is itself a convention. In the first years of the twentieth century it justified itself by analogy with science: as the scientist was making progress toward discovering the fundamental laws of nature, so the artist was progressing toward discovering the fundamental laws of representing nature. The doctrine brought with it—naturally, one might say—a critical style based on such scientific-seeming activities as definition, distinction, and the creation of syllogisms. In Beerbohm's reviews after (roughly) 1901, realism's scientific style replaces the more dandified style with which he began. The pose of supercilious trifler gives way to the pose of disinterested man of science, calmly defining the drama's laws.

The writing is more spare. It produces some of the best dramatic criticism written in this century, along with some well-written commonplace criticism. But it still allows itself on occasion to be read as a nicely controlled parody of its own tone of didactic reasonableness. An essay on 'Soliloquies in Drama' (1901), for instance, stands midway between the earlier dandy style and the newer didactic style. It begins with a careful distinction that launches several absurdities: 'Talking to oneself has this obvious advantage over any other form of oratory or gossip: one is assured of a sympathetic audience. But it also has this peculiar drawback: it is supposed to be one of the early symptoms of insanity' (*Around Theatres*, p. 184). But of course the soliloquy is not a form of talking to oneself, unless one accepts (as the essay does) that 'the aim of modern dramatists is to come as near as

possible to reality'—an aim that may seem as crazy as talking to
oneself, once the initial premises are examined. Max makes a great
show of examining those premises as he lectures the dramatist on the
allowable and non-allowable uses of the soliloquy. It should never be
used merely to give information. It should only be used when it is
inevitable. The modern mime is more resourceful than the mime of
the 'sixties; the sophisticated playwright of 1901 should therefore
resort to soliloquy only when the mime cannot convey information
without it—but neither should he expect too much of the mime. 'He
must strike the mean. As to where exactly that mean is to be struck,
he must use his own discretion.'

The scientific care for definitions and distinctions yields essays that
compare English and French mimes, essential and inessential conventions, comedy and tragedy, male and female playwrights, and so on.
And increasingly toward 1910 it produces incisive judgments both of
older playwrights from Wilde through Pinero, Jones, and Grundy, and
of newer playwrights. He finds Barrie's *The Admirable Crichton* 'the
best thing that has happened, in my time, to the British stage' (1902,
Around Theatres, p. 231); he praises Yeats and Synge, Galsworthy and
Granville Barker. He praises Barker's direction of the ensemble acting
at the Court Theatre (1905, *Around Theatres*, pp. 401–6). His opinions
of plays are, by and large, opinions shared by the other good drama
critics of the time, including Archer, A. B. Walkley, and Desmond
MacCarthy. If he had kept on as he was going, he would have become
a critic as important as William Archer for the history of the theatre in
England. Instead he quit while he was ahead.

G.B.S. had opened the door in 1898 but he continued to fill the
prospect Max surveyed. He called Max incomparable: Max replied
'compare me'[15]—and inevitably his reviews of Shaw invite a judgment
on the critic. Their mutually wary personal relationship is a drama in
its own right. Like Oscar and Max, they were too close for comfort
both by personality and circumstance. But Beerbohm had loved,
imitated, and (in his way) superseded Wilde; none of these activities
apply to his anxious relationship with Shaw.[16]

[15] Letter to Bohun Lynch printed in the Preface to Lynch's *Max Beerbohm in
Perspective* (London: Heinemann, 1921), p. ix.

[16] For a brief review of their relation, see Katherine Lyon Mix, 'Max on Shaw',
Shaw Review, 6 (September 1963), 100–4; rpt. in Riewald, *Surprise of Excellence*,
pp. 131–7.

Much of Beerbohm's response to Shaw is on the record, in reviews, parody, and caricature. He seems characteristically self-aware and in control of his feelings. He is disarmingly frank, for instance, in the Epistle Dedicatory to Gordon Craig in the 1924 *Around Theatres*:

One thing I never could, from first to last, make up my mind about; and that thing was the most salient phenomenon 'around theatres' in my day: 'G.B.S.' Did I love his genius or hate it? You, of course, survey it from the firm rock of your ideals. I wish I had had a rock of some sort. I went wavering hither and thither in the strangest fashion, now frankly indignant, now full of enthusiasm, now piling reservation on reservation, and then again frankly indignant. My vicissitudes in the matter of G.B.S. were lamentable. But they amuse me very much.

But some of his encounter with Shaw was behind the scenes, in superfluous modes like the 'improvements' he made in books by or about Shaw. There are depths to Beerbohm's elective antipathies. His public comments on Shaw are not in conflict with the private tamperings, but the latter reveal the depth of his fascination with his older, more active rival.

He couldn't leave Shaw alone. He drew more caricatures of him than of any figure beside himself and Edward VII. And he never felt that he had gotten him right. In 1920, annotating a copy of *Caricatures of Twenty-Five Gentlemen* (1896), he wrote about his original drawing of Shaw, 'This is utterly amiss, nose—hair—back of head—were never at all as I here presented them. And the lamb-like expression! I take it all back.' He then added three new profile heads: the first effort is crossed out; the second ('This is better') gives Shaw a more aggressive eye, nose, and beard; the third ('G.B.S. in 1920') adds eyeglasses and makes the features still more forward-thrusting and assertive.[17] This copy of his first collection of caricatures is extensively redrawn, but Shaw is the only figure essayed three extra times.

It was not his only effort to alter Shaw's graven image. In 1911 Professor Archibald Henderson published a copious, laudatory biography of Shaw; Beerbohm's copy is elaborately 'improved' with doctored illustrations and annotations. He attributes to Professor Henderson the following 'note': 'No man has a stronger personality,

[17] Copy in the Taylor Collection, Princeton University, and described by John Felstiner, 'Changing Faces in Max Beerbohm's Caricature', *Princeton University Library Chronicle*, 33 (1972), 73–88.

yet no man is more protean, than Shaw. His face and figure
wonderfully mould themselves in accord to his emotions. Favourable
press-cuttings make him look almost like a pig.'[18] And in the altered
photo by Edward Steichen, facing page 332, he does. Beerbohm
turned Shaw into a leering devil, and he made Professor Henderson
praise his subject's reformation from drunkenness, dandyism, and
wickedness of all sorts. Edmund Wilson was shown the Henderson
biography when he visited Rapallo in 1954; he was not amused,
'because it showed too much a jeering hatred that Max usually kept in
leash in his drawings'.[19] It reveals, says John Felstiner, 'a helpless
obsession'.[20]

'Mr Shaw's apotheosis is one of the wonders of the age', wrote A.
B. Walkley in *The Times* on 9 July 1924: Max took the line as the
caption for a caricature in which Shaw has become a vast icon; a
group of acolytes wafts incense toward his nostrils, while the critic
Walkley says in disgust, 'And calls himself a non-smoker!' (Plate 11).
Max posed G.B.S. with a different sort of admirer in a caricature
called 'The Iconoclast's One Friend', where Shaw almost wilts in
disgust as a blowzy, leering *'Member of Mrs Warren's Profession'* says,
'Mr Shaw, I have long wished to meet you and grasp you by the hand
. . . God bless you! . . . I understand that the Army and Navy, the
Church, the Stage, the Bar, the Faculty, the Fancy, the Literary
Gents, the Nobility and Gentry, and all the Royal Family, will have
nothing more to do with you. Never mind! *My* house will always be
open to you' (Plate 12).

In words as well as drawings he mocked the creation of the Shavian
image. In 1914 he wrote to Reggie Turner that the had gone to see
Shaw's waxen effigy at Madame Tussaud's:

Some days later [he writes to Turner] I was lunching at his place, and
mentioned the effigy to him; at which he flushed slightly, and waved his
hands, and said he had *had* to give Tussaud a sitting, as 'it would have seemed
so *snobbish* to refuse'! Considering that it had been the proudest day in his
life, I was rather touched by this account of the matter.

[18] In the Berg Collection, New York Public Library.
[19] Wilson, 'A Miscellany of Max Beerbohm', in *The Bit between my Teeth*: *A Literary
Chronicle of 1950–1965* (New York: Farrar, Straus and Giroux, 1965), 49.
[20] Felstiner, *The Lies of Art*: *Max Beerbohm's Parody and Caricature* (New York: Knopf,
1972), 88.

And immediately he adds: 'I am afraid he is afraid of me.'[21] Presumably Shaw was afraid because Beerbohm could see through his poses; the parodies and caricatures are the outward signs of his inner knowledge of the real G.B.S₄ In the same letter he tells Turner that 'I met him dining at Philip Sassoon's, and he seemed decidely uncomfortable at being caught by me there.' Sassoon had not provided any special dishes for the vegetarian Shaw; Beerbohm tells Turner that the 'poor man . . . got almost nothing to eat', and that Mrs Shaw was 'in fearful anxiety for him' until 'towards the end of dinner . . . he did get a potato and some beans'. In this anecdote, Shaw's embarrassment and hunger prove that he is no waxwork figure but an all-too-human poser; and Max by contrast is the self-contained, self-created icon. It is hard to say how much of the fear Beerbohm attributes to Shaw is merely projection. On the record, at least, Shaw seems perfectly unthreatened by Beerbohm. Mrs Shaw, however, was not so impassive: once 'in a fury', according to S. N. Behrman, she 'tore in two a caricature Max had done of G.B.S. and threw the pieces into the fire'.[22]

Beerbohm expresses what I would call the public explanation for his antipathy to Shaw in his further account of the dinner at Sassoon's:

. . . I talked a lot to Mrs Shaw about him, as always, and with much affection and admiration, but also, at one point, with considerable frankness. 'He is *not*,' I said, 'an artist.' At this her face beamed suddenly more than ever. 'Oh,' she exclaimed, 'how glad I am to hear you say that! That is what *I* always tell him. He's a REFORMER.'[23]

For Beerbohm, the geniuses who are unfaithful to the purity of art are distinct from those who remain steadfast, like Wilde at his best and, preeminently, like Henry James. That Shaw would allow any motive to overcome the 'artist' in him puts him in a class with Wells and Kipling. But Shaw himself claimed, like Mrs Shaw, that he was delighted to be known as a 'reformer' rather than an 'artist'. Responding to Beerbohm's original two-part critique in the *Saturday Review* in 1898, Shaw wrote to him:

[21] 14 April 1914, Beerbohm, *Letters to Reggie Turner*, ed. Rupert Hart-Davis (London: Hart-Davis, 1964), 230.

[22] Behrman, *Portrait of Max* (New York: Random House, 1960), p. 91. Behrman also gives a version of the dinner at Sassoon's, p. 25.

[23] *Letters to Reggie Turner*, p. 231.

I have read your articles on my plays with some anxiety for your salvation. You must go on a vestry at the first opportunity. You have been badly brought up, & can only taste life when it is fried in fine art. Follow my glorious example, & go into the Park every Sunday morning with a kitchen chair & red flag. That is all your genius needs to sun away the north light of the studio.[24]

It is quintessentially Shavian, a combination of self-confidence and self-mockery, untouchable superiority masquerading as the commonest of human touches. And it annoyed Beerbohm more than he wanted Shaw to know.

But there are other reasons for Beerbohm's abiding uneasiness about Shaw. They were two self-created men. Like the great self-publicists of an earlier generation, like Whistler and Wilde, they made their personalities inseparable from their work. Their iconic signatures—'Max', 'G.B.S.'—are tokens of that equivocal triumph. Repeatedly Beerbohm paid Shaw the ambiguous compliment of calling him a *personality*, 'the most distinct personality in current literature' (1903, *Around Theatres*, p. 272). It could be a way of seeming to praise the man while grudging the work from which he was inseparable: 'As a teacher, as a propagandist, Mr. Shaw is no good at all, even in his own generation. But as a personality he is immortal' (1901, *Around Theatres*, p. 175). For Max, who had (in Virginia Woolf's phrase) brought personality into literature, there are ironies within ironies in thus promoting another man of letters. In his own copy of *Caricatures of Twenty-Five Gentlemen* he wrote (August 1924), '*Aubrey Beardsley* and *G.B.S.*—these are the two most salient gentlemen of these 25, the most sharply influential, the most *surviving*'— and added: 'except of course, King Edward and the Duke of Cambridge'.[25] But Beardsley, Edward, and the Duke of Cambridge were all dead by then. Shaw went on and on.

After Wilde, Shaw was Beerbohm's only real competition as a professional ironist. But their methods were opposite. Max posed as the perfect English gentleman, modest and well-behaved, sensible and central. And under that cover he worked the black magic of

---

[24] 17 May 1898, in *Collected Letters of Bernard Shaw 1898–1910*, ed. Laurence, p. 43. Cf. 15 September 1903: 'Ten minutes on the Drainage Sub Committee of the St Pancras Borough Council, which has taken many an afternoon when the Superman took the morning, would shatter that academicism for ever' (p. 374).

[25] *Catalogue of the Library and Literary Manuscripts of the Late Sir Max Beerbohm* (London: Sotheby's, 1960) p. 6, item 5.

parody and caricature, bewitching the forms of art as well as the arts' practitioners. There was nothing covert about Shaw's practice. He advertised his outsider status and captured the English by force. Beerbohm distrusted all the big claims of systematizers and seers— and no one made bigger claims than G.B.S. His boisterousness embarrassed Max's more genteel irony. But G.B.S. the prophet was also the ironist who (Beerbohm wrote) 'contradicts and jibes at no one more than himself'. He was 'a mystery man with a big drum, and an egoist who might himself be puzzled to say exactly where his sterling affections end and his frivolous convictions begin'.[26] Shaw was his own parodist, creator of his own caricature. His ironic personality threatened to cancel Beerbohm's, and for that reason Max worked all the harder on him.

As reviewer, however, Beerbohm tried to be fair. He began with one formidable obstacle to critical judgment: until 1904, Shaw's plays were known either from occasional matinée performances (often under virtually amateur conditions) or in their published forms. The theatre managers said that Shaw was uncommercial. Beerbohm's early reviews pay Shaw the ambiguous compliment of insisting that the managers are wrong; he insists that Shaw is a master of popular formulae, and that both the managers and the playwrights should stop thinking of him as anything but an entertainer. Thus, reviewing *The Devil's Disciple* (1899, *Around Theatres*, pp. 38–41), he makes his usual objection that the characters are 'absolutely rational machines, unclogged by such accessories as flesh and blood'; but he 'offer[s] Mr Shaw my congratulations on the amazing cleverness with which he has handled the melodramatic form, and on having the loud laugh over the thirty or forty London managers who have allowed his play to go a-begging'. This was less than a year after G.B.S. had let the Incomparable step spritely through the door at the *Saturday Review*. Max recalls the fact in his review, and acknowledges the rivalry by calling attention to the difference in their ages: 'I trust that when, in the fulness of time, I leave off being a dramatic critic and become a dramatist, my successor in these columns may have reason to be half as jealous of me as I am of "G.B.S."' He gives a not very inspired

[26] The phrases are from a rejected 'Note' that Beerbohm contributed to Rothenstein's *English Portraits*. See Mix, 'Max on Shaw', in Riewald, *Surprise of Excellence*, p. 132, and Will Rothenstein, *Men and Memories 1872–1900* (London: Faber and Faber, 1931), 129.

parody of a Shavian preface, and breaks it off with an echo of the
most sublime form of artistic competitiveness:

> O most presumptuous! lay aside the pipe
> Of that sweet elder shepherd.

You Never Can Tell, performed in matinée in 1900, was another
occasion to tell the theatre managers 'to run Mr Bernard Shaw for all
he is worth': 'I have never fallen into the error of overrating the public,
but I take this opportunity of insinuating to purveyors of farce and
melodrama that the public's stupidity has its limits' (*Around Theatres*,
p. 78). And again he concludes with an ironic comparison: because
the serious acting jarred with the extravagant script, he was 'kept . . .
in mind of the author's peculiar temperament and attitude, of which
the manifold contradictions are so infinitely more delightful, even
when they make us very angry, than the smooth, intelligible consist-
ency of you or me'.

But he was not consistent, even in the matter of recommending
Shaw's commercial potential. Later in 1900 he wrote that *Captain
Brassbound's Conversion* lacks the unity of form necessary to modern
drama; and 'Without unity no play can "draw the public"' (*More
Theatres*, pp. 335–8). Coolly, confidently, Max lays down the law of
dramatic aesthetics. He turns the doctrine of realism to paradoxical
use in proving that Mr Shaw is not the realist he supposes himself to
be. Shaw is 'a very rampant idealist' who believes 'that logic, not
passion, is the pivot on which the world goes round'. Max knows that
Mr Shaw would say 'Pooh' to the law of dramatic unity; but 'I have
laid it down merely because it is true . . .' In all of this, Max preempts
Shaw's manner. His criticism of Shaw's illogical form parodies
Shavian logic. The real subject of the review is not the play but the
author: 'For my part, I am quite willing to accept Mr Shaw as he is.
But then I delight in "personality". The public does not delight in it
as I do.'[27]

His delight in Shaw's personality was greatest when he could
subdue it to his own. When *Three Plays for Puritans* (1901) was
published, Shaw was forty-five years old but Beerbohm launches an
elaborate conceit that makes Shaw 'exactly connate' with himself. And

---

[27] 'Captain Brassbound's Conversion', 29 December 1900, in *More Theatres
1898–1903*, introd. Rupert Hart-Davis (London: Hart-Davis, 1969), 335–8.

he twice reminds the reader that 'I am . . . regarded as a young writer' (*Around Theatres*, pp. 118–22). He claims that his own first publication appeared in 1888 and that Shaw's first appearance as the music critic 'Corno di Bassetto' was also in 1888; 'And thus he is as young a writer as I am.' Shaw thus becomes a prodigy, like Max, but one who is threatened with physical decrepitude before he reaches artistic maturity. Max therefore advises him 'to "slow down" at once'. Shaw's earlier *Plays, Pleasant and Unpleasant* were written, on this account, when he was 'quite young and malleable'. Shaw was not yet himself in those 'serious' plays; 'I admit that his serious plays were exceedingly good *pastiches* of Ibsen', but Max is glad that Shaw has now grown up sufficiently to stop being serious and be himself.

Beerbohm's reviews went on 'wavering', praising the Shavian personality, damning Shaw's failure to understand real human beings; criticizing his dramatic construction, but criticizing audiences and managers for not recognizing Shaw's genius. Re-reviewing *Mrs Warren's Profession*, he is 'confirmed in [his] heresy that it is, as a work of art, a failure'. But 'the failure of such a man as "G.B.S."' is better than an ordinary man's success, 'even as the "failure" of a Brummell is worthier than a score of made-up bows in the windows of a hosier' (1902, *Around Theatres*, pp. 191–5). (The bizarre comparison of Shaw to Brummel suggests how deeply Shaw had entered into Beerbohm's mythology.) Or again, reviewing the published version of *Man and Superman*, he advises the reader to 'Treasure it as the most complete expression of the most distinct personality in current literature', but not as a successful play. It has a thesis but no real characters, for 'Having no sense for life, he has, necessarily, no sense for art' (1903, *Around Theatres*, pp. 268–72).

But the tone of the reviews changed in the years from 1904 to 1907, when Granville Barker's management at the Court Theatre gave Shaw his first real opportunity for professional performance. The 'Court seasons', with Shaw personally supervising Barker's productions of his plays, led Beerbohm to recant some of his earlier objections. In 1904 came *John Bull's Other Island* and with it Beerbohm's question to the critics: 'Pray, why is this not to be called a play? Why should the modern "tightness" of technique be regarded as a sacred and essential part of dramaturgy?' (*Around Theatres*, p. 354). In 1905 there was *Major Barbara*. Beerbohm thinks it is a very funny play, but he reminds his readers that 'the purport of the play is serious'—and he seems to mean by that no dispraise. The review is broadly retrospective and essentially admiring:

I well remember that when the two volumes of *Plays, Pleasant and Unpleasant* were published, and the ordinary dramatic criticisms in this Review were still signed G.B.S., I wrote here a special article in which I pointed out that the plays, delightful to the reader, would be quite impossible on the stage. This simply proved that I had not enough theatrical imagination to see the potentialities of a play through reading it in print. (*Around Theatres*, pp. 409–14)

He says he learned the same lesson when he saw performances of *Mrs Warren's Profession*, *The Devil's Disciple*, and *You Never Can Tell*. But he learned it imperfectly, and had judged *Man and Superman* 'unsuited to any stage'. Again he recants: 'When I saw it performed, I determined that I would not be caught tripping again. I found that as a piece of theatrical construction it was perfect.'

Of course that did not end the matter between them. Beerbohm damned *Misalliance* in 1910: 'It never progresses, it doesn't even resolve, it merely sprawls' (*Around Theatres*, p. 564). But he insisted repeatedly that Shaw was not only great in himself but the reason that greatness was in other playwrights. He joined the critics who praised Galsworthy's *Strife* (1909), but added:

I observe that some of the critics have been using this play as a stick to hit Mr Shaw with. Would it not have been seemlier in them to take the opportunity of acknowledging that, but for Mr Shaw's own particular genius, which has become popular despite them, such a play as *Strife* would almost certainly not have been written, and, if written, would very certainly not have been produced? (*Last Theatres*, p. 443)

A year later he quit his job at the *Saturday Review*, but he was not done with Shaw. He continued to caricature him, for exhibition and publication as well as more privately. In a diary he made the following entry for Sunday [? 4 November] 1925: 'Shaw's *Heartbreak House* vol., which I hadn't read, is rather unreadable. Same old mechanism— steel girders without even much cement to them—cold wind just whistling through and around them, and whistling rather vulgar tunes. (He has recuperated since this vol., of course. Methuselah and Joan: a great recovery.)'[28] It may have been at about this time that his then-

---

[28] In the Berg Collection, New York Public Library.

neighbour in Rapallo, Ezra Pound, memorized the following little poem. Pound recited it to an Italian professor visiting him at St Elizabeth's Hospital, and he called it 'Maxie's epitaph' on Shaw:

> I strove with all, for all were worth my strife.
>   Nature I loathed, and, next to nature, Art.
> I chilled both feet on the thin ice of Life.
>   It broke, and I emit one final fart.[29]

When Beerbohm was asked for a contribution to Shaw's ninetieth birthday book, he replied: '. . . very fond though I am of G.B.S., and immensely kind though he has always been to me, my admiration for his genius has during fifty years and more been marred for me by dissent from almost every view he holds about anything'.[30]

The reviews are not the full extent of Beerbohm's theatrical involvement. As Herbert's brother he had virtually grown up 'around theatres'. His romantic attachments were all with actresses: first, experimentally, with Cissie Loftus; then a long, uneasy quasi-engagement to Grace Conover, whom he called 'Kilseen'; then an engagement, also unannounced, to Constance Collier. Then, in 1908, we find him writing to Shaw in praise of an American actress who specialized in Ibsen:

Have you gone to see 'Rosmersholm'? If not, do so. Two years or so ago, I wrote to Mrs Shaw, telling her about Miss Florence Kahn, who was then in England . . . A true tragedian, with a quite extraordinary beauty of 'style'. Do go and see for yourself.[31]

In 1910 he married Florence Kahn and together they left the London stage.

His few efforts at playwriting were unremarkable. His adaptation of *The Happy Hypocrite* was performed (1900) as a curtain-raiser on a program with Frank Harris's *Mr and Mrs Daventry*. In 1902 he collaborated with Harris on *Caesar's Wife*, an adaptation from a French

---

[29] *Max in Verse*, ed. J. G. Riewald (Brattleboro, Vt.: Stephen Greene, 1963), 124 and 158 n.

[30] Quoted Behrman, *Portrait*, p. 22; Cecil, *Max*, p. 463.

[31] 11 February 1908, in the Taylor Collection, Princeton University. Beerbohm adds in a postscript to this letter that he has taken to sculpture: 'Tomorrow I am going to do you. Have taken to it like a duck to water. "Plasticine—the Child's Delight" is what I am working in at present. The block of marble and the chisel may come in handy later on.'

play; and with Murray Carson on a comedy, *The Fly on the Wheel*. His one-act play, *A Social Success* (published in *A Variety of Things*) was produced in 1913 by George Alexander. It is a drawing-room comedy that puts a reverse twist on the theme of *The Happy Hypocrite*: Tommy Dixon, the social success of the title, is caught cheating at cards. But Dixon is an honourable hypocrite; the cheating was just a pretence by which he hoped to free himself from the superficial world of 'society'. Society, however, refuses to ostracize him: his disgrace increases Lady Amersham's infatuation and makes him more than ever an object for Lord Amersham's patronage. The skit ends with Dixon more 'successful' and more trapped in society than ever. As Max the satirist had reason to know, society will tolerate a lot of abuse at the hands of its paid performers.

But the theatre was not his mode. The parodic impulse that drives his work is imperialistic and privatizing—a social licensing of the impulse to control and displace. The aggressiveness of the stage is by comparison a crudely open affair. In reviews he could call actors and actresses 'mimes', but on or off the stage they would insist on their recalcitrant humanity. In 1926 Constance Collier asked for permission to revive the stage version of *The Happy Hypocrite*; his response, though couched in terms of self-deprecation, is full of anxiety about losing control over his own artistic product:

The thing must be done exactly as it is—and be done only once: once will be quite enough. Also there must be inserted in the programme a separate page containing a printed note written by me. I will write this brief note and post it to you. It will be in the form of a disparagement of the worklet, and an appeal for indulgence.[32]

He sketches the costumes; writes instructions for the actors and actresses; demands a postponement for further rehearsal: 'Good and great work can survive a little off-hand treatment. But *this* thing is gimcrack, an egg-shell, a soap-bubble. And exquisiteness of presentation is the only hope for it.' But as to 'exquisiteness of presentation'— no mime could carry off Max's act as well as Max. An actual theatre was not only uncongenial but unnecessary.

As a reviewer he had met the realistic theatre's presumption that language is a transparent medium. But the parodist's world is one of

[32] 31 March 1926, in the Taylor Collection, Princeton University.

signs representing other signs. Beerbohm's criticism is often a form of parody, as (in the more usual order of things) his parody is a form of criticism. In parody the object of imitation is itself a representation already constituted in language. When Beerbohm was finished with the theatre he turned his attention to *Zuleika Dobson*, a novel which is also (to anticipate my discussion of it) a parody of a novel. F. W. Dupee writes that *Zuleika Dobson* 'is not only about "life at Oxford"; it is about literature, above all the literature of the contemporary London stage . . .' It is—to continue quoting Dupee's description of *Zuleika*— 'life at Oxford seen through the eyes of an inveterate "play-goer", some ideally demoralized veteran of the stalls'.[33]

[33] F. W. Dupee, 'Afterword', Signet Classic edition of *Zuleika Dobson* (New York: NAL, 1966); rpt. as 'Max Beerbohm and the Rigors of Fantasy', in Riewald, *Surprise of Excellence*, pp. 175–91; quotation from pp. 183–4.

5.
The Beastly Novel

Zuleika Dobson is Beerbohm's only novel and therefore his closest brush with the contradictory fate of enduring popularity. Novels are the modern mainstream. The novel tolerates any amount of authorial distinctiveness, from Henry James to Ouida, George Meredith to George Moore. The polyglot world of the novel licenses the transgression of generic boundaries. There are more or less accessible novels, more or less artful novels, but they all tell stories. Stories require readers but readers can imagine that stories do not require authors. To become present to the reader, the novelist 'intrudes' in his own narrative.

In fact, Max is felt everywhere in *Zuleika Dobson*; the story is at times almost an intrusion on him. But there is a story, too. It tells how Zuleika came to Oxford and how all the male undergraduates drowned themselves for love of her. But no one would read it for the story. The best Beerbohm readers sometimes confess impatience with *Zuleika Dobson*. Edmund Wilson asked

What is the pattern or the point of *Zuleika*? Is it satire or parody or nonsense or what? It is full of amusing things and patches of clever writing, but it also has tiresome stretches of the thought and conversation of characters who do not even have the two-dimensional kind of life—like that of the people of Congreve or Firbank—that is possible within a comic convention.[1]

Wilson's question about 'the point' is not the sort one asks about an ordinary novel, good or bad. The 'point' of a novel is its story— whatever other points it may also have. But Wilson's question is exactly the question that a reader might ask about earlier Beerbohm writing. What is the point of 'King George the Fourth'—history or satire or parody or what? What is the point of 'Diminuendo'?

Of the various generic possibilities, parody comes closest to defining

---

[1] Wilson, 'An Analysis of Max Beerbohm', in *Classics and Commercials: A Literary Chronicle of the Forties* (New York: Farrar, Straus, Giroux, 1950), 435.

the peculiar essence of *Zuleika Dobson*. Peculiar, because the distinction between novel and parody-of-a-novel is easier to sense than to define; in some of the greatest novels it disappears entirely. Mikhail Bakhtin, distinguishing novel from epic, makes the novel's omnigeneric capaciousness its defining characteristic. The novel incorporates the other forms, and parody is its instrument:

Parodic stylizations of canonized genres and styles occupy an essential place in the novel. . . . Throughout its entire history there is a consistent parodying or travestying of dominant or fashionable novels that attempt to become models for the genre. . . . This ability of the novel to criticize itself is a remarkable feature of this ever-developing genre.[2]

Tristram Shandy is a novel and also a parody of novels; so is *Ulysses*; and so are *Pale Fire*, *The Sot-Weed Factor*, *The French Lieutenant's Woman*, *Bellefleur*, *Flaubert's Parrot*, and all the works of Peter DeVries. But differences in degree do matter. *Shamela* is more parody than *Tom Jones*, and *Tom Jones* more than *Clarissa*. *Zuleika Dobson* is so thoroughly the novel-as-parody that as novel it hardly exists.

It was published in 1911 but Beerbohm had been working at it, more off than on, since 1898. And he knew that his parody could be mistaken for the thing itself. In 1904 he had written to the publisher John Lane that his work-in-progress 'is not a "novel", but frankly the work of a leisurely essayist amusing himself with a narrative idea'.[3] And in late summer of 1911, in Rapallo awaiting the book's publication, he wrote to his friend Will Rothenstein, 'If the binders and papermakers don't play me false, the book will *look* nice: not like a beastly *novel*, more like a book of essays, self-respecting and sober and ample.'[4] *Zuleika Dobson* may not look like 'a beastly *novel*', but it could not exist without a background of novels, and of a whole repertory of other narrative modes. It is Beerbohm's 'book of essays' on the art of fiction. Like his other essays, it works by simultaneously being and parodying the thing it is. The subject of the essay—'a narrative idea' or, as it turns out, the very idea of narrative—is the object of the

---

[2] Bakhtin, *The Dialogic Imagination* (Austin: Univ. of Texas Press, 1981), 6.

[3] Quoted Viscusi, 'A Dandy's Diary: The Manuscripts of Max Beerbohm's *Zuleika Dobson*', *Princeton University Library Chronicle*, 40 (1979). 238. See also J. G. Riewald, *Sir Max Beerbohm Man and Writer* ('s-Gravenhage: Martinus Nijhoff, 1953), 125–6.

[4] *Max and Will*, ed. Mary M. Lago and Karl Beckson (London: John Murray, 1975), 87.

parody. And part of its point is to create the personality of its author out of the forms of literature.

It is his most extensive exercise in false pretences. The trick begins, as his comment to Rothenstein suggests, literally with the book's appearance. Heinemann's edition is a solid-looking affair, 350 pages long. Its very solidity seems to contradict the image its author had concocted for himself in the 'nineties. *The Works* and *More* were slim volumes; their contents were like beads, always about to slip from the reader's grasp. *The Happy Hypocrite* stood categories on their heads; it mocked mockery, laughed at a lack of seriousness. For more than a decade he had been writing theatre reviews. Week by week the essays came and went, leaving traces of the image of Max. Now Max himself had disappeared to the shores of the Mediterranean. The elusiveness was in character, but the surprisingly bulky book looked like a recantation. Yet the style is unmistakably (to some readers, objection-ably) Beerbohm's. It exuberantly reenacts the paradox that mimicry can produce a distinctively personal voice. 'Never to be yourself and yet always', in Virginia Woolf's phrase: 'This is the art possessed to perfection by Mr Beerbohm'.[5] He appears by name only once, in Zuleika's remark that 'the literary flavour' of her speech 'is an unfortunate trick which I caught from a writer, a Mr Beerbohm, who once sat next to me at dinner somewhere' (p. 100). But 'the literary flavour' is pervasive, nearly overwhelming, certainly inimical to any readerly interest in the story for its own sake. Our attention is constantly drawn to Beerbohm's manipulation of received materials, from vocabulary and syntax to the larger structures of narrative.

The variety to which Edmund Wilson objects is, then, for better or worse, exactly 'the point' of *Zuleika Dobson*. Its representational techniques range from the culturally highest to the lowest; from epic digressions, Socratic dialogue, and Greek epigrams to newspaper captions, a telegram, and the dialogue of sentimental romance and stage melodrama. Beerbohm creates a world of allusions, which repeatedly frustrate the novel reader's predictable desire to go beneath the surface of the narrative into those depths where fictive characters take on a 'life' of their own. There are moments when we are drawn into the story and are privileged to participate in the emotions of the characters. But such moments tend to end abruptly with comic

---

[5] Woolf, *The Common Reader*, 1st ser. (New York: Harcourt Brace, 1925), 222.

reminders that what we think of as lifelike in the conventional novel is in fact utterly artificial. The two books in Zuleika's personal library may be taken as ludicrous icons of this fact: 'Both books were in covers of dull gold. On the back of one cover BRADSHAW, in beryls, was encrusted; on the back of the other, A.B.C. GUIDE, in amethysts, beryls, chrysoprases, and garnets' (p. 8). The railway timetables of the geographically open world are, like Oxford itself, enclosed in a world of art. Especially in the story's latter half, Beerbohm creates scenes of real emotional power—only to remind us that scenes of real emotional power are created by imitating the techniques of melodrama. He manipulates our desire to lose ourselves in the story. Repeatedly we are made aware of the characters' absurd dependence on the least reliable narrator, Max Beerbohm.

His unreliability begins with the title itself. The two parts of Zuleika's name—the exotic Persian undercut by the bathetic English—constitute a mini-mock-heroic.(The preferred pronunciation was indicated by Beerbohm in a telegram to the BBC: 'Zuleika speaker not hiker.'[6] It chimes with Lolita.) Over and over, in small details as well as in the structure of the whole, the book performs similar pratfalling stunts. Just beneath the ornate surface of the hero and heroine is a pair of ordinary people always in danger of slipping into a plausibly realistic narrative. Zuleika, 'the omnisubjugant' (p. 23), is a petulant young woman whose insecurity (she was, after all, a governess) issues in a teasingly suppressed aggressive sexuality. She is conventional in every sense of the word: her false good manners on a date are one convention, her mystical power is another. The Duke of Dorset, ostensibly an Oxford undergraduate, is more nearly a middle-aged bachelor in the embarrassing throes of belated sexual ardour. His dandiacal magnificence is even more precariously perched than Zuleika's pose as *belle dame sans merci*. He can be discomposed by the pitcher of water Zuleika pours on his rapt face, or by an epic sneeze. Much of the book's humour derives from variations on these basic techniques of burlesque. Peeping around the edges of its lushly mythic design are traces of 'a beastly *novel*' trying with comic desperation to live up to its setting.

As indeed the setting must try to live up to itself: Oxford is the perfect location for Beerbohm's comic duplicity. '*On aurait dit* a bit of

---

[6] Quoted by David Cecil, *Max* (London: Constable, 1964), p. 472.

Manchester through which Apollo had once passed' (*Works*, p. 152), was his judgment on the city in 'Diminuendo'. The opening paragraph of *Zuleika* is compounded of several types of ambiguity, the mock-heroic being one of them:

That old bell, presage of a train, had just sounded through Oxford station; and the undergraduates who were waiting there, gay figures in tweed or flannel, moved to the margin of the platform and gazed idly up the line. Young and careless, in the glow of the afternoon sunshine, they struck a sharp note of incongruity with the worn boards they stood on, with the fading signals and grey eternal walls of that antique station, which, familiar to them and insignificant, does yet whisper to the tourist the last enchantments of the Middle Age.

The incongruity (at second reading) is less between the careless youth of the undergraduates and the 'old', 'worn', 'grey eternal . . . antique station' than it is between the phoniness of the pseudo-gothic Oxford railway station and the language in which Beerbohm dresses it. Who is the joke on, in that opening paragraph? On the undergraduates, unaware of the doom approaching; on the tourist, who mistakes a Victorian imitation for medieval originality; on Matthew Arnold, whose voice is parodied by the allusion in the last line; or on the reader, whose assumption that he is in on Beerbohm's joke is baffled as the point of the joke shifts slyly throughout the paragraph?

The best mock-heroics keep their balance on either side of the hyphen, never quite allowing the mockery to dispel the heroism. The Oxford of *Zuleika Dobson* is a middle-class academic town where 'innumerable wives and daughters around the Parks [run] in and out of their little red-brick villas' (p. 95), but it is also the visionary, vaporous, moonlit scene, 'fraught . . . with most actual magic', over which the narrator floats in the beautiful set-piece of Chapter 12. Beerbohm maintains throughout the book the double vision which begins with the cultural cacophony of the heroine's Christian and family names. That elegiac interlude in Chapter 12, for instance, ends bathetically with 'the sight of Noaks' (p. 193), the dim, bespectacled, grossly shod upstairs neighbour of the Duke of Dorset. The reader can never relax into a single point of view.

The subtitle, 'An Oxford Love Story', is no more stable than the main title. *Zuleika Dobson* is a love story set in Oxford; but it is also a story about Oxford's sort of love; and it is a story about the love of

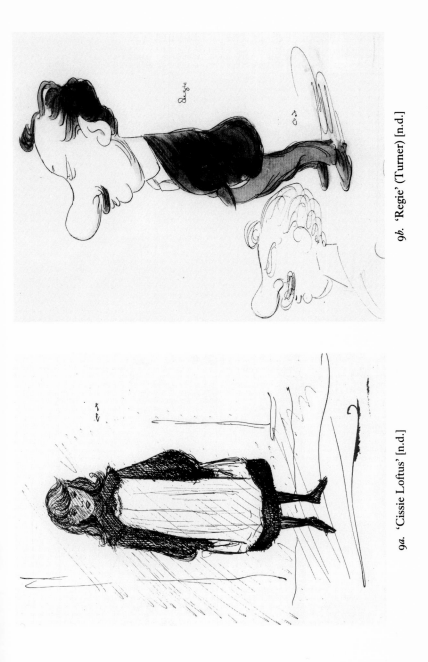

9b. 'Regie' (Turner) [n.d.]

9a. 'Cissie Loftus' [n.d.]

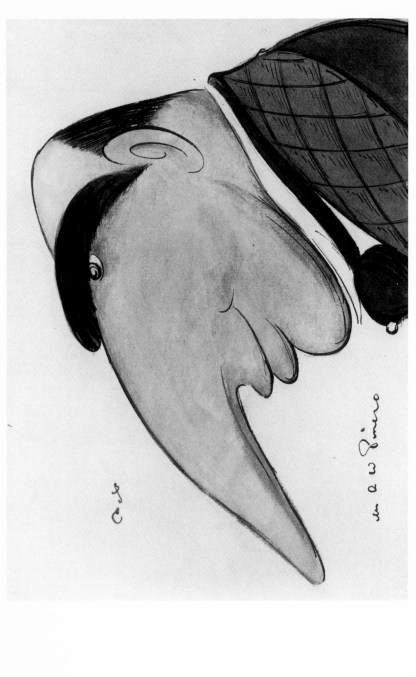

12. 'Mr. A. W. Pinero' [n.d.]

11. 'Mr Shaw's apotheosis is one of the wonders of the age. A. B. W[alkley] in *The Times* July 9, 1924: And calls himself a non-smoker!' 1924

12. 'The Iconoclast's One Friend. *A member of Mrs Warren's Profession*: "Mr. Shaw, I have long wished to meet you and grasp you by the hand . . . God bless you! . . . I understand that the Army and Navy, the Church, the Stage, the Bar, the Faculty, the Fancy, the Literary Gents, the Nobility and Gentry, and all the Royal Family, will have nothing more to do with you. Never mind! *My* house will always be open to you." (*Exit, dashing away a tear.*)' [n.d.]

THE
FINER GRAIN

BY
HENRY JAMES

METHUEN & CO. LTD.
36 ESSEX STREET W.C.
LONDON

13. 'A Memory' (James, drawn on title-page of *The Finer Grain*) 1920

14. 'How badly you wrote!/write!' (James/James in a copy of Coquelin's *Art and the Actor*) 1936

15. 'Mr. Gosse and the Rising Generation. Mr. Gosse loquitur: "Diddums!"'
[n.d.]

16. 'One fine morning, or, How they might undo me' (L. V. Harcourt, Chesterton, Kitchener, W. J. Locke, W. L. Courtney, Balfour, Curzon, Zangwill, Steer, Tonks, F. E. Smith, Lord Ribblesdale, Andrew Lang, Sargent, Walkley, Lord Burnham, Lord Spencer, Pinero, Sutro, George M... A... ld Bennett, Kipling, Rothenstein, Hall Caine, Haldane, Shaw, The Rand

Oxford. These three sorts of love are not distinct but neither are they entirely assimilable to one another. Like the main title, the idea of 'An Oxford Love Story' is, however construed, a paradox in miniature. In a theatre review in 1902—well after he had begun writing *Zuleika*—Beerbohm objected to the 'Ill-Chosen Backgrounds at Drury Lane'. The background was Oxford; and 'Poor Oxford! Will she, I wonder, ever be made successfully the background for a play, or a novel?'

What is it that prevents the serious novelist from catching the spirit of the place? I suppose it is his fear of eliminating sex. Without sex, he is sure, there can be no human interest; and so the mainspring of every Oxford story is the love of an undergraduate for Miss So-and-So; and so every Oxford story falls right out of focus. . . . But the spirit of the place, so far as the undergraduates are concerned, is still the ancient spirit of celibacy. . . . And thus, to any one who knows Oxford well, the kind of novel which has hitherto been written about Oxford rings persistently false. (*Around Theatres*, pp. 224–5)

Beerbohm first creates a technical problem for the Oxford novelist (the supposed conflict between sex and 'the ancient spirit of celibacy'), and then makes it his love story's narrative centre. 'The ancient spirit of celibacy' finds its comic apotheosis in that 'dandy without reproach', the Duke of Dorset (Zuleika's French maid mispronounces his name D'Orsay): 'He was too much concerned with his own perfection ever to think of admiring any one else. . . . he cared for his wardrobe and his toilet-table not as a means to making others admire him the more, but merely as a means through which he could intensify, a ritual in which to express and realise, his own idolatry' (p. 29). And 'Miss So-and-So' becomes the fatal Zuleika, whose less pure narcissism demands the endless tributes of her unrequited lovers.

His *donnée* would serve equally well the purposes of a Henry James or Ouida. It is potentially the stuff for an intense psychological ado or for a popular romance. Beerbohm loved James and professed, in his dedication to *More*, to love Ouida; the voices of both can be heard in the book's pastiche, and one effect of the parody is to reduce, or elevate, each to the level of the other. Zuleika cannot love any man but the one man who will not love her:

She was an empress, and all youths were her slaves. Their bondage delighted her, as I have said. But no empress who has any pride can adore one of her slaves. Whom, then, could proud Zuleika adore? . . . To be able to love once—would not that be better than all the homage in the world? But would she ever meet whom, looking up to him, she could love—she, the omnisubjugant? Would she ever, ever meet him? (pp. 22–3)

In the Duke of Dorset, a dandy so entire that all his emotion is directed to the artistic perfection of himself, Zuleika finds her immovable ideal. But only for a moment: the Duke stoops to Zuleika, and in stooping destroys her love for him. His brief defection from dandiacal sufficiency leads to the final tremendous *liebestod* when all Oxford's male undergraduates, following Dorset's lead, end the annual boat-race ('It wouldn't do', as The MacQuern tells Zuleika, 'to leave the races undecided') by drowning themselves in the Isis.

'An Oxford Love Story' is, then, in various of its constructions, a story of heterosexual desire thwarted by the more powerful appeal of narcissism. Narcissism is the Oxford kind of love; and the love of Oxford is the Oxford man's unattainable desire for the image of his own youth. 'To love oneself is the beginning of a life-long romance',[7] said Oscar Wilde. Typically Beerbohm re-ironizes an ironic Wildean dictum. In *Zuleika*'s Oxford to love oneself is the beginning of a short-lived farce.

Beerbohm makes comedy out of a situation potentially loaded with psychosexual explosiveness. But enough of the explosiveness remains so that the reader can see what is being burlesqued. The balance between the psychosexual 'reality' of the situation and its rendering in terms of literary parodies demands agility on the reader's part. Edmund Wilson objects that the characters 'do not even have the two-dimensional kind of life . . . that is possible within a comic convention', but Reggie Turner found that 'the exquisite reality of some of [the novel] occasionally makes the exquisite fantasy of the tragedy too poignant, so that my feelings are genuinely hurt'.[8] Other readers have been made uncomfortable by the language of sexual violence—of bondage and subjugation—which occasionally turns the cartoon-figure Zuleika into an almost plausible dominatrix, and which makes the Duke's sexual humiliation potentially 'poignant'. All these readers' reactions are instructive. Narcissistic love is the book's subject, and parody is its means. The parodist embraces the style of another so

[7] *Phrases and Philosophies for the Uses of the Young*, in *The Complete Works of Oscar Wilde* (London: Collins, 1948), 1206.

[8] *Letters to Reggie Turner*, ed. Rupert Hart-Davis (London: Hart-Davis, 1964), 208 n. Turner found the Katie Batch portion of the novel 'so wonderfully real that she might have stepped out of the pages of a purified George Moore.'

lovingly that it becomes himself. A parody of narcissism is itself an act of narrative perversity.

Zuleika and the Duke are fatally ill-matched by psychological and also by literary incompatibility. He comes from one mode of representation, re-represented in Beerbohm's version; she comes from another. Of the two, his mode is more obviously fantastic, less easily mistaken for 'exquisite reality'. Her mode, however, derives largely from that of the conventional modern romance (whether stage melodrama or novel) with its pretensions to realism. He is ancient, she is modern; he is epic, she is novel. Their story is the courtship of realism by heroism. It is a love story doomed for all the actors except the author.

The Duke's narcissism is expressed as a burlesque of dandyism. He masquerades, literally from head to foot, as a work of art. But his style is in unequal competition with alternative styles:

... the ducal feet were beautiful on the white bearskin hearthrug. So slim and long were they, of instep so nobly arched, that only with a pair of glazed ox-tongues on a breakfast-table were they comparable. Incomparable quite, the figure and face and vesture of him who ended in them. (p. 24)

The meatiness of that only-possible-comparison is akin in its effect to pure literary burlesque, except that the styles as well as the subject are mocked. The Latinate syntax and vocabulary allude to a style incompatible with the subject of feet, tongues, and breakfast tables. The Duke catches cold, and his epic sneezes and agitated hypochondria ruffle his perfect surface. But the descent is only from self-parody to farce.

The Duke is created largely by catalogues of his appearance, attributes, and possessions. His is the metonymic mode of the realistic novel sublimed to epic height. He is the observed of all observers including Zuleika:

Rapt, she studied every lineament of the pale and perfect face—the brow from which bronze-coloured hair rose in tiers of burnished ripples; the large steel-coloured eyes, with their carven lids; the carven nose, and the plastic lips. She noted how long and slim were his fingers, and how slender his wrists. (p. 28)

Beerbohm's actual portrait-bust of the Duke, in his privately illustrated copy of *Zuleika*, makes explicit what the verbal portrait implies:

that those carven lids and that carven nose are as unattractive as the idea of feet that look like an ox tongue on a breakfast table. For all the slenderness of his appendages, his face is gross.[9]

The Duke is most expansive in his courtship of Zuleika, which is conducted as a kind of epic Debrett. The lavish catalogue of ornaments was a decadent mode of the 'eighties and early 'nineties; borrowed from the French, it becomes native to Wilde's fairy tales and to *Dorian Gray*. The Duke's spectacular enumeration of his titles and possessions translates the style into terms that make it ridiculously liable to deflation. It is self-deflated by its excess, and punctured by Zuleika's middle-class refusal to be impressed. And it is mocked by its failure to live down to its surroundings:

Luncheon passed in almost unbroken silence. Both Zuleika and the Duke were ravenously hungry, as people always are after the stress of any great emotional crisis. Between them, they made very short work of a cold chicken, a salad, a gooseberry-tart and a Camembert. (p. 56)

Zuleika has fallen out of love with the Duke, and in this crisis 'The cold classicism of his face had been routed by the new romantic movement which had swept over his soul. He looked two or three months older than when first I showed him to my reader' (p. 56). And because the Duke's love is greater than his pride he stoops to using arguments with Zuleika:

'I, John, Albert, Edward, Claude, Orde, Angus, Tankerton,* Tanville-Tankerton,† fourteenth Duke of Dorset, Marquis of Dorset, Earl of Grove, Earl of Chastermaine, Viscount Brewsby, Baron Grove, Baron Petstrap, and Baron Wolock, in the Peerage of England, offer you my hand. Do not interrupt me. Do not toss your head.'
        *Pronounced as Tacton   †Pronounced as Tavvle-Tacton.
                                                            (p. 57)

The heroic catalogue goes on and on, a masterpiece of excess, battering ineffectually at Zuleika's indifference:

'Are you fond of horses? In my stable of pinewood and plated-silver seventy are installed. Not all of them together could vie in power with one of the meanest of my motor-cars.'

[9] *The Illustrated Zuleika Dobson*, ed. N. John Hall (New Haven, Conn.: Yale Univ. Press, 1985). This edition reproduces Beerbohm's own copy, to which he had added elaborate illustrations and decorations.

'Oh, I never go in motors', said Zuleika. 'They make one look like nothing on earth, and like everybody else.' (p. 58)

The Duke starts high and ends with the inevitable fall. Having gone through the various peerages,

'I have several titles which for the moment escape me. Baron Llffthwchl am I, and ... and ... but you can find them for yourself in Debrett. In me you behold a Prince of the Holy Roman Empire, and a Knight of the Most Noble Order of the Garter. Look well at me! I am Hereditary Comber of the Queen's Lap-Dogs. I am young. I am handsome. My temper is sweet, and my character without blemish. In fine, Miss Dobson, I am a most desirable *parti*.'

'But', said Zuleika, 'I don't love you.'

The Duke stamped his foot. 'I beg your pardon', he said hastily, 'I ought not to have done that. But—you seem to have entirely missed the point of what I am saying.'

'No, I haven't', said Zuleika.

'Then what', cried the Duke, standing over her, 'what is your reply?'

Said Zuleika, looking up at him, 'My reply is that I think you are an awful snob.' (p. 64)

Zuleika's deflation of the ducal mode is only part of the joke. The contrast in their styles is funny, but so too, here and elsewhere, is the similarity. The Duke stamps his foot as petulantly as Zuleika ever does; and she manages as good a *mot* (on the subject of motor-cars) as any of his. They could easily change parts, but his character is in danger from her realism while hers triumphs in his heroics.

The Duke's high style is mocked not only by Zuleika. Versions of realism lie everywhere in wait for it. In his courtship he recounts the fatal lore of his lineage: 'On the eve of the death of a Duke of Dorset, two black owls come and perch on the battlements. They remain there throughout the night, hooting. At dawn they fly away, none knows whither' (p. 59). But just when the Duke resolves to punish Zuleika by *not* dying for her, when he determines to teach the gods a lesson, the gods send a message:

Opening the envelope, the Duke saw that the message, with which was a prepaid form for reply, had been handed in at the Tankerton post-office. It ran thus: *Deeply regret inform your grace last night two black owls came and perched on battlements remained there through the night hooting at dawn flew away none knows whither awaiting instructions*

Jellings
(p. 217)

The telegram is one of a host of sub-literary genres, most but not all of them associated with Zuleika, that undercut the Duke's dandyism.

More effectively than the shallow waters of the Isis, Oxford's realistic setting pulls the Duke down. Mrs Batch, mother of the lovely Katie, is the Duke's landlady. (Her house seems to be located on the site of the New Bodleian Library next to the real Blackwell's bookstore.) Preparing to die, and settling his accounts with her, the Duke writes 'a testimonial to the excellence of her rooms and of her cooking . . . It had shaped itself in his mind as a short ode in Doric Greek. But, for the benefit of Mrs Batch, he chose to do a rough equivalent in English' (pp. 263–4). It was, we are told, 'one of his least happily inspired works', so only three lines are quoted of this '*Sonnet in Oxfordshire Dialect*' called 'To an Undergraduate Needing Rooms in Oxford':

> Zeek w'ere thee will in t'Univürsity,
> Lad, thee'll not vind nôr bread nôr bed that matches
> Them as thee'll vind, roight züre, at Mrs Batch's . . .

Oxford has a similarly depressing effect on the Duke's efforts to imitate other literary modes. He wants to prevent the undergraduates from following him into death. But how, from his elevated style, to address them?

Down the flight of steps from Queen's came lounging an average undergraduate.

'Mr Smith', said the Duke, 'a word with you.'

'But my name is not Smith', said the young man.

'Generically it is', replied the Duke. 'You are Smith to all intents and purposes. That, indeed, is why I address you. In making your acquaintance I make a thousand acquaintances. You are a short cut to knowledge. Tell me, do you seriously think of drowning yourself this afternoon?'

'Rather', said the undergraduate.

'A meiosis in common use, equivalent to "Yes assuredly"', murmured the Duke. 'And why', he then asked, 'do you intend to do this?'

'Why? How can you ask? Why are *you* going to do it?'

'The Socratic manner is not a game at which two can play. Please answer my question, to the best of your ability.' (p. 230)

Failing in the Socratic manner, the Duke wavers 'between the evangelic wistfulness of "Are you saved?" and the breeziness of the recruiting sergeant's "Come, you're fine upstanding young fellows.

Isn't it a pity," etc.' (p. 282). He tries preaching in the manner of John Knox. But nothing can shake the undergraduates' resolve to drown themselves for Zuleika.

Caught in the ridiculousness of his proper style, the Duke can put on no other style that is not more ridiculous. 'Nature, fashioning him, had fashioned also a pedestal for him to stand and brood on, to pose and sing on. Off that pedestal he was lost . . . For him, master-dandy, the common arena was no place' (p. 269). And Beerbohm is the parodist of the Nature that fashioned the Duke, which is the nature of the most common arena, the modern novel.

No fashioning hand is exempt from Beerbohm's parody. Dressed in the panoply of a Knight of the Garter, 'the perfect seal of his dandyism' (p. 270), the fourteenth Duke resembles 'Mr Sargent's famous portrait of him':

Forget it [the narrator tells the reader trying to remember Sargent's portrait]. Tankerton Hall is open to the public on Wednesdays. Go there, and in the dining-hall stand to study well Sir Thomas Lawrence's portrait of the eleventh Duke. Imagine a man some twenty years younger than he whom you there behold, but having some such features and some such bearing, and clad in just such robes. Sublimate the dignity of that bearing and of those features, and you will have seen the fourteenth Duke somewhat as he stood reflected in the mirror of his room. (pp. 272–3)

The failure of Sargent's portrait, compared with Sir Thomas Lawrence's portrait of the Duke's ancestor, is the occasion for a criticism of Sargent which requires the creation in Beerbohm's words of the prototypical Sargent portrait:

Marvellous, I grant you, are those passes of the swirling brush by which the velvet of the mantle is rendered—passes so light and seemingly so fortuitous, yet, seen at the right distance, so absolute in their power to create an illusion of the actual velvet. Sheen of white satin and silk, glint of gold, glitter of diamonds—never were such things caught by surer hand obedient to more voracious eye. Yes, all the spendid surface of everything is there. Yet must you not look. The soul is not there. An expensive, very new costume is there, but no evocation of the high antique things it stands for; whereas by the Duke it was just these things that were evoked to make an aura round him, a warm symbolic glow sharpening the outlines of his own particular magnificence. Reflecting him, the mirror reflected, in due subordination, the history of England. There is nothing of that on Mr Sargent's canvas. Obtruded instead

is the astounding slickness of Mr Sargent's technique: not the sitter, but the
painter, is master here. (p. 273)

The painter whose technique is obtruded here is Max Beerbohm.
The passage of pure Sargent is pure Max. He catches the surface and
soul of a Sargent portrait in order to give us the surface and 'warm
symbolic glow' of his character, the Duke, whose existence is even
more tenuous than that of the imaginary portrait.

Tenuous, and threatened by all the modes of representation that
mock his epic pose. Even in the Sargent portrait 'there is . . . a hint of
something like mockery—unintentional, I am sure, but to a sensitive
eye discernible. And—but it is clumsy of me to be reminding you of
the very picture I would have you forget' (pp. 273–4). The Duke
shakes off a moment of self-doubt and determines to be true to
himself in death: 'A dandy he had lived. In the full pomp and radiance
of his dandyism he would die' (p. 274). Hence the regalia of a Knight
of the Garter: 'Well, what he loved best he could carry with him to
the very end; and in death they would not be divided' (p. 274). The
line recalls the often-recalled epitaph of Saul and Jonathan. It had
high literary associations: Pater used it to retell the story of *Amis and
Amile*, a 'monkish miracle of earthly comradeship, more faithful unto
death—"For, as God had united them in their lives in one accord, so
they were not divided in their death"'.[10] But it had a low life too: the
epitaph often fed the omnivorous sentimentalism of popular fiction,
homoerotic and otherwise. Ouida was especially fond of the line; it is
her valediction on the little boy and his dog in the tear-jerking novella
'A Dog of Flanders':

All their lives they had been together, and in their deaths they were not
divided; for when they were found the arms of the boy were folded too closely
around the dog to be severed without violence, and the people of their little
village, contrite and ashamed, implored a special grace for them, and, making
them one grave, laid them to rest there side by side—forever.[11]

[10] Walter Pater, *The Renaissance* ('Two French Stories'), in *Walter Pater: Three Major
Texts*, ed. William E. Buckler (New York and London: New York Univ. Press, 1986),
91.
    [11] *A Leaf in the Storm; A Dog of Flanders, and Other Stories* (Leipzig: Tauchnitz, 1872),
71. The same allusion serves for mother and son in 'A Leaf in the Storm': 'The death
was fierce but swift, and even in death she and the one whom she had loved and reared
were not divided' (p. 298).

In popular fiction, anything and anything else can in death be not divided—a little boy and his dog, or the Duke of Dorset and his dandyism. The biblical echo therefore echoes its own parodies, redoubled on the head of the Duke.

The Duke is hopeless in the democratic, polyglot world of the novel-as-parody. As he passes through Radcliffe Square on his way to die, visiting aunts and sisters stare and an undergraduate named Harold suffers agonies of embarrassment. The very stones of Oxford rebuke his high style: at the entrance to the Bodleian, pausing in full Garter regalia, the Duke feels 'for the last time the vague thrill he had always felt at sight of the small and devious portal ... "How deep, how perfect, the effect made here by refusal to make any effect whatsoever!" thought the Duke. Perhaps, after all ... but no: one could lay down no general rule. He flung his mantle a little wider from his breast, and proceeded into Radcliffe Square' (pp. 276–7).[12]

But all styles become Zuleika. She can rise to the height of her exotic forename and descend comfortably to 'Miss Dobson'. She is as adaptable as the novel itself is; she swims through the parodies that drown the Duke. Her triumphal tour of America, for instance, is recorded as a bunch of newspaper clippings:

All the stops of that 'mighty organ, many-piped', the New York press, were pulled out simultaneously, as far as they could be pulled, in Zuleika's honour. She delighted in the din. She read every line that was printed about her, tasting her triumph as she had never tasted it before. And how she revelled in the Brobdingnagian drawings of her, which, printed in nineteen colours, towered between the columns or sprawled across them! (p. 18)

It is not only Zuleika who revels 'in the Brobdingnagian drawings': Beerbohm translates the newspapers' visual effects into language that forwards his narrative while also serving as virtuosic self-display:

There she was, measuring herself back to back with the Statue of Liberty; scudding through the firmament on a comet, whilst a crowd of tiny men in evening-dress stared up at her from the terrestrial globe; peering through a microscope held by cupid over a diminutive Uncle Sam; teaching the

---

[12] The obscure old entrance to the Bodleian has been superseded by a grand entrance through the former School of Theology. The new entrance is much more the sort of thing tourists expect.

American Eagle to stand on its head; and doing a hundred-and-one other things—whatever suggested itself to the fancy of native art. (p. 19)

The passage continues on with the joy of comic invention, well beyond the requirements of a plot. It ends ('At present she was, as I have said, "resting"') only to make room for the invention of other narrative ideas—in this case, for a flight in the style of Greek pastoral ('She was as pure as that young shepherdess Marcella, who, all unguarded, roved the mountains and was by all the youths adored' [p. 20]).

Zuleika is the very soul of popular fiction. She is an orphan and she was a governess. She is sexually irresistible. By profession she is a magician. She is not a good magician; anyone can see through her corny tricks—but her failure to illude only makes her art more potent because it makes her seem to her audience more vulnerable, more pathetic, and therefore more desirable. Zuleika makes good reading: she is all potential, all deceit, and like the page on which she is written she is eternally available and never to be had.

Unlike the epical Duke, Zuleika knows all the novelistic tricks. Her first sleight of hand is simply to seem to be. Mikhail Bakhtin, tracing the novel's derivation from 'parodying-travestying' modes of writing, notices that 'Language in the novel not only represents, but itself serves as the object of representation'.[13] What we see in Beerbohm's conjuration of Zuleika are the various languages, now made 'the object of representation', that give us the illusion of Zuleika. She manifests herself as a sort of disappearing act; what her disappearance reveals is the language itself, which is the real object represented. The trick is most apparent when it pretends to hide itself. Thus the Duke asks Zuleika whether she has not 'dipped into the Greek pastoral poets, nor sampled the Elizabethan sonneteers?' 'No, never', says Zuleika. 'You will think me lamentably crude: my experience of life has been drawn from life itself.' The claim is a conventional claim of realism; it is immediately exposed by her admission that the 'literary flavour' of her speech 'is an unfortunate trick which I caught from a writer, a Mr Beerbohm ...' (p. 100). Apart from that 'flavour' and that 'trick', there is no Zuleika.

This was William Empson's point about Beerbohm's style. Empson analyses the description beginning 'Zuleika was not strictly beautiful' and ending 'She had no waist to speak of', where 'we are left in doubt

[13] Bakhtin, *Dialogic Imagination*, p. 49.

whether ... her beauty was unique and did not depend on the conventional details, or that these parts of her body were, in fact, not good enough to be worth mentioning, or that they were intensely and fashionably small':

This contradiction as to the apparent subject of the statement seems very complete: it is not obvious what we are meant to believe at the end of it. But it cannot be said to represent a conflict in the author's mind; the contradiction removes the reader from the apparent subject to the real one, and the chief 'meaning' of the paragraph, apart from the criticism in its parody, is 'believe in my story; we have to take it sufficiently seriously to keep it going.' I hope [Empson concludes] I need not apologise, after this example, for including Mr Beerbohm among the poets.[14]

We watch a similar trick when Zuleika proceeds in triumph to the boat race:

She swept among them. Her own intrinsic radiance was not all that flashed from her. She was a moving reflector and refractor of all the rays of all the eyes that mankind had turned on her. Her mien told the story of her days. Bright eyes, light feet—she trod erect from a vista whose glare was dazzling to all beholders. She swept among them, a miracle, overwhelming, breath-bereaving. Nothing at all like her had ever been seen in Oxford. (p. 94)

The literal truth of the conclusion ('Nothing at all like her had ever been seen in Oxford') caps a paragraph full of the illusion of substance. Zuleika, the reflector and refractor, exists by being seen; what the beholder causes to exist 'told the story of her days'. The brightness and lightness of her putative being is indistinct in the dazzling glare of the vista. At the same instant she yields herself and takes herself away, 'a miracle, overwhelming, breath-bereaving'. The hyperbole creates absence: Zuleika disappears in the language that describes her. But Beerbohm's act continues: the next paragraph begins with a sentence that ostensibly brings us back to earth—'Mainly architectural, the beauties of Oxford'—while actually bringing us back to Max.

The Duke always sounds like literature. Zuleika reveals her novelistic soul by imitating the sounds of life as they are conventionally supposed to sound. Thus their dialogue frequently creates the two halves of mock-heroic, with her realistic style comically undercutting his heroic:

[14] Empson, *Seven Types of Ambiguity*, 3rd ed. (London: Chatto and Windus, 1963), p. 177.

'When I shall have sunk forever beneath these waters whose supposed purpose here this afternoon is but that they be ploughed by the blades of these young oarsmen, will there be struck from that flint, your heart, some late and momentary spark of pity for me?'

'Why of course, of *course!*' babbled Zuleika, with clasped hands and dazzling eyes. 'But', she curbed herself, 'it is—it would—oh, you mustn't *think* of it! I couldn't allow it! I—I should never forgive myself!' (p. 106)

Zuleika 'babbles' elsewhere in the story. When she learns that the other undergraduates intend to imitate the Duke and die for her, 'Zuleika babbled like a child going to a juvenile party' (p. 158). To cap her great success (and outdo the Duke, whose performance of the *Marche Funèbre* has just been applauded by the shades of Chopin and Georges Sand), Zuleika will perform her magic-show. The MacQuern will carry her box of tricks and the Duke will be her announcer. She sees the chance that a group of doomed lovers may soon grow to a multitude: 'With such hopes dimly whirling in the recesses of her soul, her beautiful red lips babbled' (p. 158).[15]

Those babbling lips mimic the sounds of novelistic life. They manage also, however, to speak for Max Beerbohm. Realism's babble is repeatedly infiltrated by the narrator's knowingness. The results can be strange. Playing the Duke off against his Celtic friend The MacQuern, '*You*, dear Mr MacQuern—' Zuleika begins, then breaks off and continues: 'does one call you "Mr"? "The" would sound so odd in the vocative. And I can't very well call you "MacQuern"—*you* don't think me unkind, do you?' (p. 157). The sliding from a social concern about the proper mode of address into a fastidious concern for Latin grammar and back into the style of the vamp is a trick from Max's Wildean period. '"The poor darlings!" murmured Zukeika', seeing the overflow crowd outside the hall (p. 159): the perfect novelistic *femme fatale* sounds like a female impersonator. She is, in fact, like Max, a mimetic marvel.

So, at her most intense, threatened with the possibility that the Duke will *not* kill himself for her, Zuleika speaks with a sincerity so deep that it can only have been borrowed from the contemporary

[15] In his own illustrated copy, Beerbohm drew a picture of those babbling lips—too conventionally red, perfectly toothed, mockingly laughing—at the end of Chapter 9; and at the following chapter head he drew a picture of Zuleika with her 'magic' barber's pole in her mouth.

stage. At the end of Chapter 15 she makes the appropriate melodramatic entrance to the Duke:

As he threw open the door to his sitting-room, he was aware of a rustle, a rush, a cry. In another instant, he was aware of Zuleika Dobson at his feet, at his knees, clasping him to her, sobbing, laughing, sobbing. (p. 239)

And in Chapter 16 she continues in perfect Pinerorobertsonian vein:

'Oh John', she cried, turning to him and falling again to her knees, 'I do so want to forget what I have been. I want to atone. You think you can drive me out of your life. You cannot, darling—since you won't kill me. Always I shall follow you on my knees, thus.' (p. 244)

Beerbohm had objected that Henry James's characters failed on the stage because they sounded just like Henry James's characters on the page. Zuleika convincingly imitates the sounds of a good novelistic idea translated into bad stage dialogue. The Duke tells her to use her sense of proportion:

'If I do that', she said after a pause, 'you may not be pleased with the issue. I may find that whereas yesterday I was great in my sinfulness, and to-day am great in my love, you, in your hate of me, are small. I may find that what I had taken to be a great indifference is nothing but a small hate. . . . Ah, I have wounded you? Forgive me, a weak woman, talking at random in her wretchedness. Oh, John, John, if I thought you small, my love would but take on the crown of pity. Don't forbid me to call you John. I looked you up in Debrett while I was waiting for you. That seemed to bring you nearer to me.' (p. 246)

And so on, in a parody that works, as Beerbohm's best formal parodies do, not only by making us laugh at the thing parodied but also by giving us the parodied thing's proper pleasures. This love-taking-on-the-crown-of-pity business is melodrama confessing itself, yet for a moment a reader may be threatened, as Reggie Turner was, by the 'exquisite reality' of the fantastic situation.

In the second half of the book, especially, there are scenes which have an oddly embarrassing sexual intensity. The intensity is odd because these scenes are also very funny. The embarrassment comes from being a sophisticated reader indulging in the most absurdly melodramatic pleasures: our readerly susceptibility exposes us to Beerbohm's satire. These scenes tend to be heavy with the language of submission and shame. Chapter 16 begins with Zuleika on her knees, stroking the carpet, crooning 'Aye, happy the very woman that wove the threads that are trod by the feet of my beloved master. But hark! he bids his slave rise and stand before him!' (p. 241). Chapter 22 is the high, or low, point in that vein. The dim Noakes, too cowardly to kill himself for Zuleika, is Oxford's sole surviving male undergraduate. Katie Batch, the landlady's lovely daughter, mistakes his survival for self-sufficient strength: 'And impulsively she abased herself, kneeling at his feet as at the great double altar of some dark new faith' (p. 317). Their plans for marriage are interrupted by the appearance of a cloaked woman, the miserable Zuleika, searching the desolate city for a man to love. She too mistakes the embarrassed little man's cowardice for mastery: '"Hush", she cried, "man of my greater, my deeper and nobler need! Oh hush, ideal which not consciously I was out for to-night—ideal vouchsafed to me by a crowning mercy! I sought a lover, I find a master"' (p. 325). Zuleika bows to the will of her master and bids him chasten her with his tongue—while Noakes, suspecting irony, tries desperately to excuse himself. The spurned Katie enters, and she too contributes to Zuleika's abasement; she throws Noakes's engagement ring down: 'Crawl for it. . . . Grovel for it, Miss Dobson.' Both women now realize that they have been mistaken about Noakes, and joined by Mrs Batch and her son Clarence they turn on him, all crying 'Shame!' Young Clarence rushes up to the room to thrash Noakes, but Noakes has climbed onto the window-sill; and then:

Down on the road without, not yet looked at but by the steadfast eyes of the Emperors, the last of the undergraduates lay dead; and fleet-footed Zuleika, with her fingers still pressed to her ears, had taken full toll now. (p. 329)

The sadomasochistic vocabulary is a parody that has some of the real thing's power to make a reader queasy. *Zuleika Dobson* is not in fact an easy book to read; part of the difficulty comes in negotiating the distance between the elegant surface and the substrate of narcissism destructively turned toward dominance and shame. Our own act of reading implicates us in the characters' fantastic problem. Like Zuleika herself, *Zuleika Dobson* makes its readers desire what they can never possess. It illudes us with our own desiring for a reality beneath its narrative surface. Yet Zuleika, whom all men love, needs to abase herself before the man who is unmoved by her. She seeks the lover/reader who will know her as fiction. But the embrace of such a lover would be her death: like the novel, she lives as illusion, and end-lessly—or at least as far as Cambridge—she will find new readers to drown in her mirroring depths.

Beerbohm began *Zuleika Dobson* as early as 1898, the year he started regular work on the *Saturday Review*. Not much got done; the extant manuscripts suggest that only four chapters existed by 1904.[16] He made a more concerted effort around 1904, when he wrote to John Lane describing the book as 'the work of a leisurely essayist amusing himself with a narrative idea'. Everything from chapter 9 through the end seems then to have been written between 1908 and 1911, when he was planning marriage and right after the move to Rapallo. And from Rapallo in 1911 he wrote to Will Rothenstein, 'I am really very glad I found it impossible to go on writing the book in London years ago. I have developed since then; and the book wouldn't have had the quality it has now. It really is a rather beautiful piece of work . . .'[17]

The change in the latter half of the book is most evident in the narrator's greater prominence. Not that he had anywhere been effaced. He constantly risks stylistic excess, and usually gets away with it. 'He becomes', as Robert Viscusi points out, 'the central character in the work'; in the first half he achieves that centrality especially through the narrative excess of the digressions—about the history of Judas College, the origins of the Junta, the love of the Duke's ancestor for a dairy-maid, and so on.[18] He obtrudes himself in the supernatural 'machinery'—the pearls that change colour in sympathy with the characters' passions, the chorus of Emperors' busts outside the Sheldonian—which keeps the author as prominent as his characters. He is there in the virtuosic mimicking of the modes of representation from newspaper captions through portrait painting. But these are all more-or-less indirect ways of grabbing attention compared to what goes on in the latter half of the book. There, Max achieves for himself the seductively elusive presence of a Zuleika Dobson.

'A text', says Roland Barthes, 'is made up of multiple writings, drawn from many cultures and entering into mutual relations of dialogue, parody, contestation'. It is, Barthes says, 'a multi-dimensional space in which a variety of writings, none of them original,

[16] The MSS are in the Taylor Collection at Princeton University.
[17] 28 August 1911, in *Max and Will*, p. 87.
[18] Viscusi, 'A Dandy's Diary', p. 248.

blend and clash. The text is a tissue of quotations drawn from innumerable centres of culture.'[19] This is a reasonable description of *Zuleika Dobson* and, insofar as *Zuleika Dobson* is an effective parody of the novel, an accurate description of the genre generally. But it would require a caricature by Max to explicate Barthes' conclusion. From the belatedness of all efforts to be original Barthes concludes that the author is dead. The defunct author is now, at best, a copyist of what culture dictates.

The author in *Zuleika Dobson* jauntily refutes the rumour of his death. But the comedy of Max's presence in his text's pastiche is not unequivocally reassuring. He manifests himself as a wraith-like vaporous being, literally a kind of ghost. His narrative powers of 'invisibility, inevitability, and psychic penetration, with a flawless memory thrown in' were granted him by Zeus as a boon to Clio, the muse of history. Clio, whose servant Max is, had grown restive with history's limitations: 'One Sunday afternoon—the day before that very Monday on which this narrative opens—it occurred to her how fine a thing history might be if the historian had the novelist's privileges' (p. 182). She selected Max 'because she knew me to be honest, sober, and capable, and no stranger to Oxford' (p. 183). Zeus, 'with a majesty of gesture which I shall never forget', endowed him with the novelist's gifts, and thus Max found himself on the platform of Oxford station: 'It was fun to float all unseen, to float all unhampered by any corporeal nonsense, up and down the platform' (p. 184).

The account of Max's dealings with Clio and Zeus is a preposterous version of the fiction-writer's conventional claim to be a recorder of historical actuality. This mock-effort to illude actually draws more indelibly the line between fiction and reality. Claiming to be Clio's servant, Max fictionalizes even his own historicity as narrator.[20] The myth of the historian's acquisition of novelistic powers occurs in

[19] Barthes, 'The Death of the Author', in *Image-Music-Text*, trans. Stephen Heath (New York: Hill and Wang, 1977), 148, 146.

[20] Cf. John Felstiner, *The Lies of Art: Max Beerbohm's Parody and Caricature* (New York: Knopf, 1972), 177: '*Zuleika Dobson* stands between Beerbohm's *Yellow Book* period, with its quasi-historical essays "George IV" and "1880," and his mature work, *The Mirror of the Past* and *Seven Men*, in which he mediates as a character between the given and the improbable. In his novel he claims to fall for the elaborate pageant of Dorset and Zuleika. He calls attention to the reality of his story ('They are still vivid to us, those headlines') instead of tacitly taking it for granted as normal fiction does. An artifice like this tends to prejudice the credibility of the story, and at the same time to rediscover the assumptions behind any technique in literature.'

Chapters 11 and 12, midway through the twenty-four chapters that give the book its epically correct dimensions. It leads to the book's most splendid set piece, Max's nostalgic overview of Oxford. The historian-cum-novelist floats through the closed doors of his old college room, up through the floor, then over Merton Wall to Christ Church Meadow; higher he floats until Oxford lies beneath him 'like a map in grey and black and silver' (p. 191):

All that I had known only as great single things I saw now outspread in apposition, and tiny; tiny symbols, as it were, of themselves, greatly symbolising their oneness. There they lay, these multitudinous and disparate quadrangles, all their rivalries merged in the making of a great catholic pattern. And the roofs of the buildings around them seemed level with their lawns. No higher the roofs of the very towers. Up from their tiny segment of the earth's spinning surface they stood negligible beneath infinity. (p. 191)

Oxford, the site of his love story, is now explicitly a set of signs or symbols. The whole section, with all its absurdity, is genuinely moving, not least because 'Oxford' at its most intensely realised is expressly a fiction, a representation, a word:

. . . there is nothing in England to be matched with what lurks in the vapours of these meadows, and in the shadows of these spires—that mysterious, inenubilable spirit, spirit of Oxford. Oxford! The very sight of the word printed or sound of it spoken, is fraught for me with the most actual magic. (p. 191)

Like Zuleika's less actual magic, Oxford's—and the novel's—requires an audience willing to be illuded by what it knows to be illusory. ('Inenubilable', as far as I can make out, means 'incapable of being made clear or uncloudy'.)

This fantastic middle of the book, populated by Clio, Zeus, and the dematerialized Max, is immediately framed by its most novelistically intense sections. This is the part of the book, beginning at Chapter 9, that Beerbohm wrote just during and after the move to Rapallo. The earlier half of the book had been written under the aegis of Oscar Wilde, but the latter half under the oddly combined aegis of Ouida and Henry James: it is less disdainful of the conditions under which 'a beastly *novel*' exists, and for that reason it is also a better parody of the turn-of-the-century psychological novel. As in 'The Mote in the Middle Distance', James's intense psychologism is invested in an absurd situation; but the intensity redeems the situation as much as the situation burlesques the intensity. In the process, psychological realism is revealed as near kin, or even another name for, popular romance. Realism and fantasy are amusingly, disquietingly married in Max's narration.

In Chapter 9, the Duke performs Chopin's *Marche Funèbre* in the Judas College Hall. The narrative atmosphere, like the Chopin music, could make one in love with death—except that it is shot through with nicely deflationary touches. These include the satire on mob-psychology ('You cannot make a man by standing a sheep on its hind-legs. But by standing a flock of sheep in that position you can make a crowd of men' [pp. 150–1]), and the narrator's hesitance between the modes of romance and realism ('The moon, like a gardenia in the night's button-hole—but no! why should a writer never be able to mention the moon without likening her to something else—something to which she bears not the faintest resemblance?' [p. 152]). Zuleika Dobson, like her own name, embodies this odd mix. She is an annoyingly prosaic babbler, repeatedly telling people 'that she knew nothing about music really, but that she knew what she liked' (p. 150), yet transfigured by the wan light of the moon, 'how nobly like the Tragic Muse' (p. 153). To compete with the Duke's performance, she decides to perform her magic-show on the moonlit lawn of Salt Cellar. She is crude and inept; her patter— 'Well, this is rather queer!'—is dreadful. Yet it is indeed a magic-show, as engaging to its willingly beguiled audience of lovers as any manipulative romantic novel is to its readers. Max is faithful to Clio: he tells the historical truth that 'the climax of Zuleika's entertainment was only that dismal affair, the Magic Canister' (p. 166). But: 'At a distance, she might have been a wraith; or a breeze made visible; a vagrom breeze, warm and delicate, and in league with death' (p. 164).

Along with the obvious joke that the Tragic Muse is a silly vamp, the doubleness creates a situation at least potentially moving and actually complex. The characters' incompetence at inhabiting their own fictive forms is comic—we keep seeing the prissy bachelor behind the Duke's magnificent dandy, and the neurotic tease behind Zuleika's *femme fatale*—but it also figures as a psychological problem. Chapter 10 builds in sexual tension. The Duke, forced to watch Zuleika's magic-show, experiences the masochistic component of his love: 'He thrilled with that intense anxiety which comes to a man when he sees his beloved offering to the public an exhibition of her skill, be it in singing, acting, dancing, or any other art' (p. 162). Helplessly, he must stand and watch as Zuleika incompetently displays herself to the 'great dense semicircle' of young men disposed around her (p. 162). 'It was especially her jokes that now sent shudders up the spine of her lover, and brought tears to his eyes, and kept him in a state of terror as to what she would say next' (p. 163). The impassive dandy is caught in an agony of contradictory emotions: 'Bitter his heart was, but only against the mob she wooed, not against her for wooing it. She was cruel? All goddesses are that. She was demeaning herself? His soul welled up anew in pity, in passion' (pp. 164–5).

The Duke's anxiety at Zuleika's performance has the intensity of a voyeuristic dream, or of one's earliest, most engrossing experiences as a reader of fiction. It leads him to his third great mistake: the first was falling in love with Zuleika, and thereby losing her; the second was promising to die for her; the third is trying to win her love and live. He will fight for Zuleika, fight with Zuleika; he will have her, not as an ungraspable fiction but as a woman. Nowhere in the book is he more magnificent, and more laughable, than here at the end of chapter 10; nowhere is he more stickily enmeshed in the traces of fictional being than when he tries to break free.

He struggles with his rival, The MacQuern, for possession of Zuleika's casket of tricks. The imminence of battle thrills Zuleika, who wants to create the appropriately artistic conditions: 'It occurred to her—a vague memory of some play or picture—that she ought to be holding aloft a candelabra of lit tapers; no, that was only done indoors, and in the eighteenth century. Ought one to hold a sponge?' (p. 172). The Scotsman yields, 'Cowed by something daemonic in the will-power pitted against his . . .' And the Duke, in the excitement of his masculine pride ('Does the stag in his hour of victory need a diploma from the hind?'), feels himself in a new relationship with Zuleika:

. . . with a pang he remembered his abject devotion to her. Abject no longer though! The victory he had just won restored his manhood, his sense of supremacy among his fellows. He loved this woman on equal terms. She was transcendent? So was he, Dorset. To-night the world had on its moonlit surface two great ornaments—Zuleika and himself. Neither of the pair could be replaced. Was one of them to be shattered? Life and love were good. He had been mad to think of dying. (pp. 172–3)

Dying for love is a motif in art; living belongs to, well, life—which explains why Zuleika will have nothing to do with it.

In fact, however, the Duke's idea of life is as deeply sunk in fiction as was his idea of a *liebestod*. Zuleika and the Duke have crossed Front Quad and reached her stairway. She makes him put her box down inside the door—a good thing, since holding it 'was fatal to self-expression . . . the soul needs gesture; and the Duke's first gesture now was to seize Zuleika's hands in his':

She was too startled to move. 'Zuleika!' he whispered. She was too angry to speak, but with a sudden twist she freed her wrists and darted back.

He laughed. 'You are afraid of me. You are afraid to let me kiss you, because you are afraid of loving me. This afternoon—here—I all but kissed you. I mistook you for Death. I was enamoured of Death. I was a fool. That is what *you* are, you incomparable darling: you are a fool. You are afraid of life. I am not. I love life. I am going to live for you, do you hear?'

She stood with her back to the postern. Anger in her eyes had given place to scorn. 'You mean', she said, 'that you go back on your promise?'

'You will release me from it.'

'You mean you are afraid to die?'

'You will not be guilty of my death. You love me.'

'Good night, you miserable coward.' She stepped back through the postern.

'Don't, Zuleika! Miss Dobson, don't! Pull yourself together! Reflect! I implore you . . .' (pp. 174–5)

Trying to break from romance into realism, the Duke can do no better than borrow Zuleika's own accents ('you incomparable darling . . . Pull yourself together!'). The narrator takes the novelistic privilege of moving between centres of consciousness. First, he gives us the Duke: 'And he hadn't even kissed her! That was his first thought. He ground his heel in the gravel.' Then Zuleika: 'And he had hurt her wrists! This was Zuleika's first thought, as she came into her bedroom' (p. 175). In the bedroom, the narration moves into free indirect style; joint property of narrator and character, it is a style which gives the illusion of innerness. Appalled by the Duke's assault ('Yes, there were two red marks where he had held her'), Zuleika struggles to preserve her status as ungraspable fantasy, while Beerbohm presents that struggle in a narrative style which conventionally illudes the reader with a character's actuality:

No man had ever dared to lay hands on her. With a sense of contamination, she proceeded to wash her hands thoroughly with soap and water. From time to time such words as 'cad' and 'beast' came through her teeth.

She dried her hands and flung herself into a chair, arose and went pacing the room. So this was the end of her great night! What had she done to deserve it? How had he dared?

There was a sound as of rain against the window. She was glad. The night needed cleansing.

He had told her she was afraid of life. Life!—to have herself caressed by *him*; humbly to devote herself to being humbly doted on; to be the slave of a slave; to swim in a private pond of treacle—ugh! If the thought weren't so cloying and degrading, it would be laughable. (p. 175)

Zuleika's disgust at the Duke's handling has a barely repressed sexual edge that would do honour to James's heroine Isabel Archer, in *Portrait of a Lady*; it brings to mind the nervous collapses she suffers from the physical demands of Caspar Goodwood. For an instant, the reader caught in the psychologism of the free indirect narration is tempted to forget the absurdity of the situation—a fictional figure protesting the effort of another fictional figure to give it 'life'.

But Zuleika is not to be had, by Duke nor reader. The scene segues into one of the book's moments of perfect farce as Zuleika shows that she is as much kin to Chaucer's Alisoun as to any woman in modern fiction:

She thrust her head out [the window] again. 'Are you there?' she whispered.

'Yes, yes. I knew you would come.'

'Wait a moment, wait!'

The water-jug stood where she had left it, on the floor by the wash-stand. It was almost full, rather heavy. She bore it steadily to the window, and looked out.

'Come a little nearer!' she whispered.

The upturned and moonlit face obeyed her. She saw its lips forming the word 'Zuleika'. She took careful aim.

Full on the face crashed the cascade of moonlit water, shooting out on all sides like the petals of some great silver anemone. (p. 176)

Zuleika's farcical action shatters the Duke's preposterous attempt to become psychologically realistic or, in novelistic terms, to 'live'. She puts him back where he belongs—and to confirm his position the telegram arrives from Tankerton Hall telling him that the fatal owls have hooted and flown away 'none knows whither'. He is doomed to his place in the story. In the following two chapters, Max takes centre stage. He tells us about his relation to Clio and spends an hour floating around Oxford. The hour is intended to give the Duke a decent interval in which to recompose himself: Max feigns a more-than-Jamesian respect for the independent existence of a character whose fate is dictated by the gods of the '*beastly* novel'.

Among the last things Beerbohm ever wrote—possibly the last—is the brief BBC talk he called, simply, 'An Incident' (*Mainly on the Air*, pp. 131–3). In it he tells about a meeting with Henry James. It has special poignancy as his unintended valedictory. And it makes, I think, a fitting coda to my discussion of *Zuleika Dobson*, and an introduction to a discussion of parody.

He says that the incident, which occurred 'in the early Spring of (I think) the year 1906', seemed to him afterwards 'strangely and exactly like the basis of a short story written by [James] himself—one of the many stories he wrote on the theme of an elderly and very eminent great writer in relation to an earnest young admirer and disciple'. Max was on his way to his club, the Savile, in Piccadilly, where he intended to read a story James had published in a new monthly review. Hurrying against the wind, 'I encountered a slowly ascending figure that seemed to me vaguely familiar. I must explain [Beerbohm continues] that hitherto it was only in drawing-rooms and dining-rooms that I had seen Henry James, and that his magnificently massive and shapely brow was what had always impressed me there.' That brow was now covered by a hat. James, however, recognized Beerbohm, 'and he accosted me in the deeply ruminating manner that was his'. He had just come up to London from Rye. He asked whether there were any new exhibitions of pictures to see. Beerbohm recommended the one at the Grafton Gallery, but when James, 'with much circumlocution', asked Beerbohm to accompany him there, Beerbohm to his great surprise heard himself saying 'Well, I'm afraid I can't. I have to be in Kensington at half-past three'.

'What had prompted me to tell that fib?' The answer, of course, is his impatience to be reading James's story:

And here I was now at the Savile, reading it. It was, of course, a very good story, and yet, from time time, I found my mind wandering away from it. It was not so characteristic, not so intensely Jamesian a story as James would have founded on the theme of what had just been happening between us— the theme of a disciple loyally—or unloyally?—preferring the Master's work to the Master.

We may have expected the opposition between 'Master's work' and 'Master'; it is turned into a conundrum by the question of loyalty versus disloyalty and also by the difficulty in saying whether this is an instance of life imitating art (the meeting is like a James story) or art feebly imitating life (the James story is not as intensely Jamesian as the incident was).

The story was 'The Velvet Glove'. It adds a related series of opposing pairs to the oppositions between author and work, life and art, inherent in Beerbohm's own anecdote: John Berridge is a playwright who has had a belated success with a play called *The Heart of Gold*. At a grand party in Paris he sees the beautiful Princess and her handsome Prince. Berridge imagines she is one of the Olympians who lives a life of pure Romance. The prince urges Berridge to read a new novel called *The Top of the Tree*, by one Amy Evans—and eventually reveals that the Princess *is* 'Amy Evans'. She offers Berridge a ride home from the party. In her carriage she asks him to write a preface to puff her novel. He refuses not only to write the preface but ever to see her again:

'Then you don't like me—' was the marvellous sound from the image.

'Princess', was in response the sound of the worshipper, 'Princess, I adore you. But I'm ashamed for you.'

'Ashamed—?'

'You *are* Romance—as everything, and by what I make out every one, about you is; so what more do you want? Your Preface—the only one worth speaking of—was written long ages ago by the most beautiful imagination of man.'[21]

The Princess *is* Romance; she mustn't write it: 'Don't attempt such base things. Leave those to us. Only live. Only be. *We'll* do the rest.' Standing by the carriage, Berridge grips her hands. Again she urges him to write the preface. Their faces are close:

'You *are* Romance!'—he drove it intimately, inordinately home, his lips, for a long moment, sealing it, with the fullest force of authority, on her own; after which, as he broke away and the car, starting again, turned powerfully across the pavement, he had no further sound from her than if, all divinely indulgent but all humanly defeated, she had given the question up, falling back to

[21] *The Compete Tales of Henry James*, ed. Leon Edel, vol. 12: *1903–1910* (London: Hart-Davis, 1964), 233–65 (quote on p. 263).

infinite wonder. He too fell back, but could still wave his hat for her as she passed to disappearance in the great floridly-framed aperture whose wings at once came together behind her.[22]

The ending destabilizes an intricate series of oppositions that Berridge wants to keep intact. The Princess disappears like a painted goddess, but she is also 'humanly defeated'. The carriage is the scene of 'Romance', but it also calls to mind the place of Emma Bovary's assignations; just as the party, which for Berridge is the playground of the Olympians, turns out to be also a literary marketplace. 'Romance' with a capital R, the creation of 'the most beautiful imagination of man', merges with 'romance', the novels written by the likes of Amy Evans. Berridge wants the Princess only to 'live'; the writers will do 'the rest'. But writing/living, romance/Romance, divine/human are, in James's bitter story, inextricable. Because Berridge will have none of Amy Evans, he cannot have the Princess either.

Zuleika Dobson makes slapstick out of such overburdened pairs. It is (among other things) a fantastic satire on the condition of fiction. The Duke tries to redeem Zuleika from her status as the unattainable object of fantasy; the result is the drowning of Zuleika's undergraduate lovers in the shallow waters of the Isis. Max himself, ubiquitous and omniscient narrator, takes (unlike James's Berridge) a comically cheerful attitude to the old problem of life and art. In *Zuleika Dobson* you get both romance and Romance, both the babbling woman and the fatal goddess, the ridiculously human and the equally ridiculous divine. Parody thrives on them all, alike.

[22] Ibid. pp. 264–5.

6.

Their Habits as They Lived

DESPITE his thousands of drawings and hundreds of essays, reviews, and stories, Beerbohm is semi-famous for having published so little. Compared with the writers of his own constant observation, with Henry James or George Meredith, with Wells, Kipling, or Shaw, the reputation is well earned. But sheer volume doesn't account for the sense of artistic parsimony. It is lapidary work (*Zuleika Dobson* dangles a pearl or two too many); and, more, it is tightly held by a sense of privacy that contradicts the very notion of publication, of publicity, of going public. Beerbohm seems to take in at least as much as he gives out. He is an observer and collector; the artists, politicians, and royalty of his childhood and young manhood became exhibits in his art. His publications are the occasional reflux of what he had made his own. If you were famous, you could go and see yourself biennially at his Leicester Gallery exhibitions.

Thus the public's fascination with his retreat to Rapallo. The Villino Chiaro is an ordinary little house, but it became the place where Max was really to be read. The books and exhibitions that slipped out hinted at what was within; publicity made the privacy more interesting. Inside were the 'improved' books, reworked with infinite cunning for an audience of one or none. The Villino was decorated with frescoes.[1] On one wall, twenty-one men march along in a compact mass. There are the fat (Chesterton) and the thin (Strachey), the tall (hatchet-faced Edward Carson) and the short (John Davidson). Edmund Gosse, seriously determined, paces briskly; Shaw, prominent in the middle of the pack, is serenely self-assured; Asquith and Balfour move along with the rest. No one takes notice of anyone else: they are possessed by Max's composition of vertical lines and diagonal planes. In a fresco arching over a doorway parade the heads and shoulders of another

---

[1] The frescoes I describe are now at the Humanities Research Center, Austin, Texas. Two others, one of characters from *Zuleika Dobson* and the other of Swinburne and Rossetti with an artist's model, are at Merton College, Oxford.

group. Edward VII leads this pack, and Winston Churchill brings up the rear. Between them are the Marquis de Soveral, Henry James, Joseph Chamberlain, Lord Rosebery, Reggie Turner, Arthur Wing Pinero, Will Rothenstein (barely tall enough to make it into the picture), George Moore, Rudyard Kipling, and Lord Burnham. Overlapping or abutting one another, they make a fascinating abstract design; their noses are its main structural element. Each is locked in the style he had previously assumed in caricatures by Max, instantly recognizable, not as in himself he really was, but as he had become in Beerbohm's mythology.

The frescoes are an amusing but also slightly disturbing joke. (Florence Beerbohm thought they were unseemly.) They express the same privatizing impulse as the parodies in *A Christmas Garland*. In that book, as in the frescoes, Max's contemporaries display themselves with bewitched unself-consciousness; the eery simulacra of their self-representations make a fascinating pattern of contrasts and complements. R*d**rd K*pl*ng shrieks 'Frog's-march him! . . . For the love of heaven, frog's-march him!' as his friend Constable Judlip ('P.C., X, 36') applies his knuckles to the cervical vertebrae of a little foreigner named Santa Claus. The voice is familiar: it sounds like Rudyard Kipling's blind hero Dick Heldar who 'stretched himself on the floor, wild with delight at the sounds and smells' of machine-guns firing at the 'fuzzies', and cried 'God is very good—I never thought I'd hear this again. Give 'em hell, men. O, give 'em hell!'[2] Most of us have to take it on faith that A. C. B*ns*n sounds like his unasterisked original; but it is still amusing to turn from the explosive K*pl*ng and find, on the next leaf of *A Christmas Garland*, 'Chapter XLII' of B*ns*n's *Out of Harm's Way*: 'More and more, as the tranquil years went by, Percy found himself able to draw a quiet satisfaction from the regularity, the even sureness, with which, in every year, one season succeeded to another' (*Christmas Garland*, p. 23). And to turn from that to H. G. W*ll's utopia where, on 'General Cessation Day', a procession of all who have 'reached the age-limit' avail themselves of 'the Municipal Lethal Chamber' and joyfully perform the ceremony of 'Making Way'. And then comes Ch*st*rt*n lecturing on 'Some Damnable Errors about Christmas'.

A Christmas Garland teems with stories and clashes of authorial

[2] Kipling, *The Light that Failed* (New York: Doubleday & Page, 1900), 327.

temperaments, but it engrosses what it discloses. It contains the world of words. It is the basis of Beerbohm's reputation as the greatest English parodist. The distinction is dubious, like being the greatest pole-sitter or goldfish-swallower: the trade is very specialized. I suspect that *A Christmas Garland* is praised more often than read. Partly this is because what the parodies propose is too obviously *fun*: it is exhausting to respond to cleverness in such intense doses. In *The Works* or *Zuleika Dobson*, even in the drama reviews, parody serves some other, more easily accommodating genre. *A Christmas Garland* is parody pure. I am going to discuss it at sober length because of its centrality to his career and also because, like any freak-show, it has as much to do with the supposedly 'normal' as with anything pathological. Good parody, of which Beerbohm's is the uncanny best, exhibits some of art's scandalous features without embarrassment.

Parody is a subversive form. It can dissolve boundaries between one author and another, one work and another, while also calling into question cherished ideas about the integrity of personality and artistic product. So it is fitting that even the title *A Christmas Garland* has an elusive referent. Presumably a garland can be strung as long as there are leaves to weave it with. Beerbohm began weaving early and continued late. The original 'Christmas Garland', seven parodies of contemporary authors including 'Max Beerbohm', appeared in England in 'the First Illustrated Supplement' of the *Saturday Review* and in America in *The Chap-Book* in December 1896. This was within six months of the publication of *The Works*, which had satirized the very idea of a literary career and included covert parodies of various authors including (again) 'Max Beerbohm'. Ten years later he used the title for another series in the *Saturday Review*, two parodies a week from 8 December through 29 December 1906. The volume called *A Christmas Garland*, published by Heinemann in 1912, contained one parody (revised) from the first series, seven from the second, and nine 'printed for the first time'. He added one more parody for a revised edition in 1950. Beerbohm called parody 'a speciality of youth' (*Last Theatres*, p. 66): he specialized in it during a life that had neither youth nor age but as it were a perfect mimicry of both.

As a parodist Beerbohm is an apparent contradiction in terms: an original artist in the mode of mimicry, creating a distinct personality through the imitation of others. He is distinguished from his nineteenth-century parodistic precursors less by the quality of his parody than by its place in his entire career. James Smith's parody of Wordsworth in *Rejected Addresses* (1812), James Hogg's of Wordsworth in *The Poetic Mirror* (1817), C. S. Calverley's of Browning in *Fly Leaves* (1872) are individually as good as any parody of Beerbohm's. But except for the remarkable Hogg, these writers exist *only* as parodists. Their antics confirm the distinction between artist and mimic. And then there were the real poets who happened also to write parody—which is exactly the point: they practised it like a secret vice or at least kept it distinct from their 'original' work. Swinburne's *Heptalogia*, published anonymously (1880), is the clearest example of this parodic self-segregation, and Byron's self-parodic *Don Juan* a spectacular exception that proves the rule. (Keats however is a tougher case: his imitations of Chaucer, Spenser, Milton, and Wordsworth slide between parody and pastiche, apprenticeship and mastery, until they become indelibly 'Keatsian'.) *A Christmas Garland* is not separate from Beerbohm's 'original' work. It completes the logic of that work, and therefore undermines distinctions the nineteenth-century parodists tended to confirm.

And because his parody transgresses the line between original and copy it questions the issue of artistic ownership. In the romantic ideology of the nineteenth century the literary work is an extension of the author, even the site where the author is most truly his or her own self. Beerbohm manages both to affirm that ideology and, because he affirms it in *parody*, to undermine it.[3] Virginia Woolf's claim that in his essays Beerbohm 'has brought personality into literature' can be made about his parodies too, but in an oddly doubled sense, since the 'personality' is both his own and that of the parodied other. The parodist challenges the very idea of a singular, self-possessed personality even as he seems to conjure it into being. Henry James's comment about *A Christmas Garland* sums the matter up in an uncharacteristic nutshell: '. . . he says [Edmund Gosse reported to Beerbohm] you have destroyed the trade of writing. No one, now, can write without incurring the reproach of somewhat ineffectively imitating—*you*!'[4]

The paradox of Beerbohm's whole act of writing therefore emerges

---

[3] Cf. Linda Hutcheon, who writes that parody 'forces a reassessment of the processes of textual production' (*A Theory of Parody* [New York and London: Methuen, 1985], 5).

[4] Quoted in Evan Charteris, *The Life and Letters of Sir Edmund Gosse* (London: Heinemann, 1931), 350 and cited in S. N. Behrman, *Portrait of Max* (New York: Random House, 1960), 231–2.

most intensely in his parodies. 'Literary style', he says, 'is the exact expression of a writer's self through means of written words. Some people—most people—die inarticulate' (*Around Theatres*, p. 287). But this definition of style as self-expression appears in an essay that begins as a parody of Pinero's style and modulates into a fine self-parody of his own academic-critical style. The 'writer's self' that Beerbohm expresses both in essays and in parodies is 'a kind of freehand circle of voices, drawn without reference to a fixed center'.[5] The proliferation of self-expressive styles, each original and personal yet each demonstrably imitable, raises questions about any act of writing: What is 'personality' in literature? How 'original' can anyone be? When are we truly ourselves?

Often in this book I have used the word parody in an extended sense to refer to Beerbohm's witty manipulation of the mass of prior texts that presses on a writer. All Beerbohm's writing, from the flashy insincerity of 'King George the Fourth' to the equally played-up sincerity of 'William and Mary', is parodic in that extended sense. Usually parody is thought of as just one of the techniques used by the more general class called satire; but for my purposes the order is reversed, since satire is only one of the possibilities of Beerbohm's parody. (For instance, an essay like 'The Golden Drugget', as I showed in Chapter 1, is parodic but only incidentally satiric.) And I prefer parody to the modish term 'intertextuality': as used in recent criticism, the latter term suggests a condition of all discourse, that signs refer to other signs, that language is in effect always quotation. Beerbohm's parodies, both general and specific, acknowledge the second-handedness of discourse but they also constitute a peculiar strategy for encountering that condition. And it is the peculiarity I want to indicate by the term 'parody'.[6] But as I move from parody in

---

[5] The phrase is from the essay by John Felstiner, 'Max Beerbohm and the Wings of Henry James', *The Kenyon Review*, 29 (1967), 449–71; rpt. in J. G. Riewald, *The Surprise of Excellence: Modern Essays on Max Beerbohm* (Hamden, Conn.: Archon, 1974), where the quotation is on p. 193. See also Felstiner's *The Lies of Art: Max Beerbohm's Parody and Caricature* (New York: Knopf, 1972).

[6] The term 'intertextuality' owes its currency to the work of the French critic Julia Kristeva. The idea is developed by Gerard Genette with special reference to parody, pastiche, burlesque, and other forms of what he calls *hypertextualité*. Genette distinguishes five types of transtextual relations, which he lists in the following order: (1) *intertextualité*; (2) *paratextualité*; (3) *metatextualité*; (5) *architextualité*; (4) *hypertextualité*. The fourth and last sort refers to the transformative relation between a 'hypertext' and its anterior 'hypotext'. Despite this formidable taxonomy, Genette's discussion of parody is interesting and relatively accessible. See *Palimpsestes: La litterature au second degré* (Paris: Editions du Seuil, 1982).

the extended sense to the specific parodies of *A Christmas Garland* I encounter two problems: first, and lesser, is the problem of definition; second is the problem of talking about a mode which has often seemed too *déclassé* to be noticed by the high cultural mode of literary criticism.

Parody is a phenomenon that looks very specific and distinct until one tries to specify its distinctions. Then it spreads and spills; it includes imitation, pastiche, allusion, quotation, burlesque, satire, irony—until we are back in some general realm called, simply, writing.[7] Margaret A. Rose defines parody 'as a literary work perceived by the reader as juxtaposing preformed language material with other linguistic or literary material in an incongruous manner in a new context, to produce a comic effect'.[8] Definitions of parody tend to sound like parodies—this one less than many. One virtue of the definition is that it acknowledges the reader's role: since it is notoriously difficult to tell a really bad poem from a good parody many texts become parodies by virtue of the reader's perception rather than the author's intention; conversely it is a question whether a parody acts parodically unless a reader thinks it does. In parody, then, the reader's active role in the creation of meaning is especially prominent—and again, therefore, the supposedly specialized case of parody makes explicit something that is in fact common to all writing.

Recent criticism has done much to repair parody's past neglect. There are several related reasons for this new interest.[9] Because parody is self-conscious and reflexive it is peculiarly responsive to the critical temper of the times. The art that hides its art is likely today to be called no (serious) art at all; we expect artists to acknowledge the material, social, and historical dimensions of their work. Often that

[7] Hutcheon, *Theory of Parody*, lists some of these terms but thinks that parody 'remains distinct from them' (p. 43).

[8] Rose, *Parody/Meta-fiction* (London: Croom Helm, 1979), 79. Another helpful definition is by G. D. Kiremidjian: 'A parody is a kind of literary mimicry which retains the form or stylistic character of the primary work, but substitutes alien subject matter or content.' Like most theorists of parody, Kiremidjian stresses the element of 'incongruity'. ('The Aesthetics of Parody', *Journal of Aesthetics and Art Criticism*, 28 [1969], 232.) Interestingly, several of Beerbohm's parodies—for instance those of Shaw and Moore—do *not* substitute 'alien subject matter or content'. They are about just the sorts of things these authors really would write about. The more alien the subject matter, the closer to burlesque or travesty.

[9] Hutcheon, *Theory of Parody*, provides an excellent overview of the relevant theorists, as does Rose, *Parody/Meta-fiction*. Hutcheon is especially good at canvassing recent European criticism, and Rose at canvassing other theories of parody.

acknowledgement takes the form of parody; far from disabling the work of art, parody is now a way to guarantee its high cultural status. (The *New York Times* reports the case of a Greenwich Village resident who 'dropped into a neighborhood magazine-book-newspaper store known for its impressive line of intellectual publications. "Do you have *USA Today*?" [he] asked the clerk. "No, sir," replied the clerk. Then, with a tone of pomposity, he added, "*We* carry only the parody." '[10]) And recent criticism tends to call into question the objective, unified text that served the purposes of older literary history and the older New Criticism. Proceeding either from the microscopic evidence of linguistics or the coarser-grained evidence of political theory, such criticism tends to see all writing as a cultural rather than an individual act and all texts as intertexts. From such points of view a book of parodies '*woven by* Max Beerbohm' may seem an exemplary case of 'textual production' rather than a mere sport.

But it is also the fact that Beerbohm's text presents itself as unique, inalienable, and in every sense the self-possessed expression of the personality it reciprocally creates. In 'Enoch Soames' Beerbohm jokes about proper names and their possessors: 'After all [Max says to Soames], the name "Max Beerbohm" is not at all an uncommon one, and there must be several Enoch Soameses running around—or rather, "Enoch Soames" is a name that might occur to anyone writing a story.'[11] There *are* 'several Enoch Soameses running around', since Soames is the type of the failed decadent poet, one standing for many. The idea of multiple 'Max Beerbohms', however, is ridiculous not only because those particular syllables sound unusual to English ears but because the author exists with a real individuality that his creation, Soames, can never attain. But the story that asserts the author's uniqueness consigns him literally to the same page as Soames; and the type-character Soames emerges as vividly and personally from the page as the individual Max. Similarly, the weaver of *A Christmas Garland* both defies and gives evidence for the death of the author: as the creator of such effaced originals as H*nry J*m*s and R*d**rd

---

[10] *New York Times*, 5 November 1986. Parody's cultural elevation is most apparent in visual art, from dada through pop to upscale versions of subway graffiti.

[11] *Seven Men* (New York: Knopf, 1924), 44. In this edition the name is misprinted as 'Max Beerbolm', which gives an interestingly different point to the joke.

K*pl*ng he asserts the uniqueness of his parodied authors even as he proves that there must be 'several of them running around'.

There is a political dimension to the current interest in parody. Like satire, parody has often been seen as a conservative force. For instance, George Kitchin's *A Survey of Burlesque and Parody in English* (1931)—virtually unreadable but the only such survey there is—makes the parodist seem like a bullying prefect defending the old school against anything foreign or new. Kitchin's English parodist dislikes excessive displays of emotion or pessimistic talk that might weaken the troops in wartime; mockery is the parodist's defence of the literary realm. The 'golden age of parody', in this view, was inaugurated by the *Anti-Jacobin* which 'reaps the golden honours of having materially helped to stem the rising tide of revolutionary feeling'.[12]

But in more recent theory the parodist is enlisted in the forces of progressivism. Parody has become useful in explaining the process of historical change in styles and genres; that usefulness—along with the political implication of a mode that is now seen to be always hastening change—is another reason for criticism's new interest in parody. Partly for that reason parody moves to the centre of Bakhtin's theory of the novel. As in the conservative view, so too in this one, 'parodic-travestying literature introduces the permanent corrective of laughter', but now it forms 'a critique on the one-sided seriousness of the lofty direct word, the corrective of reality that is always richer, more fundamental and most importantly *too contradictory and heteroglot* to be fit into a high and straightforward genre'.[13] From this point of view, parody resists repression, including the ultimate social repressiveness of language itself.

Beerbohm's parody cannot easily be enlisted in either camp. Explicitly he is an artistic conservative. Writing to Virginia Woolf in 1927 about her essay 'Mr Bennett and Mrs Brown' Beerbohm disagrees with her 'argument that a new spirit extracts a new method':

There seems to me to be only one good method of narrative—Homer's and Thackeray's method, and Tolstoi's, and Tom's, Dick's, Chaucer's, Maupas-

---

[12] Kitchin, *A Survey of Burlesque and Parody in English* (Edinburgh and London: Oliver & Boyd, 1931), 176. Dwight Macdonald, citing Kitchin, echoes the point: 'Parody is conservative and classical' (*Parodies: An Anthology from Chaucer to Beerbohm—and After* [London: Faber and Faber, 1961], 560).

[13] Bakhtin, *The Dialogic Imagination* (Austin: Univ. of Texas Press, 1981), 55.

sant's, and Harry's; all of them very different men spiritually, and employing the method in very different ways, but not imagining that a new method is needful, or couldn't be unhelpful, and wouldn't certainly play the deuce and all, in its own time, and might by dint of various alterations and improvements become a sure and shining instrument in the hands of the Hereafter.[14]

When he wrote this, Beerbohm's own best work was finished. The notion of parody as carnivalesque promoter of change seems grotesquely inappropriate to a parodist who was in nostalgic retreat from the twentieth century. Still, the objects of Woolf's attack in 'Mr Bennett and Mrs Brown'—the Edwardian novelists Bennett, Wells, and Galsworthy—had all been parodied in *A Christmas Garland*; and whatever Beerbohm's announced intentions, those parodies reveal (as Linda Hutcheon claims all parody does) an 'ambivalence [that] stems from the dual drives of conservative and revolutionary forces that are inherent in [parody's] nature as authorized transgression'.[15] Beerbohm did not hurry along any change in the history of literary styles. But the very act of alienating those styles from their proprietors makes them part of the general store of styles. It pays homage but it also superannuates.

The disarming title *A Christmas Garland* stamps all the parodies— each style, each personality—as Max's own; they share his image. The idea of 'seasonal tributes' provides an occasion and gives form to a miscellany, like the Smith brothers making the dedication of the new Drury Lane Theatre the occasion for their *Rejected Addresses*. Even more than that collection, though, this one seems to present itself as an act of friendliness, homey and personal. But Christmas is not only the time of gift-giving: in England it is the time for pantomime, with its cross-dressing, *double entendre*, and broad burlesque. In its traditional form (now much eroded) panto is carnivalesque rather than specifically satiric; it attacks no particular social form but undermines, in a temporary and licensed way, all forms and distinctions. It dissolves differences between sexes and ages, performers and audiences. It aims to be in thoroughly bad taste. *A Christmas Garland* is a much more decorous affair than the Christmas panto, but it shares the anarchic tendency.

Beerbohm's parodies exemplify various things parody can be.

---

[14] 30 December 1927, in the Taylor Collection, Princeton University.
[15] Hutcheon, *Theory of Parody*, p. 26.

Instead of searching for a unified field theory I am going to look at specific examples.

In the late works of Henry James, as in an illuminated fog, everything glows but hardly anything is distinctly visible. Clarification, if it comes, may be disappointing or, more likely, deceptive—another brilliant false light. The experience can be frustrating, but also both luxurious and comic. The luxury is that of sinking into the plenitude of language: here is a style that can expend and replenish itself infinitely. It is comic by the same token: like a figure in a Steinberg cartoon, the Jamesian narrator stands on a promontory made out of his own words. The surrounding words uphold him from vacuity. The dense Jamesian circumlocution revolves around a revelation it endlessly postpones.

In 'The Mote in the Middle Distance', by H*nry J*m*s, the non-revelation is of the contents of the Christmas stockings at the foot of the beds of Keith and Eva Tantalus. Beerbohm thought that James's 'The Velvet Glove' was insufficiently Jamesian; his parody suffers no such defect. The parody provides many of the pleasures of an authentic James story. There is, first of all, the perfect mimicry of the style itself. By this I mean not only that Beerbohm successfully imitates James, but that James himself, at his most characteristic, seems to be imitating James; the parody is like the original because, in both, part of the reader's pleasure comes from discovering those inherently caricatural touches where the style proclaims itself as Jamesian. The parody also provides the matter to go with the Jamesian manner: with Keith and Eva, as with Merton Densher and Kate Croy, the reader peers through the density of language to discover that phantom—something *beyond* language—that the language itself withholds in the creation. (And as James himself seems to be peering in the caricature Max added to the title-page of James's *The Finer Grain* [Plate 13].) In James, the phantom may be some moral question; in Beerbohm's parody it is burlesqued as the question whether the children should 'peer' or not 'peer'.

In J*m*s as in James the moral question is also a dramatic question which elicits more questions with each potential response. Is Eva heroic or, as her name suggests, merely devious? Did she, for all her moral stringency, actually peer into her stocking before Keith woke up? Does Keith really understand his sister, who is, after all, the most 'telephonic of her sex'?

In talking to Eva, you always had, as it were, your lips to the receiver. If you didn't try to meet her fine eyes, it was that you simply couldn't hope to: there were too many dark, too many buzzing and bewildering and all frankly not negotiable leagues in between. Snatches of other voices seemed often to intertrude themselves in the parley; and your loyal effort not to overhear these was complicated by your fear of missing what Eva might be twittering. (*Christmas Garland*, p. 5)

Does the J*m*sian narrator himself know what really went on that morning? Or is his 'impression' that his friends never 'peered' the product of his own timidity, his failure to ' "come up to the scratch" of yielding to [the] temptation' to ask them?

Beerbohm loved James's 'late manner', though like anyone else he sometimes found it unreadable.[16] But he disliked James's habit of revising his earlier work into that manner, as he did for the New York Edition. Or as he did for an Introduction to Coquelin's *Art and the Actor*: a printed footnote says that 'The substance of this paper appeared in the *Century Magazine* in January 1887', to which Beerbohm added in his copy, 'and was very obviously—or, rather, deviously and circuitously—revised in the great dark rich fulness of time, for republication in 1915'. And on the facing page he drew a double caricature in which an old James confronts a middle-aged James, each accusing the other, 'How badly you wrote!/write!' (Plate 14)[17] The revisionary process reanimated a fixed specimen; it was a nightmare for the parodist like the one the caricaturist depicts in his drawing 'One fine morning, or How they might undo me', in which a group of Max's favourite subjects has each revised his appearance (Plate 15). The familiar figures parade past, as they do in the Villino's frescoes, but here Max starts back in alarm at the sight of an elegantly dressed G.B.S., a smiling Rothenstein, a Pinero without eyebrows, and so on. What has entered the public domain (including Max's own published images) should stay put, the better for Max to privatize it.

But in his privacy Max gave himself revisionary licence. Long after the publication of *A Christmas Garland* he sent Gosse—himself one of the book's parodees and the man who reported James's comment that Max had destroyed the trade of writing—some additional manuscript pages to add to the printed version of 'The Mote in the Middle

---

[16] 18 May 1920, *Letters to Reggie Turner*, ed. Rupert Hart-Davis (London: Hart-Davis, 1964), 248

[17] Copy at the Houghton Library, Harvard University.

Distance'.[18] In them, Keith and Eva now debate the question of the stockings' contents in even darker Jamesian circumlocution:

Well, [Keith] had got *tout bonnement* the measure of it now. But he had not yet covered, as was to appear, the span of his insistence. 'You know then, by blest induction, what there *is* in them?'

'I know', she had a high gesture for it, '*only* that.'

He hardly hesitated. '*What's* in them?'

'Everything', she gave back to him. She had closed her eyes. '*More* than everything', she passionately, she all but inaudibly now breathed.

What it came to, then, *was* precisely the thing to which it came.

Keith, like the reader, still wonders what's inside this passionate circularity. Eva clarifies the nature of her 'vision':

'What we have to hold on to—but with a tenacity—is not so much what you perhaps saw as what you have all along, *caro*, foreseen—the impossibility, simply, of our *not* being able not to. *That's* all that counts. It's the lamp in our darkness and the seal of our good faith. It's the end of our journey and the garland at the feast.'

In the addition, then, Eva thus pays a little tribute to Beerbohm's own *Garland*. The burlesque aspect of the parody is made even wilder as the children become more sophisticated, more intensely Jamesian moral connivers. Eva's 'vibrant' judgment (in the published version) that 'One doesn't . . . violate the shrine, pick the pearl from the shell' becomes an even more perfectly reflexive judgment on the figure in James's carpet.

In 'The Mote in the Middle Distance', the unasterisked author is present by implication in the style, the contents (like the contents of the stockings, a more-than-everything that comes to precisely what it comes to), the 'vision'. But Beerbohm later wrote another parody of James, 'The Guerdon' (1916), in which the name itself (almost) appears. It is a story *about* James in the Jamesian manner, and it therefore shades into another sort of Beerbohm parody in which personal satire is more prominent than it is in 'The Mote in the Middle Distance'. 'The Guerdon' was written for private circulation—a joke between Max and a couple of friends, who copied it for other friends who copied it and so on until it was pirated into print and at

---

[18] Note to Gosse on additional MS pages for 'Mote' (in the Taylor Collection, Princeton University).

last included, seemingly by default, in *A Variety of Things* (pp. 193–6). Thus Beerbohm simultaneously authorizes and disclaims its publication: he calls it 'stolen goods' that should have been 'put into the fire', like the earlier pirating of 'A Peep into the Past'.[19] And as with that 'squib about Oscar Wilde', his apparent reluctance to go public indicates that there is anxiety as well as pleasure in parodying an author of his deepest regard.

'The Guerdon' is the story of how James was awarded the Order of Merit despite the fact that neither Lord Chamberlain nor King had 'the beginning of a notion ... who the fellow, the so presumably illustrious and deserving chap in question *was*'. The infinitely probing Jamesian style makes a mountain of nervous hesitation out of his 'dim bland' molehill of a character, 'Poor decent Stamfordham', who has come to the palace to present the honours list. At the gates of the palace, Stamfordham 'all peeringly inquire[s]' of one of the sentries: 'To whom do you beautifully belong'. (The question is an authentic Jamesianism, quoted from his play *The High Bid*; it contained, according to Beerbohm the drama reviewer, the 'quintessence of Mr James': 'the sound [of the spoken line] ... sent innumerable little vibrations through the heart of every good Jacobite in the audience'.[20]) Stamfordham presents his list to 'the Personage' and waits in 'perspirational agony' for the moment 'when, at long last, the finger *was* placed, with a roll towards him of the blue, the prominent family eye of the seated reader'; then, 'it was with a groan of something like relief that he faintly uttered an "Oh well, Sir, he *is*, you know—and with all submission, hang it, just *isn't* he though?—of an eminence?"'

In 'The Guerdon', as in 'The Mote in the Middle Distance', the dramatic and moral question is whether to peer or not to peer: Will 'the royal eye' look into 'the fat scarlet book of reference' (*Who's Who*) and find 'What *sort*, my dear man, of eminence?' is being proposed? In the silence of the ensuing pause Stamfordham experiences something like revelation: 'It never, till beautifully now, had struck our poor harassed friend that his master might, in some sort, be prey to those very, those inhibitive delicacies that had played, from first to last, so eminently the deuce with *him*.' Inhibitive delicacy triumphs over

---

[19] See the prefatory Note to *A Variety of Things*.

[20] 'Mr Henry James' Play', 27 February 1909, in *Around Theatres* (New York: Simon and Schuster, 1954), 541. See John Felstiner's excellent discussion of this and other aspects of Beerbohm on James in *Lies of Art*, pp. 141–56.

blatant revelation: 'there *was* no recourse to the dreadful volume', which 'somewhat confirmed for [Stamfordham] his made guess that on the great grey beach of the hesitational and renunciational he was not—or wasn't all deniably not—the only pebble'.

He was to form, in later years, a theory that the name really *had* stood in peril of deletion, and that what saved it was that the good little man, as doing, under the glare shed by his predecessors, the great dynastic 'job' in a land that had been under two Jameses and no less than eight Henrys, had all humbly and meltingly resolved to 'let it go at that'. (*Variety of Things*, p. 196)

In 'The Guerdon', James is mimicked, directly quoted, and finally named—though dimly—as one in a list of English kings. The American author gets his Order of Merit despite, or because of, the fact that the royal reader is reluctant to open a book.

The usual question about the parodist's relation to the parodee— love or hate, homage or envy?—is too crude for the case of Beerbohm and James. In his little reminiscence of 'An Incident' Max touches the question in an elegiac manner; he wonders about his sense of loyalty in having given up the Master's presence in order to have the Master's work. It is, as Beerbohm says, a question sufficiently complicated to be a Jamesian subject. James has pride of place in *A Christmas Garland*, but the question of motivation is equally complicated with other Beerbohm parodees. Edmund Gosse, for instance, was a personal friend, despite the twenty-three-year difference in their ages. In 1896, Gosse signalled the success of *The Works* by inviting Beerbohm to his weekly literary salon. They kept up their friendship, in person and correspondence, through many years. Gosse was one of the correspondents with whom Beerbohm played the 'sonnet game', in which the two participants write alternate lines. It is impossible without external evidence to know which lines of their joint sonnet 'To Henry James' belong to Gosse and which to Beerbohm.[21] But their personal affinities also accentuate the differences. They were a pair of the sort Beerbohm liked to create in his comic art: little and big, ironic and stolid, supple and stiff. Gosse laboured over Scandinavian literature while Max played in the Mediterranean sun.

There was another contrast between them. Beerbohm was an artist in misrepresentation, dazzling with misquotation, false attribution,

---

[21] See J. G. Riewald, ed. *Max in Verse* (Brattleboro, Vt.: Stephen Greene, 1963), p. 19 and n. pp. 137–8.

controlled inaccuracies of all sorts, including the trenchant inaccuracy of parody. Gosse was also inaccurate, but he was a scholar, not a satirist. His career had been dogged by the vicious, sometimes niggling but accurate attacks of a less successful scholarly rival, John Churton Collins.[22] Gosse and the angrily accurate Churton Collins played out in real life one of the central relationships of late Victorian literature. They were *doppelgängers* like Jeckyll and Hyde, like Conrad's secret sharers, like Beerbohm's own Maltby and Braxton. Churton Collins knew Gosse's scholarly sins.

Beerbohm's parody makes no overt allusion to the embarrassing scandal of Gosse's exposure by Churton Collins. It simply makes embarrassment the theme of G*sse's 'Recollection' (*Christmas Garland*, pp. 133–43) of the social disaster he engineered when he brought about a meeting between his heroes Browning and Ibsen. G*sse's ostentatious humility and busy deference mark him out as one of the 'dim' characters who need to batten on more powerful 'personalities': 'My use of the first person singular, delightful though that pronoun is in the works of the truly gifted, jars unspeakably on me; but reasons of space baulk my sober desire to call myself merely the present writer, or the infatuated go-between, or the cowed and imponderable young person who was in attendance.' The self-portrait of G*sse in a prospect of greater authors depends less on mimicry of a style than on situation. It is parody as extended verbal caricature. 'A Recollection' could, in fact, easily have been a Beerbohm caricature. It brings to mind the embarrassment of Gosse's Old Self when, in the company of his distinguished literary and political friends, he is accosted by his fervent Young Self crying, 'Are you saved?' (Hart-Davis, *Catalogue*, no. 616, *Observations*, 1925); or his discomfort as he tries to quiet a squalling infant called 'the Rising Generation' ('Mr Gosse loquitur: "Diddums!"' [Plate 15]). It would be a caricature like the comic confrontations in *Rossetti and his Circle*: in 'A Recollection', Browning and Ibsen fail to connect, like Carlyle and Whistler (in the drawing 'Blue China' [Plate 17]), or like Jowett and Rossetti ('And what were they going to do with the Grail when they found it, Mr Rossetti?' [Plate 24]). In the verbal caricature of 'A Recollection', young G*sse, all nervous good will, stands translating between the

[22] The Collins-Gosse affair is recounted by Ann Thwaite, *Edmund Gosse: A Literary Landscape* (London: Secker & Warburg, 1984).

tremendously hearty Browning, with his torrential energy and talk, and 'the great Scandinavian', Ibsen, 'closely buttoned in his black surcoat and crowned with his uncompromising top-hat'. The scene is the Palazzo Rezzonico in Venice. Browning and Ibsen have never heard of one another. ('It was one of the strengths of [Ibsen's] strange, crustacean genius that he had never heard of anybody', says G*sse.) The meeting has been a series of contretemps. Now the conversation takes another bad turn when Browning declares his 'unshakeable belief in the authenticity' of some newly discovered verses supposed to be by Sappho:

> To my surprise, Ibsen, whom I had been unprepared to regard as a classical scholar, said positively that they had not been written by Sappho. Browning challenged him to give a reason. A literal translation of the reply would have been 'Because no woman ever was capable of writing a fragment of good poetry'. Imagination reels at the effect this would have had on the recipient of 'Sonnets from the Portuguese'. The agonised interpreter, throwing honour to the winds, babbled some wholly fallacious version of the words. Again the situation had been saved; but it was of the kind that does not even in furthest retrospect lose its power to freeze the heart and constrict the diaphragm. (*Christmas Garland*, p. 142)

G*sse mistranslates in order to save the social situation. The scholar throws honour to the winds, and thinks he has escaped. But his *doppelgänger* knows—and in this case the double is not Churton Collins but Gosse's good friend Max Beerbohm.

Parody is a logical artistic end of the *doppelgänger* theme, and the uncanny relationship of secret sharers is one possible relationship of parodist to parodee. The parodist is the double who threatens to supplant the self. Freud links the literary theme of the double to the unconscious fear of castration and the forbidden knowledge of one's own mortality; the meeting with the double produces a sensation he characterizes as 'uncanny' (*unheimlich*).[23] I will return to Freud's account when I discuss the doubles of *Seven Men*; here I'll only say that *uncanny* is the perfect word to describe the best Beerbohm parodies, where the impression is not of satire but of possession. Like a voodoo-man, Max manipulates something supposedly external—a

---

[23] 'The Uncanny' (1919), in *The Standard Edition of the Complete Psychological Works*, trans. and ed. James Strachey with Anna Freud (London: Hogarth Press, 1953–74), xvii. 218–54.

literary style—and by sympathetic magic captures a person's essence. He intrudes on space that seemed already occupied—a different sort of aggression against reality than that of the fiction-writer who erects his creation in empty space. Beerbohm's victims seldom protested publicly; this is partly because Max's pose of infinite good humour would have made protest seem merely crabbed, but partly, no doubt, because they were afraid to provoke him further. The uncanny parodist finds out the parodee's most vulnerable place and makes him impotent.

Beerbohm's masterpiece in the vein of uncanny parody is 'Dickens' by G**rge M**re. The parody is funny even for a reader who knows nothing about George Moore, but funnier, and maybe scarier, for one who can compare the caricature with the sitter. Read Moore's *Confessions of a Young Man* after reading Beerbohm's parody and you have the shock of seeing an original in the act of imitating its copy. Beerbohm's satire is sharp, personal, and malicious, but the mimicry is also perfect.[24]

'Luminous vagueness' is how Beerbohm characterized Moore's presence: 'There was always an illusory look about him—the diaphanous, vaporous, wan look of an illusion conjured up for us, perhaps by means of mirrors and by a dishonourable spiritualist.'[25] M**re's 'Dickens' (*Christmas Garland*, pp. 179–85) weaves from irrelevance to irrelevance with a similar vaporous vagueness. The plodding style is wildly contradicted by the random wandering of the thought, the air of reasonable retrospection by the bizarre factual errors:

[24] Compare Beerbohm's parody with this typical passage from *Confessions of a Young Man* (London: Swan Sonnenschein & Co.; New York: Brentanos, n.d.), in which Moore is talking about a woman's face in a miniature painting:

'She is a woman of thirty,—no,—she is the woman of thirty. Balzac has written some admirable pages on this subject; my memory of them is vague and uncertain, although durable, as all memories of him must be. But that marvellous story, or rather study, has been blunted in my knowledge of this tiny face with the fine masses of hair drawn up from the neck and arranged elaborately on the crown. There is no fear of plagiary; he cannot have said all; he cannot have said what I want to say.

'Looking at this face so mundane, so intellectually mundane, I see why a young man of refined mind—a bachelor who spends at least a pound a day on his pleasures, and in whose library are found some few volumes of modern poetry—seeks his ideal in a woman of thirty.

'It is clear that, by the very essence of her being, the young girl may evoke no ideal but that of home; and home is in his eyes the antithesis of freedom, desire, aspiration. He longs for mystery, deep and endless . . .' (pp. 100–1)

[25] 'George Moore', in *Mainly on the Air* (New York: Knopf, 1958), 81; written 1913, broadcast 6 October 1950.

I had often wondered why when people talked to me of Tintoretto I always found myself thinking of Turgeneff. It seemed to me strange that I should think of Turgeneff instead of thinking of Tintoretto; for at first sight nothing can be more far apart than the Slav mind and the Flemish. But one morning, some years ago, while I was musing by my fireplace in Victoria Street, Dolmetsch came to see me. He had a soiled roll of music under his left arm. I said, 'How are you?' He said, 'I am well. And you?' I said, 'I, too, am well. What is that, my dear Dolmetsch, that you carry under your left arm?' He answered, 'It is a mass by Palestrina.' (*Christmas Garland*, p. 179)

And so on through a paragraph that forgets all about Turgeneff or the Flemish Tintoretto and ends with a reflection on Renoir's 'subfusc palette'.

In his essay 'The Spirit of Caricature'—a self-parodic dream-vision of a learned lecture—Beerbohm claims that 'Such laughter as may be caused by caricature is merely aesthetic' (*Variety of Things*, p. 125). In the Moore parody, Beerbohm seems to recreate Moore's wispy egotism with a caricaturist's comico-aesthetic pleasure. But 'the aesthetic' is a dubiously honorific category, since what is 'merely aesthetic' is often also useless, or contains some defect (moral or otherwise) that is tacitly recognized by being dismissed under the label. Thus it is a basic tenet of the pseudo-Aristotelianism Max draws on for 'The Spirit of Caricature' that things horrible to behold in real life become pleasurable when represented in art—that is, when they are bracketed in the category of the aesthetic. In contemplating George Moore in parody and caricature, Beerbohm pretends not only to accept this old-style aestheticism, but (in the Wildean vein) to take it a step further; he finds its properties not only in artistic representations but in the man himself. Like Max's George IV, George Moore is an unself-conscious work of comic art.

That is how 'my friend' Moore appears in the reminiscence Max delivered on the BBC in 1950 (written in 1913); it is a kind of spoken caricature which devastates Moore by taking ironic delight in his aesthetic fineness. Moore's 'peculiar personality was an entirely natural product', appreciated especially by artists 'who had the wit to enjoy in the midst of an artificial civilisation the spectacle of one absolutely natural man' (*Mainly on the Air*, pp. 82, 83). The chatty essay is in Beerbohm's mature style, but it retains from earlier days the transvaluations implied by calling Moore 'natural' and then contemplating him aesthetically. Aesthetically contemplated, the 'absolutely natural man' is a monstrosity. Moore's vague face and droning voice, the conversational *gaffes* which elevate the obvious to the level of revelation and reduce the bizarre to the pedestrian, his fickleness in art and literature, his sexual adventuring, even his misappropriations of other people's work, all are fondly remembered and made ridiculous by the essayist-as-caricaturist.

In 'The Spirit of Caricature', Max claims that 'Caricature consists merely in exaggeration':

You ask me [he goes on in his role as Professor of Caricature], 'How about a subject who is neither handsome nor ugly?' In that case, merely, it is the lack of features that must be exaggerated. Through intensification of its nullity, such a subject may be made as ridiculous as any other. (*Variety of Things*, p. 127)

In the broadcast reminiscence, he intensifies Moore's mental nullity. Moore's silences in company were 'unutterably blank', and 'His face was as a mask of gauze through which Nothing was quite clearly visible' (*Mainly on the Air*, p. 83). 'His face, too, while he talked, had but one expression—a faintly illumined blank' (p. 84). Always intensely himself, nonetheless 'In public he simply evaporated' (p. 87). And in the *Christmas Garland* parody, M**re's efforts to write about Dickens (or Turgeneff, Tintoretto, or anything else) dissolve repeatedly as he wavers from one private association to another. Most often, M**re's 'roving thoughts' rove to women and sex. As Dolmetsch reads Palestrina's semibreves to him, M**re wonders 'what girl Palestrina was courting when he conceived them. She must have been blonde, surely, and with narrow flanks' (*Christmas Garland*, p. 180). And with unself-editing confidence, M**re wanders from Palestrina to Tintoretto to the statement 'There never was a writer except Dickens' (p. 181). He has read only one chapter of one book, *Pickwick Papers*, but it is enough to set going his lecture on 'the erotic motive' in Dickens and a fantasy of Mr Winkle and the knock-kneed Miss Arabella—a fantasy which immediately leaves Dickens behind as it imagines how Miss Arabella would look in a painting by Hals or Winchoven and how Manet would 'have stated the slope of the thighs of the girl' (p. 184). And because 'Strange thoughts of her surge up vaguely in me as I watch her—thoughts that I cannot express in English', M**re switches to French and produces (without acknowledgement) a translation of Pater's famous description of the *Mona*

Lisa, 'Elle est plus vieille que les roches entre lesquelles elle s'est assise; comme le vampire elle a été fréquemment morte . . .' (p. 184). As the parody ends, M**re foreswears French and all European languages ('one can say in them nothing fresh') and vows to become a Mexican: 'On a hillside, or beside some grey pool, gazing out across those plains poor and arid, I will await the first pale showings of the new dawn . . .' The manuscript of the parody concludes with a sketch of the wispy Moore, wearing sombrero and spurs, watching the sunrise in Mexico (Plate 18).

I don't doubt Beerbohm's sincerity when he describes the subject of this parody as his 'friend'. He *liked* George Moore for being (as he saw it) so absurd. *A Christmas Garland* contains parodies of some closer friends, notably Fr*nk H*rr*s, G. K. Ch*st*rt*n, and H*l**re B*ll*oc; in them too mimicry goes beyond satire to capture the parodee's personality. And the more self-assured the personality, the greater the gift to the parodist, on the principle that the bigger they come the harder they fall. One thing he can do is explode the personality into fragments. Thus H*l**re B*ll*c writing 'Of Christmas' is a hysterical bundle of digressiveness, jumping in theme and style from energetic archaism to irrelevant topicality, breaking into verse and Latin tag-phrases, indulging every impulse. He gives us a little self-caricature in verse:

> One Christmas Night in Pontgibaud
> *(Pom-pom, rub-a-dub-dub)*
> A Man with a drum went to and fro
> *(Two merry eyes, two cheeks chub)* . . .

This is the Belloc who is seen in Max's caricature 'Revisiting the Glimpses' (Plate 20), where in a group of literary tub-thumpers the chubby-cheeked little Belloc is gesticulating with special intensity. The *Christmas Garland* parody makes a joke of Belloc's sectarian fanaticism and nothing of his anti-Semitism; those matters are subsumed, as it were, under the crazily energetic dispersedness of the style itself. B*ll*c is satirized less for his particular ideas than for the undisciplined personality that spins out his undisciplined writing.

Frank Harris's self-assurance was almost maniacal; as Beerbohm told S. N. Behrman, 'When you believe yourself omnipotent, it is hard, don't you know, to reconcile yourself to mere potency'. Behrman asked if Harris ever told the truth: '"Sometimes, don't you know—

when his invention flagged," Max said.'[26] In 'Shakespeare and Christmas' (*Christmas Garland*, pp. 77–82) H*rr*s is made to tell the unconscious truth about his fanatically over-compensated 'mere potency'.

His essay is literally threatening:

That Shakespeare hated Christmas—hated it with a venom utterly alien to the gentle heart in him—I take to be a proposition that establishes itself automatically. If there is one thing lucid-obvious in the Plays and Sonnets, it is Shakespeare's unconquerable loathing of Christmas. The Professors deny it, however, or deny that it is proven. With these gentlemen I will deal faithfully. I will meet them on their own parched ground, making them fertilise it by shedding there the last drop of the water that flows through their veins. (*Christmas Garland*, p. 77)

Its most glaring stylistic peculiarity, the joining of two adjectives as in 'lucid-obvious', 'feeble-cold', or 'inevitable-final', produces a violent collision. And H*rr*s's theory is threatening because it is crazily self-involved. It is circularity masquerading as syllogism: Anne Hathaway was born on Christmas day; Shakespeare hated Anne Hathaway; therefore he hated Christmas. H*rr*s proves these propositions by discovering what is *not* in the text; it is a rough exercise in pseudo-Freudian literary criticism: 'If you find, in the works of a poet whose instinct is to write about everything under the sun, one obvious theme untouched, or touched hardly at all, then it is at least presumable that there was good reason for that abstinence' (p. 77).

H*rr*s acknowledges that Shakespeare 'did mention [Christmas] now and again, but in grudging fashion, without one spark of illumination—he, the arch-illuminator of all things'—which he takes as 'proof positive that he detested it'. Shakespeare also 'never says a word about the birthdays of the various shrews and sluts in whom, again and again, he gave us his wife':

It is clear that Shakespeare cannot bring himself to write about Anne Hathaway's birthday—will not stain his imagination by thinking of it. That is entirely human-natural. But why should he loathe Christmas Day itself with precisely the same loathing? There is but one answer—and that inevitable-final. The two days were one. (pp. 81–2)

[26] Behrman, *Portrait*, pp. 123, 124.

Filling in the Shakespearean lacunae, H*rr*s reveals his own obsession. Specifically, Beerbohm is parodying Harris's exercise in biographical criticism, *The Man Shakespeare* (1909). The parody's violence and illogic hint at a fear of women that the sexual swaggering in Harris's *My Life and Loves* denies in literally incredible detail—a denial that may be said, in the spirit of H*rr*s's argument, to confirm its own negation. A caricature Max drew on the subject of Harris, Shakespeare, and homosexuality makes the same point. In it a slightly built and very startled Shakespeare, in full Elizabethan dress, looks at the back view of a totally naked Frank Harris. Harris is muscular, broad-shouldered, manly-thighed, but with an infantile rotundity of buttocks; his face, in profile, is thoughtful and he strokes his spectacular moustache. The caption reads 'Had Shakespeare asked me . . .'— which is supposed to be the one exception Harris made in denying any interest in homosexuality (Plate 19).

Beerbohm appended a note to the parody: 'Mr Fr*nk H*rr*s is very much a man of genius, and I should be sorry if this adumbration of his manner made any one suppose that I do not rate his writings about Shakespeare higher than that of all "the Professors" together— M. B.' (p. 82). It is the only apologetic note in *A Christmas Garland*, except for one justifying the parody of a dead author (Meredith). There are several possible reasons for Beerbohm's unusually tender regard for Frank Harris's feelings. Harris had been editor of the *Saturday Review*; he hired Beerbohm and, despite his eccentricities, he was a good editor. They had collaborated on a play. So Beerbohm had reason to be loyal. He also had reason to be prudent. In 1912 Harris was far along on his descent from respectability, but he was always capable of making trouble. (The chapter called 'Max, "The Incomparable"' in Harris's *Contemporary Portraits* [4th Ser., 1924], shows that Beerbohm had good reason to be cautious.[27]) Libel and

---

[27] Harris begins the portrait by saying that the young Beerbohm reminded him 'of one of those lunar creatures, visitants from some other planet, with more brains than we earth-born folk, and no passions' (p. 127). He damns with faint praise: Max 'has done two or three charming little sketches and one astonishing picture, "No. 2, the Pines" . . .' and as a caricaturist he ranks with Forain and Sem; but *The Happy Hypocrite* left Harris cold and *Zuleika Dobson* floored him (p. 130). He describes Max as just one in a family of equally gifted siblings. He reminds us that there were only two apologies in *A Christmas Garland*, to 'Meredith and my humble self' (p. 129). His nearly direct response to the parody comes in the form of an apocryphal anecdote about Max's wedding day: As the wedding party broke up, Max's 'marvellous self-possession broke

lying were Harris's stock-in-trade. More delicately named, those were Beerbohm's own weapons in his operations as parodist and caricaturist. So Beerbohm's solicitude may also suggest sympathy for a fellow-artist. And there was concern for the feelings of a man whose blustering inadequately covered a self-destructive lack of insight. Harris's compulsive unreliability made him as dangerous to himself as to others.

But above all, Frank Harris was a distinct personality—few more distinct; that put him in a class that transcended ordinary canons of liking and disliking. In the unfinished *Mirror of the Past* there is an imaginary conversation between the prudent, dullish narrator, Sylvester Herringham, and his friend Rossetti, on the subject of Rossetti's friend Charles Augustus Howell. Howell was a rogue like Frank Harris: he was a forger, swindler, double-dealer, sexual athlete, and companion to artists. Rossetti's interest in Howell is like Beerbohm's in Harris. Herringham recalls:

I once said to Rossetti, 'If I were you, I wouldn't see so much of that man. I don't think he's to be trusted.' Rossetti laughed. 'Sylvester', he said, 'whenever a man says to me *If I were you*, I pay no attention, because I know that what he means is *If you were I*; and because I happen to be myself. If I happened to be you, I daresay I should forbid Howell the door, and live in terror of him, and surround myself with a loyal bodyguard of dreadful dullards. You're young, Sylvester. When you're as old as I am, you'll realise its the *dull* friends that one has to avoid, not the untrustworthy ones. You'll come to me and say in a hollow voice, *If I were you, I wouldn't see so much of So-and-So: he's dull.* And I shall look up and say, *Is he? Why, I do believe you're right! Yes, I am conscious that he's been exhausting me all this time. Many thanks for your warning.*—A man who's got work to do, Sylvester, can't afford not to have amusing people about him. Charles Howell is the most amusing fellow I know. He gives me something all the time. As for the chance of his doing me mischief around the corner—why, that's all the more reason for not letting him out of my sight. I must see more of Howell.'[28]

The 1896 'Christmas Garland' barely exists any more. The magazines that published it have become the rarest of rare books. A pirated

---

down; frantically he seized' a guest by the arm and cried 'You're not going to leave me *alone* with her' (p. 131). This is typical Harris hatchetry, but it suggests that he understood the point of the parody as I do.

[28] *Mirror of the Past*, typescript page with Beerbohm's corrections; in the Taylor Collection, Princeton University.

edition appeared in America in 1926: seventy-two copies were printed, and the type distributed. The parodied authors have proved little more substantial than the printed parodies. Any educated reader—and what other sort would there be?—should know H. G. Wells. But even the finely literate may have forgotten Marie Corelli, Richard LeGallienne, Ian Maclaren, Alice Meynell, and Max Beerbohm. The authors in the 1912 volume have fared better, overall, but some of them—G. S. Street and A. C. Benson, for instance—have gone the way of the popular authors in the earlier collection. The 1950 edition added a parody of Maurice Baring. If parody necessarily depended on the reader's knowledge of the parodied author, then many of the 'Christmas Garland' parodies, from 1896 through 1950, were doomed.

That they remain funny, or are indeed readable at all, shows that parody is not entirely in thrall to its originals. Some, like the J*m*s, are parodies of novels or stories; others, like the G*sse, M**re, B*ll*c, and H*rr*s, are parodies of essayists writing in the first person. These first-person parodies extort ironic self-revelation. They are directly manipulative: the parodee is made to confess things that he or she would never, presumably, want to confess. The resulting spectacle remains comic despite the obscurity of its subject.

The first-person confessional parody fails, not when the parodee is too obscure, but when the parodist is too prominent and his manipulations too obvious. 'John Oliver Hobbes' was the *nom de plume* of Mrs Craigie, and under that name in 1904 she published *The Artist's Life*, a collection of her essays and speeches. On the endpapers of his copy, Beerbohm wrote a parodic lecture called 'Isaiah, Watteau, and Strauss'.[29] There are some good touches. It nails the style of a public speaker who has nothing important to say and a stupidly digressive way of saying it. Its basic technique is the factitious comparison and personal intrusion:

Isaiah was a Prophet, Watteau was a Painter, Strauss is a musical composer. Strauss was born in the 19th century, Watteau in the 18th; but Isaiah was born so long ago as the 7th century B.C. Thus between Isaiah and Watteau there is a far greater interval than between Watteau and Strauss. There have been very few feminine Prophets. In the nature of women there seems to be (I say it with a giggle) something that prevents them from prophesying. But Isaiah was not a woman. Isaiah was a man. About his parentage and his early

[29] In the Berg Collection, New York Public Library.

education little is known. It is likely enough that, in his boyhood, people did not foresee his future eminence. There were people who did not foresee mine.

Beerbohm's surprisingly bad ear for American speech (notorious from the case of Abimelech V. Oover, in *Zuleika Dobson*) is only part of the problem—as in 'I've got culture but I'm a right smart Amuurican gurl, and don't you make no darned error about it.' Worse is the fact that his personal animosity keeps bubbling to the surface so that we hear an actually angry Beerbohm rather than a plausibly parodied Mrs Craigie.

The giggly femininity, for instance, does not mimic her actual style; rather, it expresses Beerbohm's masculine antipathy. Mrs Craigie confesses that

my private motive (between you and me and Papa's Little Liver Pills) is that I have nothing whatsoever to say about Isaiah or Watteau or Strauss—nothing, that is, to say above the level of any high school girl who has dipped into a popular encyclopedia ... and when at length I suddenly resume my seat I shall smile round on you so sweetly, with such a modest brilliance, that you really won't be able to realise that I have merely succeeded in making fools of you, and a fool of myself. My hat, at which so many of you are looking, cost 17 guineas.

This parody is only a not-for-publication marginal tampering; but its privacy discloses things that Beerbohm's published parodies keep hidden. The main drama going on in it is the contest between parodist and parodee, as Beerbohm almost literally tries to take the book away from Mrs Craigie. In better parodies the parodist's strength is his invisibility; signs of struggle have been eliminated, and the contest is already over.

In first-person parodies the satire can be at odds with other parodic values. But that problem can be overcome if the object of the self-confessional parody is an author, like Moore or Harris, who actually specializes in outrageous self-confession. G**rge B*rn*rd Sh*w begins 'A Straight Talk (*Preface to "Snt George: A Christmas Play"*)' with a prefatory confession:

When a public man lays his hand on his heart and declares that his conduct needs no apology, the audience hastens to put up its umbrellas against the particularly severe downpour of apologies in store for it. I won't give the customary warning. My conduct shrieks aloud for apology, and you are in for a thorough drenching. (*Christmas Garland*, p. 155)

And he proceeds immediately to the major confession: 'Flatly, I stole this play.' But unlike Mrs Craigie's confession, Sh*w's is perfectly in character. Sh*w tells us, 'flatly', that he stole the plot of 'Snt George' because, like Shakespeare, he was 'too lazy' to make up his own plot. Only a baker's dozen of the possible plots in the world have got themselves told:

The reason lies in that bland, unalterable resolve to shirk honest work, by which you recognise the artist as surely as you recognise the leopard by his spots. In so far as I am an artist, I am a loafer. And if you expect me, in that line, to do anything but loaf, you will get the shock your romantic folly deserves. The only difference between me and my rivals past and present is that I have the decency to be ashamed of myself. (p. 156)

The final sentence could as plausibly be attributed to Shaw as to Sh*w; and in either case we would know that the writer was *not* ashamed of himself. The idea of Shaw as a loafer is so wildly Shavian that it serves the mimicry rather than, directly, the satire. What then is being satirized? The style pretends to take us into its confidence but actually speaks from the heights of self-secure superiority. The style says about Shaw what Beerbohm's reviews often say—that for all his cleverness and technical competence Shaw has no sympathy for real people. Sh*w borrows plots, not out of laziness or because there are only a limited number of plots, but because he is not in contact with the real human emotions his voice tries to mimic. His bluffly honest self-confession is the dishonest act of a man who is always on stage.

But the parody is still limited in comparison to some in *A Christmas Garland*. Beerbohm does a preface rather than a play. We get the Shavian voice and an agile deployment of ironies around a supreme ironist; but, as with other self-revelatory first-person parodies, we remain aware of Max manipulating G.B.S., and the interest is of a different kind than the interest we have in watching Max become the author of an absurd story by Henry James or George Meredith, by Conrad, Galsworthy, or Arnold Bennett. The first-person parody is a clever turn by a ventriloquist and his dummy; by contrast, J*m*s's 'The Mote in the Middle Distance' is a full-dress comic drama. In 'A Straight Talk', as in his dozen years of drama reviewing, the urgency of Beerbohm's competition with Shaw keeps him from really getting his man.

There was no such urgency in the case of Arnold Bennett. The result is 'Scruts', one of the more amiably entertaining of the *Christmas Garland* parodies yet in its way as trenchant a criticism as Virginia Woolf's in 'Mr Bennett and Mrs Brown'. The parodist first met his parodee in 1909: Beerbohm wrote to Bennett praising *The Old Wives' Tale* and inviting him to lunch at the Savile: 'Do come—I know I should like you, in my humble way; and you'd probably like me—c'est mon metier to be liked by the gifted: I somehow understand them.'[30] In fact he needed to meet Bennett so that he could draw him. The kittenish tone is professionally Max. In return for lunch Bennett will donate his 'gifts' to Max's gallery of caricatures and parodies.

'Scruts' is only slightly taller than some of the tall tales in Bennett's own *Tales of the Five Towns.* Beerbohm manages to exaggerate the intentional comedy of a Bennett tale as well as the unintentional comedy of B*nn*tt's effort to wring universal significance out of supposedly documentary realism. Emily Wrackgarth is a fiercely independent Bursley woman keeping house for her brother Jos. Albert Grapp is a meek Hanbridge bank clerk who has been invited to Christmas dinner by Jos. 'Scruts' is the story of how Albert woos and wins Emily by calmly eating every scrutty scrap of her Christmas pudding. The narrator explains that *scruts* are discarded fragments of flawed pottery:

The dainty and luxurious Southerner looks to find in his Christmas pudding a wedding-ring, a gold thimble, a three penny-bit, or the like. To such fal-lals the Five Towns would say fie. A Christmas pudding in the Five Towns contains nothing but suet, flour, lemon-peel, cinnamon, brandy, almonds, raisins—and two or three scruts. There is a world of poetry, beauty, romance, in scruts—though you have to be brought up on them to appreciate it. . . . Of Emily Wrackgarth herself people often said, in reference to her likeness to her father, 'Her's a scrut o' th' owd basin'. (*Christmas Garland*, p. 89)

The angry Emily loads her pudding with scruts; Albert rises to her challenge:

Without a sign of nervousness he raised his spoon, with one scrut in it, to his mouth. This scrut he put between two of his left-side molars, bit hard on it,

[30] 9 May 1909, in the Berg Collection, New York Public Library.

and—eternity of that moment!—felt it and heard it snap in two. Emily also heard it. He was conscious that at sound of the percussion she started forward and stared at him. But he did not look at her. Calmly, systematically, with gradually diminishing crackles, he reduced that scrut to powder, and washed the powder down with a sip of beer. (p. 97)

Scrut by scrut, and despite 'a slight abrasion inside his left cheek', Albert advances in heroism: 'He knew that what he was doing was a thing grandiose, unique, epical; a history-making thing; a thing that would outlive marble and the gilded monuments of princes.'

While Albert chews he talks calmly to Jos about 'the Borough Council's proposal to erect an electric power-station' and about 'a first edition of Leconte de Lisle's "Parnasse Contemporain" that he had picked up for sixpence in Liverpool . . .' Emily's eyes on him 'were collective eyes—that was it! They were the eyes of stark, staring womanhood.' Albert swallows the last of Emily's scruts: '"Happen", he said without a quaver in his voice, "I'll have a bit more, like"'. Emily flings her arms forward on the table and buries her face in them: 'It was a gesture wild and meek. It was the gesture unforeseen and yet incredible. It was recondite, inexplicable, and yet obvious. It was the only thing to be done—and yet, by gum, she had done it.' B*nn*tt's anthropological pretensions are mocked by the juxtaposition of the Bursley vernacular with the 'recondite' ('and yet obvious'), as they are by the wilder juxtaposition of the Borough Council with Leconte de Lisle, and by the Shakespearean allusion to marble and gilded monuments. Emily's elevation to the status of collective womanhood, like the narrator's exclamations throughout the story ('Fantastic!' 'Impossible!' 'Odd!'), is a hard lump of pretension, a scrut in the pudding of his tale.

The parodies of Conrad and of Hardy's *Dynasts* are similarly ingenious burlesques, but like the Bennett they still lack the wilder inventiveness of the James parody. The comparison suggests that it may in fact be preferable to love what one mocks. But these parodies also lack the vigour of the Wells and Kipling parodies—which shows that contempt is another good motive for parody. In a letter in 1910 Beerbohm laid out his reasons for despising Kipling:

The schoolboy, the bounder, and the brute—these three types have surely never found a more brilliant expression of themselves than in R.K. (Nor, I will further grant, has the nursery-maid.) But as a poet and seer R.K. seems to me not to exist, except for the purpose of contempt. All the ye-ing and the Lord-God-ing and the Law-ing side of him seems to be a very thin and trumpery assumption; and I have always thought it was a sound impulse by which he was driven to put his 'Recessional' into the waste-paper basket, and a great pity that Mrs Kipling fished it out and made him send it to *The Times*. I think (absurd though it is to prophesy) that futurity will give him among the poets a place corresponding exactly with the place reserved for Theodore Roosevelt among statesmen.[31]

His animus was formed during the Boer War and had a specifically political focus; but it outlasted the original occasion and its focus broadened. Even the famous caricature in *The Poets' Corner* (1904), 'Mr Rudyard Kipling takes a bloomin' day aht, on the blasted 'eath, along with Britannia, 'is gurl', goes beyond the immediate political point by making Kipling a hyperactive little monster of uncontrollable enthusiasm.

It would be no paradox to say that what Beerbohm hated in Kipling was Kipling's hatred, his fierceness of feeling that only made itself more dangerous when it appeared in the service of chauvinism or sentimentality. Kipling's fictional men show the ugly side of sentimentality, a quality Beerbohm devastatingly mocked in his 1903 review of a stage adaptation of *The Light that Failed*. He toys with the idea that 'Rudyard Kipling' is the pseudonym of a woman writer, since only women are so 'permanently and joyously obsessed' with 'the notion of manhood, manliness, man'. Real men writers take virility for granted; women writers dwell on the lurid fact that their 'male characters are men'. But 'Kipling' cannot be a woman, in fact, because he lacks a woman's redeeming squeamishness. He relishes whatever is ugly: 'Writing of George Sand, Mr Henry James once suggested that she, though she may have been for all intents and purposes a man, was not a gentleman. Conversely, it may be said that Mr Kipling, as revealed to us in his fiction, is no lady. But he is not the less essentially feminine for that.'[32]

[31] 30 October 1910 to Holbrook Jackson; in the Taylor Collection, Princeton University.
[32] 'Kipling's Entire', 14 February 1903, in *Around Theatres*, pp. 245–8. Cf. 'An Aside' 8 April 1899, in *Around Theatres*, pp. 28–30, in which Beerbohm imagines Kipling as a Frenchman: '. . . he would never have extricated himself from the necessity of journalism, and would at this moment be known to us only as a particularly virulent Anti-Semite, Chauvinist, and fulminator against "*perfide Albion*". Luckily he was not born under the French standard of literary taste.'

So, in 'P. C., X, 36', from which I quoted at the beginning of this chapter, K*pl*ng fawns over a stupid, strapping constable and dances in hysterical joy as the foreigner, Santa Claus, 'squealing and whimpering', is beaten and dragged away. The parody is excessive and unfair, and means to be so. It meets a threat with a threat. And, to move finally to the other object of Beerbohm's undisguised loathing, the parody of H. G. Wells is similarly remarkable both for its accuracy and its anger. I will say more about his relations with Wells in my next chapter. Here, the measure of W*lls's 'Perkins and Mankind', which was published in the 1912 *Christmas Garland*, can be taken by comparing it with the earlier parody Beerbohm published in the 1896 series. In 1896 Wells was the author of *The Time Machine*; the socialist utopian writing was still to come. In 'The Defossilized Plum-Pudding' W*lls's narrator is having his annual Christmas dinner with Simpson, 'the most brilliant Pantaeschrologist of his day'. Simpson has a club-foot, long, bony fingers, and a 'scar that runs vertically from his forehead to his chin'. He mutters, serves middling sherry, and sends the narrator to sleep before he is half-way through his annual true story. In past years the narrator has slept through 'The Carniverous Mistletoe', 'The Secret of the Sinister Crackers', and 'The Microbes in the Yule Log'. This year Simpson begins to talk about the plum pudding they have just eaten, which 'was originally a cannon-ball. It was picked up on the field of Naseby. Never mind how I came by it. It has been under treatment in my laboratory for the last ten years.' And so on as the narrator drifts into unconsciousness.[33]

'The Defossilized Plum-Pudding' is a funny parody that takes off a typical Wells narrative situation, his descriptive realism, and, of course, his early brand of science-fantasy. 'Perkins and Mankind', by contrast, is a more elaborate and less genial affair. It begins with the young reformer Perkins at the Duchess's party, to which he has come in response to 'a three-page wire in the hyperbolical style of her class, conveying a vague impression that she and the Duke had arranged to commit suicide together if Perkins didn't "chuck" any previous arrangement he had made'. Perkins's scheme to found 'a Provisional Government of England by the Female Foundlings' has not fared well in Parliament:

[33] In *Leaves from the Garland Woven by Max Beerbohm*, pirated ed. (New York: Max Harzof [G. A. Baker & Co.], 1926).

What was the matter with the whole human race? He remembered again those words of Scragson's that had had such a depressing effect on him at the Cambridge Union—'Look here, you know! It's all a huge nasty mess, and we're trying to swab it up with a pocket handkerchief.' Well, he'd given up trying to do that.... (*Christmas Garland*, p. 35)

After dinner, Perkins finds a book on the shelf by his bed: '*Sitting Up For The Dawn*! It was one of that sociological series by which H. G. W*lls had first touched his soul to finer issues when he was at the Varsity'. The rest of 'Perkins and Mankind' is W*lls's Fabian pamphlet within a W*llsian novel, a parody within a parody. Beerbohm thus does Wells in several voices: the narrator's, Perkins's, and the pamphleteer's. And the pamphleteer cites other pamphleteers, by quotation and footnote. Part of the parody's grim humour is the contrast between this proliferation of voices and the literally deadly uniformity they advocate.

The pamphlet proposes a way to rid the social organism of that canker called 'Sunday' and yet 'to secure for the human units in the Dawn—these giants of whom we are but the foetuses—the holidays necessary for their full capacity for usefulness to the State ...' (p. 41). W*lls's solution is to divide the community into ten sections and to assign to each section one day of the decimal week as its 'Cessation Day'. And 'The five-hundredth and last day of each year shall be a General Cessation Day' to be observed by 'all those who shall in the course of the past year have reached the age-limit':

You figure the wide streets filled all day long with little solemn processions— solemn and yet not in the least unhappy.... You figure the old man walking with a firm step in the midst of his progeny, looking around him with a clear eye at this dear world which is about to lose him. He will not be thinking of himself. He will not be wishing the way to the lethal chamber was longer. He will be filled with joy at the thought that he is about to die for the good of the race—to 'make way' for the beautiful young breed of men and women who, in simple, artistic, antiseptic garments, are disporting themselves so gladly on this day of days. They pause to salute him as he passes. And presently he sees, radiant in the sunlight, the pleasant white-tiled dome of the lethal chamber. You figure him at the gate, shaking hands all round, and speaking perhaps a few well-chosen words about the Future ... (pp. 45–6)

Perkins has read enough. The chambers of his soul have been swept clear of cynicism and lethargy, and he goes off to meet the Dawn as a character in W*lls's novel.

I don't know why Beerbohm chose—if that is the word—to hate Kipling and Wells rather than, say, Belloc or Chesterton, both of whom were eligible to be hated, not only on my own scale of values but on what I understand of Beerbohm's. Ordinary political standards do not apply. I am tempted to explain his loathings by saying that beyond all the vocal shape-shifting, and despite his claims that he was too unsystematic to be held to any belief, Beerbohm did in fact stand for a few irreducible values—civility and good grace, tact, kindness. The claim is true, I have no doubt, but it depends for its interest on Beerbohm's *performance*, since only in the variety-act did the stable centre of values become available. And to rest too much on the claim may deprive the act of all that is not civil, tactful, or kind in it; it falls into Max's tender trap.

More pertinent than the question of his affinities is his choice of parody as the means to express them. The born parodist, like the born musician, has a technically expert ear; only he hears a social consort, a community of voices. It begins as a genetic quirk. And even then it is usually 'a speciality of youth' that diminishes as the personality hardens and becomes deaf to other possibilities. But 'the mimetic marvel' continues to hear, and continues to keep open the more mysterious passage from reception to re-creation. It is a strange instance of the ordinary way in which we can be both ourselves, alone, and also entertain the possibility of otherness.

Max the parodist is closely related to 'Max the essayist', and both to 'Mr Beerbohm the man'. He stands in the tradition of essayists who use words to stop the gap made *by* words between artifice and artificer. According to Hazlitt, Montaigne's great merit is that he 'was the first to say as an author what he felt as a man'; therefore, 'we know not which to be most charmed with, the author or the man'.[34] Hazlitt thus creates precisely the distinction he, like Montaigne, wants to overcome. Not sincerity, but presence is at stake. And the *illusion* of it is success, even when that illusion is accomplished by quotation, misquotation, allusion, and similar tools of the parodic trade, as so spectacularly it is in both Montaigne and Hazlitt, as well as in Lamb and Beerbohm. Max the essayist brings his personality to literature, and Max the parodist brings another's. And then he brings more and more, all of them, like the men in the frescoes on the Villino's walls, at home in the engrossing intimacy of Max's art.

[34] William Hazlitt, 'Of the Periodical Essayists', in *The Complete Works*, ed. P. P. Howe (London and Toronto: J. M. Dent, 1933), vi. 92, 93.

7.
Men of Letters

IT is hard to say where the volume called *Seven Men* properly begins or ends. Published by Heinemann in 1919, it is a collection of five stories about six men who happened to cross paths with the unassuming seventh, Max Beerbohm. An enlarged edition, published in 1950, included one more story and two more men. Like *A Christmas Garland*, *Seven Men* seems to be a collection that could grow indefinitely. Characters who verifiably exist without the author's aid—Will Rothenstein and Arthur Balfour, for instance—walk in and out of its weirdly permeable space. Seven of the eventual nine men are authors: their inventions infiltrate Beerbohm's invention, making the borders that separate creation from creator eerily indistinct. The whole affair has a ghostly indeterminacy. The characters' precarious existence depends on their being perceived by that seventh man who exists, like them, as a character in the stories of Max Beerbohm.[1] This conundrum of representation links the stories of *Seven Men* to the parodies of *A Christmas Garland*.

Some of them actually are ghost stories and, perhaps needless by now to say, also parodies of ghost stories. The connection between *Seven Men* and *A Christmas Garland* goes deeper than the obvious fact that 'Enoch Soames' (for instance) contains parodies of the decadent writing of the 1890s or ' "Savonarola" Brown' a parody of Stephen Phillips's pseudo-Elizabethan verse drama. The author-characters in

---

[1] In Knopf's American edition of *Seven Men*, the volume's illusory 'realism' was reinforced by the addition of sketches purporting to have been made at the time of Max's original encounters with his six men. His portrait of A. V. Laider, for instance, is done on stationery from the (fictitious) Beach Hotel, Linmouth, Sussex (Propr. R. Garrow); a page of rough sketches of Enoch Soames at the Cafe Royal also contains a sketch of Will Rothenstein. In a letter to the Century Company about American publication (at the Houghton Library, Harvard University), Beerbohm wrote: 'The form of the stories is biographical and autobiographical. They pretend to be *memories*. I would suggest, therefore, that in America, as in England, the book's format should be unlike that of ordinary fiction.' He suggests, as he had about *Zuleika Dobson*, that the type and binding 'should be of a kind suitable to a book of *essays*'.

Seven Men are shadowy doubles, taking and giving life. As the parodist is to the parodee—a double whose mimicry threatens to undo the original—so, in various configurations, the author-characters of *Seven Men* are to one another.[2] They are alter egos asserting individuality in a world of words where authors are the product of their all-too-imitable writing. *A Christmas Garland* presented parody under the aspect of a Christmas cracker, a little package with a harmless explosion and funny hat. *Seven Men* presents it as black magic. Actively or passively, aggressively or shyly, the men in Max's collection try to overcome their rivals by curious acts of imaginative or even protoplasmic engorgement. Some of them die in the process, others just fade away.

Beerbohm wrote the original five stories between 1914 and 1918. These are the same years in which he wrote the best essays in *And Even Now* (1920), including 'The Golden Drugget', 'No. 2 The Pines', 'Hosts and Guests', 'Quia Imperfectum', and 'A Clergyman'. Also from this period is the ambitious but uncompleted project called *The Mirror of the Past* and the related drawings that would be gathered as *Rossetti and his Circle*. It is strong work from a man barely in his middle age, but it is also his last strong work.

The style prances less than in *Zuleika Dobson*; it has been chastened by the twelve years labour at the *Saturday Review*. Beerbohm is now a writer with a personality so assured that he can seem by his relative stylistic restraint to be taking its existence for granted. He seems to feel no need to impose himself. He wins our confidence not with daring stunts on the verbal trapeze but with comradely demonstrations of how much we, his discerning readers, have in common with him, our talented friend. Of course it was only through his 'painful carefulness', as he told Reggie Turner, that 'the public [was] beginning to regard [him] as really rather a wit'.[3] And a theme that links all this work suggests how far from nonchalance he actually was about his status. The stories, the essays, even the collection of caricatures suggest 'that mankind is divisible into two great classes'.[4] There is war

---

[2] See Ira Grushow, *The Imaginary Reminiscences of Sir Max Beerbohm* (Athens: Univ. of Ohio Press, 1984). Grushow makes the *Seven Men*-type of story the centre of his interesting analysis.

[3] 10 July 1920, *Letters to Reggie Turner*, ed. Rupert Hart-Davis (London: Hart-Davis, 1964), 252.

[4] 'Hosts and Guests', in *And Even Now* (New York: E. P. Dutton, 1921), 128.

between these classes, though it may be undeclared or it may seem merely playful. The contestants may be labelled hosts and guests, but they can also be servants and masters ('Servants'), talkers and listeners ('A Clergyman'), artists and hangers-on ('Quia Imperfectum'), writers and readers ('The Crime'), distinct personalities and dim. And it is unclear who has the advantage.

There was another war, a declared war, in the years that saw the writing of these stories and essays. 'The Golden Drugget' is unusual in making anything explicit of the fact. But the reformed style and the anxiety which (I believe) informs much of this work reflects the Great War's influence. The War is part of the real, emotional background for the imaginary conflicts fought by the seven men. The stories also reflect Beerbohm's personal situation: he was now doubly deracinated, an expatriate Englishman of foreign extraction driven back to England and living as a guest in temporary quarters, uncertain if he would ever see his Villino Chiaro again. These were years of loss for him in other ways, too. His brother Herbert died in 1917, his mother less than a year later. He had achieved the status he claimed proleptically in 'Diminuendo': he was 'a classic'. By the same token he was in danger of being 'outmoded', fading away, losing that personal distinction he had won by writing well. *Seven Men* and the essays in *And Even Now* are assured performances, but motivated in part by a paradoxical uncertainty about the value of imaginative endeavour in a world of loss and death and apparently endless conflict.

'What a world! What a period to have been born into!' he wrote to Turner in September 1914. 'It is very epical and all that; but the horror and the sadness and absurdity of it! The horror duly horrifies me, and the sadness saddens, whereas by the absurdity "we are," like Queen Victoria, "not amused."'[5] The guns of August were only the beginning: *if* Germany is beaten, still, he predicts, 'we shall have in the not very distant future the epical business all over again'. His pose of ironic detachment has become hard to maintain: 'My breadth and delicacy of mind, and my far-sighted misgivings, come out only when I set pen to paper. They are part of my literary style.' And what to write in times like these? This is no Boer War, with its invitation to satire and caricature. 'Dear England has behaved with all the fineness one expects of her; and I love to think of her fleet and its magnificent

[5] 6 September 1914, *Letters to Reggie Turner*, p. 234.

success the world over, and its superb little raid on the Heligoland ships ... the *spirit* of England is beautiful.' The sentiment does honour to the English gentleman but was a danger for the ironist.

Moral fineness and delicacy of judgment had always guided Beerbohm's careening humour. His wildest irony was ballasted by a bottom of good sense. These qualities had carried him through the various crazinesses of the *Yellow Book* period, the Boer War, and into the Edwardian world. Now they threatened to silence him. David Cecil quotes his letter (December 1914) to Gosse:

It seems absurd to write to anyone about anything but the war. It seems to argue a lack of sense of proportion. But if I wrote anything about the war, not less guilty should I seem of that lack. What could I write that would not seem utterly trivial in proportion to this theme?[6]

He tells the proprietors of the Leicester Galleries that an exhibition of his drawings, scheduled for spring, must be cancelled:

My caricatures, exhibited while England is in the throes of a life-and-death struggle, would not merely fall flat: they would be an offence against decency. In time of peace, they are delightful, no doubt; but imagine a nation being called on, in the midst of a whole world's tragedy of suffering and horror, to enjoy my little jokes about Mr Hall Caine and Sir Gilbert Parker and Mr Bonar Law and Mr Sydney Webb and other people whose foibles, in time of peace, are very good fun, but whose very existence is forgotten in time of war. The idea is inconceivable. ...

The war is no laughing matter; and the war is *the only matter* in the present and in the near future.[7]

Nonetheless he continued to write and draw. In spring 1915 he and Florence left Italy. For most of the next two years they lived as Will Rothenstein's guests in the village of Far Oakridge, Gloucestershire. There, too, he wrote and drew. What to write in time of war? He wrote *Seven Men*, a book full of *trompe l'oeil* high jinks which is also a record of covert aggressions, lies, deadly gambles, thwarted ambition, and artistic bad faith.

I begin with 'James Pethel' and 'A. V. Laider', the two stories that seem anomalous in the collection. Neither is about an artist—except insofar as they are about the seventh man, Max Beerbohm. 'A. V. Laider' toys with the idea of the supernatural only to reject it, and

---

[6] Cecil, *Max* (London: Constable, 1964), 336.   [7] Ibid. pp. 336, 337.

'James Pethel' is keyed so low that it seems to be a mere slice of remembered life. Their central characters are physically unremarkable. James Pethel 'was inconspicuous . . . there was nothing at all odd about him' (*Seven Men*, p. 108). A man of 'moderate' age, size, and colour, he had 'so very usual a face' that it gave him 'a sort of frank inscrutability' (p. 119). A. V. Laider too 'was enigmatic' by virtue of being nothing very definite: 'he did not look soldierly nor financial nor artistic nor anything definite at all. He offered a clean slate for speculation' (p. 141). Because these characters do not declare themselves they must be read into. Max the writer therefore becomes a reader, trying to interpret the characters and their stories. But they are, of course, *his* characters in *his* stories: speculating on the text, Max holds up a mirror that reflects a multiple image of the reader in the author in the character.

We are familiar with unreliable narrators. What to make, however, of an unreliable reader reading his own unreliable text? Pethel and Laider are as ordinary as the language of everyday; but they turn out to be as slippery, too. The ironies with which Beerbohm teased the reader in *The Works* now tease the author.[8] In the early essays Max never lied because he never asserted; in a world of supposition he could mean what he said and its opposite, and let the reader sort it out. The more companionable, older and wiser Max now participates with us in our readerly dilemmas. He can no longer float over his text as he did in *Zuleika Dobson*.

'James Pethel' begins with an obituary: 'Though seven years have gone by since the day when I last saw him, and though that day was but the morrow of my first meeting with him, I was shocked when I saw in my newspaper this morning the announcement of his death' (p. 107). The newspaper's last word on 'him' immediately prompts the recollection. It was on Max's annual August holiday in Dieppe that he saw amidst the grotesquely fat or harrowingly thin gamblers at the Casino, 'the man whose memory I here celebrate': 'My gaze was held

---

[8] In places, *Seven Men* seems to me to step over the line Wayne Booth sets between 'stable' and 'unstable' ironies. For the most part, however, Beerbohm's irony is of the sort Booth attributes to 'many of the great personal essayists [who] provide experience in the art of deciding when to stop . . . [T]hey develop a tone which becomes known as their true style and which includes frequent stable ironies.' Beerbohm is Type 11 in Booth's (ironic) anatomy of ironic genres: 'The Comic Apotheosis of the Coping Self (Max Beerbohm)'. *A Rhetoric of Irony* (Chicago: Univ. of Chicago Press, 1974), 185, 212.

by him for the very reason that he would have passed unnoticed elsewhere' (p. 108). Though he was holding the bank at the principal table, 'Everything about him, except the amount of money he had been winning, seemed moderate' (p. 108). This is the first of several negatives or blanks in the reminiscence that demand readerly filling in. Why is Max's gaze held by this 'moderate' man, whose eyes had neither unnatural brightness nor unnatural dulness, who appeared neither nonchalant nor grim? In *The Works* he had defined the aim of dandyism as 'the production of the supreme effect through means the least extravagant'. The dandy has the power of his unsullied potential, a vacuity irresistible to the beholder's narcissism. At the Casino in Dieppe, one middle-ageing dandy has his self-regarding gaze held by another, his opposite and his double.

Who is he? Max learns from his friend Grierson that this is James Pethel: 'Oh, he's a great character. Has extraordinary luck. Always' (p. 110). Pethel is a member of the Stock Exchange, where his luck is even more spectacular than at baccarat. He hunts and shoots, also with great luck. He had married a barmaid at Cambridge when he was nineteen, and the marriage seems to have worked out well. 'Altogether, a great character' (p. 111).

They are introduced. 'He spoke to me with some *empressement*, saying he was a "very great admirer" of my work' (p. 111). Pethel disparages his own gambling, and Max, without saying how pleased he is to be seen talking with a rich admirer, allows that baccarat is as good a way of wasting time as another. 'Ah, but you despise us all the same!' Pethel says; and he adds 'that he always envied men who had resources within themselves' (p. 112).

Pethel collects his winnings, and Max (for all his enviable inner resources) fantasizes a scene in which Pethel insists on giving him the money 'as a very small return for all the pleasure your work has given me, and . . . *There*! PLEASE! Not another word!' But 'Nothing of the sort happened. Nothing of that sort ever does' (p. 113). So Max returns from fantasy to reality. The two men walk on the windy terrace and Pethel, looking 'at the black and driven sea', says that it would be great fun to be out in a sailboat. Indoors, they order drinks, beer for Max, plain water for Pethel: 'Pethel asked me to tell him who every one was. I told him no one was any one in particular, and suggested that we should talk about ourselves. "You mean", he laughed, "that you want to know who the devil I am?"' (p. 114). Max tells us that 'indeed, since he had *not* handed his winnings over to me, I did hope he would at any rate give me some glimpses into that "great character" of his' (p. 114).

A reader must feel by now that if James Pethel is to be 'a great character' Beerbohm had better set to work making him one. But the absence of anything remarkable in Pethel continues to be the main mystery. The reader (Max in the story, and the reader of Max's story) tries to supply the character Pethel withholds. Pethel explains that he never touches alcohol while he is gambling: 'It—takes the edge off' (p. 115). He wants 'the full sensation of gambling', the 'tremors . . . throes . . . thrills' (p. 115). His voluptuous dedication to risk-taking seems at odds with his moderation and his previous deprecation of gambling, and makes his motivation a puzzle. Max asks how a man who takes risks on Pethel's scale can get any thrill out of baccarat; and the stockbroker replies like an artist, 'While I'm playing a game like this tonight, I *imagine* the stakes are huge, and I *imagine* I haven't another penny in the world' (p. 117). But he preserves his mystery. When Max says, 'Ah! So that with you it's always a life-and-death affair?', Pethel looks away: 'Oh, no, I don't say that' (p. 117). And when Max mentions the nearly-magical aspect of Pethel's reputation, 'you have extraordinary luck—always', Pethel denies that he is always lucky: '"Good heavens", he exclaimed, "if I thought I had any more chance of winning than of losing, I'd—I'd—"' (p. 118). Max fills in the blank for him: 'Never set foot in that baccarat room tonight.' But Pethel re-opens the interpretive gap: he was, he replies, 'thinking of—oh, lots of things; baccarat included, yes' (p. 118).

Pethel invites Max to lunch with him and his wife and daughter the next day. He mentions that he has a new car, that his daughter is keen on motoring, that they will be starting the day after tomorrow on a spin through France and Switzerland. Does Max care about motoring? Would he join them for a spin after lunch? Arm in arm they pass into the corridor:

He asked what I was writing now, and said that he looked to me to 'do something big, one of these days', and that he was sure I had it 'in' me. This remark (though of course I pretended to be pleased by it) irritated me very much. It was destined, as you shall see, to irritate me very much more in recollection. (p. 119)

Pethel's remark links his putative greatness as a 'character' with Beerbohm's bigness as an author. Though Max is annoyed by the patronizing tone, he implicitly accepts its challenge:

Though you may think me very dense for not having thoroughly understood
Pethel in the course of my first meeting with him, the fact is that I was only
conscious, and that dimly, of something more in him than he had cared to
reveal—some veil behind which perhaps lurked his right to the title so airily
bestowed on him by Grierson. I assured myself, as I walked home, that if veil
there were I should tomorrow find an eyelet. (p. 119)

Pethel's wife turns out to be small and grey, not the golden-haired
barmaid Max expected. Their 'little' daughter is tall, attractive, and
'absurdly' like her father. Like him she enjoys rough water and high
speed. 'Whenever he was looking at her (and it was seldom that he
looked away from her) the effect, if you cared to be fantastic, was that
of a very vain man before a mirror. . . . No one who ever saw that
father with that daughter could doubt that he loved her intensely'
(p. 122). Mrs Pethel seats Max in the front seat of the car with Pethel,
herself with her daughter behind: 'a person in the front seat was less
safe in case of accidents than a person behind. And of course [Max
tells us] I did not expect her to prefer my life to her daughter's'
(p. 126). The ride begins. It is exactly the hair-raising race the reader
expects. And suddenly Max understands—or thinks he understands—
his character's mystery: 'Here was the real thing—the authentic game,
for the highest stakes! And here was I, a little extra-stake tossed on to
the board' (p. 128).

Satisfaction at understanding—and at getting safely to Dieppe—
gives way to moral outrage. The language is unusually severe. Max
feels 'hatred' for Pethel. It is 'utterly abominable' that in order 'to
secure for himself the utmost thrill of gambling' he risks the lives of
his wife and daughter and of an author who has it in him to do
something big. He wants to stop Pethel, save the women, do *something*.
He fantasizes a confrontation. But the story ends in a series of
anticlimaxes. He never sees Pethel again, only sends a note declining
an invitation to join the family on the trip to Switzerland. And then we
are back at the obituary, which tells us that Mr James Pethel, the very
popular all-round sportsman and amateur pilot, suddenly fell dead of
a heart attack after returning from a flight 'which despite an extremely
high wind he had made on his new biplane and on which he was
accompanied by his married daughter and her infant son' (p. 133).
His doctor said that he had been warned repeatedly 'that any strain
on the nervous system might prove fatal' (p. 133). Max concludes that
Pethel's heart disease 'had its origins in his habits' and that he

17. 'Blue China' (Whistler and Carlyle) 1916

18. George Moore in Mexico, drawn on MS of 'Dickens by G**rg* M**r*' [n.d.]

19. 'Had Shakespeare asked me . . .' (Frank Harris) [unsigned, n.d.]

20. 'Revisiting the Glimpses. Shade of R. L. S[tevenson]: "And now that you have shown me the new preachers and politicians, show me some of the men of letters." Mr. Gosse: "But my dear Louis, these *are* the men of letters."' (Cunningham Graham, Wells, Chesterton, Galsworthy, Shaw, Zangwill,

21. 'N.E.A.C.' (Steer in middle, surrounded by Sickert, Orpen, W. G. de Glehn, Augustus John, MacColl, Tonks, Rothenstein [standing on table], Sargent, L. A. Harrison, Walter Russell, Albert Rutherston [under table]) 1907

The handwritten note in the image reads: "an. H. G. Wells and his patent mechanical New Republic; and the Spirit of Pure Reason crowning him President. (View of Presidential Palace in background) max"

22. 'Mr. H. G. Wells and his patent mechanical New Republic; and the Spirit of Pure Reason crowning him President. (View of Presidential Palace in background)' [1903]

23. 'At the Pines' (Swinburne and Watts-Dunton) [n.d.]

24. 'The sole remark likely to have been made by Benjamin Jowett about the mural paintings at the Oxford Union: "And what were they going to do with the Grail when they found it, Mr. Rossetti?"' 1916

therefore did not 'live his life with impunity': 'Let not our hearts be vexed [the story ends] that his great luck was with him to the end.'

The invitation to the reader to become an author, rewriting the story by an act of interpretation, is most obvious in that understated ending. Did Pethel's heart disease come (as Max says) from his gambling? Or did he gamble (as I might rewrite the conclusion) because he had heart disease? Was his luck with him when the plane didn't crash? Or was he playing a game he could only win by dying? While the reader is becoming active in the story, the author (we remember) remained passive despite being prompted to action by his moral feelings. Is Max's anger directed only at Pethel for using others, or partly at himself for having failed to stop him? But what difference would his intervention have made? The daughter did not die, while Pethel was bound to die in any event. To ask such questions is to make a solemn affair out of the joke hatched by the story's realistic pretence, as though the fictional Max's actions could matter, as though anyone could change the course of a story already written. But the fictional Max is also the real Mr Beerbohm; and for him, as author-reader, and for us, as reader-authors, the question whether to act or not can be a troubling question, in 1914 or now. There may be no way to defeat the Pethels of the world at their mad game. But how should the artist play?

'A. V. Laider' similarly invites unanswerable questions about fate, foreknowledge, and fiction. On their own and together, the two stories suggest a mirror-play of shifting identities among author, character, and reader. I will take up the 'A. V. Laider' invitation (more briefly) in a moment, but the suggestion of character doubles in 'James Pethel' deserves some thought, especially since one of the matters left untouched by the anticlimactic ending is the odd similarity between Jimmy Pethel the death-dealer and Max Beerbohm the humorous writer.

The sense that there is an unspoken affinity between these two figures begins as soon as Max's gaze is held by Pethel's blankness. What he sees is, like himself, a 'moderate' man. But Pethel is a villain who selfishly uses the people he loves and admires. Artists also use the people they love and admire, and no artist more so than the caricaturist or the parodist. (James Pethel was modelled on a man named Arnold Hannay, whom Beerbohm had in fact known in

Dieppe.[9]) Pethel and Max are attracted to each other as antagonists in a risky game. Max is an extra-stake in Pethel's gamble. But Pethel risks letting Max know who the devil he is: if they aren't killed in that car ride, Pethel will become one of Beerbohm's seven or nine or however many men. Max risks his life with Pethel, and Pethel his character with Max.

The unexpected connections between them contribute to the story's uncanny flavour. 'Uncanny' (*unheimlich*) is Freud's word to describe the feeling one has when encountering one's double—an experience, Freud acknowledges, more common in fiction than life.[10] Freud's essay on the uncanny appeared in 1919, not long before the publication of *Seven Men*; needless to say, Beerbohm did not read it. But Freud's essay is in large part an exercise in literary criticism; his main text is a story by E. T. A. Hoffmann, but he could have found equally fertile texts in some of Beerbohm's favourite authors, from Hawthorne to Stevenson to Conrad and James. James's 'The Jolly Corner' is one of the masterpieces of the uncanny and the subject of one of Max's best caricatures of James. Beerbohm did not need Freud to write his (parodic) tales of the uncanny. But Freud's analysis of the uncanny illuminates them.

Freud builds on Otto Rank's idea that the double is the projection of our own guilty feelings. What self-love rejects is embodied in this personified return of the repressed. But the double is only part of the experience of the uncanny. Freud draws on his recently developed idea of a repetition-compulsion: 'whatever reminds us of this inner "compulsion to repeat" is perceived as uncanny'. The uncanny is experienced, then, as something always-already happening, a first-time meeting with our familiar repressed desires. An otherwise innocent event takes on the appearance of fatefulness because of the 'omnipotence of thoughts', the irrational sense that desire (even repressed) can cause an event to happen.

Envy is therefore an emotion that often translates into the uncanny: 'Whoever possesses something that is at once valuable and fragile is afraid of other people's envy, insofar as he projects on to them the envy he would have felt in their place.' More generally, Freud says

[9] *Letters to Reggie Turner*, p. 240 and p. 145 n.

[10] 'The Uncanny' (1919), in *The Standard Edition of the Complete Psychological Works*, trans. and ed. James Strachey with Anna Freud (London: Hogarth Press, 1953–74), xvii. 218–54.

that 'an uncanny effect is often and easily produced when the distinction between imagination and reality is effaced, as when something that we have hitherto regarded as imaginary appears before us as real, or when a symbol takes over the full functions of the thing it symbolizes, and so on'. Whatever effaces the line between the living and the dead fulfils this requirement. Knowledge of our own mortality (the knowledge we most strictly forbid ourselves) comes upon us as the return of the repressed. The appearance of the double is therefore felt as a harbinger of death.

Explicitly, Max seems unaware of anything uncanny about 'good old Jimmy Pethel'. His impercipience is eloquent in the story's several anticlimaxes, which leave space for the reader's own recognitions. In effect, Beerbohm demystifies his story and tempts the reader to remystify it. Pethel is the *Erlkonig* disguised as an English stockbroker, taking his daughter on a deadly ride by motor car and biplane. He has 'extraordinary luck—always'; his gambling seems to go beyond compulsion into the magical realm where thoughts are omnipotent. His wealth is fabulous. He has a beautiful daughter who is so much like him that, 'if you cared to be fantastic', she is his mirror-image. He loves her with the intensity of his vanity; the narcissism increases the thrill of death. Discovering Pethel's perversity, Max feels personally threatened, and helpless. Only the obituary, the announcement that Death has died, frees Max to tell this story.

Freud's essay leads me to this interpretation, but it can also lead to a different one. Freud says that the death-dealing double is a projection of repressed desires. Max envies Pethel's wealth and worldliness. His envy projects malevolent intentions on to Pethel (for we only have it on Max's word, after all, that Pethel was gambling on death in the ride to Dieppe). His guilt at harbouring an unworthy emotion returns to him as an intimation of his own death, which he then rejects by refusing to acknowledge the uncanny aspect of the story. Writing the story satisfies his desire for revenge on the successful but otherwise innocent Pethel, and exorcises the destructive envy which threatens his own life.

My piling interpretation on interpretation and indeterminacy on indeterminacy unfortunately brings to my own mind an anecdote Edmund Wilson tells about his visit to Rapallo. Wilson asked Beerbohm 'what he thought of the theory that the governess in *The Turn of the Screw* was intended to be a neurotic case, suffering from hallucinations. This aroused him: he denounced this theory, starting out

with a sentence which began, "Some morbid pedant, prig and fool."'
Wilson then admitted that *he* was the morbid author of the theory.[11]
The incident easily forms itself into a caricature by Max. Indeed the
psychologically bizarre always converts to caricature and parody at his
touch, as it does in his caricature of Henry James's 'The Jolly Corner'
(Hart-Davis, *Catalogue*, no. 808). In James's story, Spencer Brydon
feels compelled to confront his alter ego—the self he would have
been had he remained in his native America. Max caricatures the
climactic moment when Brydon's double reveals its face: 'Horror,
with the sight, had leaped into Brydon's throat . . . for the bared
identity was too hideous as *his*, and his glare was the passion of his
protest.'[12] In Max's version, a very severe, surprised but quite
unterrified Henry James looks down on his other self, an American
plutocrat in evening dress with pearl button and gold watch-guard.
The *doppelgänger* is missing two fingers from one of his hands, as the
story requires, but his splendid moustache is Max's invention. Original
and double both have the great, glaring Jamesian eyes. There is
nothing spectral about the portly double, and nothing morbid about
that 'marmoreal darling of the Few', Henry James.[13] Max catches the
comedy of Brydon/James's 'protest' against the vulgarity of the ghostly
presence, and converts the horror into humour.

What Beerbohm does to 'The Jolly Corner' he does, preemptively,
to 'James Pethel'. No one could read that story for its narrative and
psychological subtleties, as I have tried to do, without feeling like a
morbid pedant, prig, and fool. But the story invites the reading. It is
an exemplary instance of authorial peek-a-boo: if you enter into it,
Max will tell you it was only a game; but if you stay outside you miss
the fun.

'A. V. Laider' more openly makes a joke out of the conditions of its
own narration. And it is more openly a story about the deviousness of
writing. The title character is a liar of the Cretan persuasion: A. V.

[11] Wilson, 'A Miscellany of Max Beerbohm', in *The Bit between my Teeth: A Literary Chronicle of 1950–1965* (New York: Farrar, Strauss, Giroux, 1965), 47; and *The Fifties*, ed. Leon Edel (New York: Farrar, Strauss, Giroux, 1986), 198.

[12] 'The Jolly Corner', in *The Complete Tales of Henry James*, ed. Leon Edel, vol. 12: *1903–1910* (London: Hart-Davis, 1964), 225.

[13] The phrase 'marmoreal darling of the Few' is from the sonnet written jointly by Beerbohm and Gosse, probably in 1908. It is printed in *Max in Verse*, ed. J. G. Riewald (Brattleboro, Vt.: Stephen Greene, 1963), 19.

Laider says that everything A. V. Laider says is a lie. That paradox is one of the things that makes him seem another of Beerbohm's authorial *alter egos*. In 'James Pethel' it was Max the author who failed to act on his knowledge; in 'A. V. Laider' it is Laider the character who takes the role of passive author—if we can believe the tale he authorizes. Both stories ask whether a person's actions matter, or whether we are characters in a story already written; and both ask what responsibility we have for the fictions in which we play our roles. Pethel is a risk-taker, Laider a risk-avoider. Yet both tempt fate. Both are uncanny characters masquerading as the most ordinary of Englishmen.

It is mid-February and Max is back at a familiar seaside hotel, once again convalescing from influenza. On the letter-board a few hopeful new envelopes keep company with their dusty unclaimed elders. One of the old envelopes 'was vaguely familiar':

It was mine. I stared, I wondered. There is always a slight shock in seeing an envelope of one's own after it has gone through the post. It looks as if it had gone through so much. But this was the first time I had ever seen an envelope of mine eating its heart out in bondage on a letter-board. (*Seven Men*, p. 140)

It is addressed to A. V. Laider. After a comforting dinner, Max recalls in detail the circumstances of the letter's writing.

They had been the only two guests in the hotel: '[H]e was just the right kind of guest. He was enigmatic . . . a clean slate for speculation. And thank heaven! he evidently wasn't going to spoil the fun by engaging me in conversation later on. A decently unsociable man, anxious to be left alone' (p. 141). Max could tell that Laider, too, was recovering from influenza. 'Anywhere but in England it would be impossible for two solitary men, howsoever much reduced by influenza, to spend five or six days in the same hotel and not exchange a single word. That is one of the charms of England' (p. 142). But the pleasure of noncommunication ends when Laider picks up a weekly review that Max had bought. 'It was a crisis. We faced it like men. . . . The social code forced us to talk now' (p. 143). They talk about a correspondence that was raging in the weekly review on the subject of Faith and Reason.

They discover that they both believe in palmistry, the grotesque idea (as Max describes it) that one's past and future are neatly mapped on one's hands. But Max knows that his belief is unreasonable, while

Laider says he has evidence. The discussion turns to the question of free will, in which Max believes more strongly than he believes in palm-reading: 'I'll be hanged if I'm an automaton', he says. Laider questions him:

> 'And you believe in free will just as in palmistry—without any reason?'
> 'Oh, no. Everything points to our having free will.'
> 'Everything? What, for instance?'
> This rather cornered me. I dodged out, as lightly as I could, by saying 'I suppose *you* would say it was written in my hand that I should be a believer in free will.'
> 'Ah, I've no doubt it is.' (p. 148)

But when Max holds out his palms Laider turns away: 'There was agitation in his voice as he explained that he never looked at people's hands now. "Never now—never again." He shook his head as though to beat off some memory' (p. 148).

So it comes out. The mild, reticent A. V. Laider says that he is a murderer, not in any bald sense of the word, but morally a murderer. With wonderful good breeding, the two uncommunicative Englishmen settle back in their chairs while Laider prepares to tell his story—a story, he says, that will shake Max's belief in free will.

The murders (for there were many of them) that he committed fourteen years ago were all 'due to the wretched inherent weakness of [his] own wretched self' (p. 150). He was 'twenty-six—no, twenty-seven years old, and rather a nondescript person'; a man of means, but desultory, aimlessly pursuing his hobbies, including the study of palmistry. And palm-reading told him that when he was *about* twenty-six he would have a narrow escape from a violent death. He became very cautious, 'very circumspect, very lamentable!' (p. 151). If a railway journey could be avoided, he avoided it. But one November, not long after his twenty-seventh birthday, he was travelling by rail from his uncle's place in Hampshire with several other guests. There were six of them in the carriage. And at their excited request he agreed to read their hands. He read Mrs Elbourne's hand and saw that she would die violently, very soon. He did not tell her. He read Mrs Blake's hand and saw the same fatal text. He read it in Mrs Elbourne's daughter's hand too. He desperately wanted to pull the communication cord to stop the train. Nothing easier: 'I was quite at liberty. I was going to do what I had to do. I was determined, yes' (p. 156).

He awoke in hospital, with a racking headache. He had been unconscious for forty-eight hours after the collision.

Max reacts angrily to this fatalistic story: 'Do you really mean', he asked, 'that because you didn't pull that cord, you *couldn't* have pulled it?' (p. 158). He is angry at Laider's self-pity. When Laider again calls himself a very weak man, Max demands to know whether he is too weak to believe in the possibility of free will. Laider says it is marked in his hands: he was destined to suffer.

Back in London an idea occurred to Max. It was 'an ingenious and comfortable doubt. How was Laider to be sure that his brain, recovering from concussion, had *remembered* what had happened in the course of that railway journey? How was he to know that his brain hadn't simply, in its abeyance, *invented* all this for him?' (p. 160) He wrote to tell Laider his idea; that was the letter still waiting on the letter-board when Max returned a year later. Except that when he looks again, the envelope is gone: 'Resourceful and plucky little thing—it had escaped!' He has a vision of his envelope 'skimming wildly along the coastline . . . dodging past coast-guards, doubling on its tracks, leaping breakwaters, unluckily injuring itself, losing speed, and at last, in splendour of desperation, taking to the open sea' (p. 161). Or perhaps it was only that Laider has returned?

They meet again on the sands. 'Influenza, of course?' they ask simultaneously. There is a long silence before Laider mentions the letter. It has not comforted him. It has made him feel very guilty. Max's theory was right, in a way, only it didn't go far enough. Laider hadn't seen the signs in those hands. In fact, he hadn't been in Hampshire, ever. Trying to take an imaginary load off Laider's conscience, Max has laid a real one on it. Laider explains that his weakest point is his will, and that influenza fastens on one's weakest point. But he has a strong imagination. Ordinarily his will keeps his imagination under control, but when it is weak, as with influenza, his imagination invents the most preposterous fables. 'Until I've thoroughly shaken off influenza, I'm not fit company for anyone' (p. 163); so he comes to this hotel to protect his friends from his unrestrainable fiction-making. The whole story about his belief in palmistry 'was a sheer improvisation' (p. 164). He feels his weakness and his guilt: 'I simply can't help telling what I've made up, and telling it to the best of my ability. But I'm thoroughly ashamed all the time' (p. 165).

Laider suggests that they keep their original distance from one another. He turns away with a smile. Once or twice in the following week it occurs to Max 'that perhaps Laider had told the simple truth at our first interview and an ingenious lie at our second' (p. 166). On the last evening of his stay they venture some small talk. A casual remark reminds Laider 'of something—rather an awful thing—that once happened to [him] ...' 'It was', writes Beerbohm, 'a very awful thing indeed' (p. 167), and the story ends by threatening to begin all over again.

In 'A. V. Laider' Max comforts himself with the sort of interpreta-tion I read into 'James Pethel', or Edmund Wilson into 'The Turn of the Screw'. *He* now has the ingenious idea that Laider's story about the train-wreck is the projection of an unsound mind, and therefore an untrustworthy fiction. But the least morbid interpretation could not return this story to a healthy state. In 'A. V. Laider' fiction itself is tainted: imagination figures as a symptom of influenza, and story-telling as a weakness of the will. I began by likening the story to the paradox of the Cretan who says that all Cretans are liars. In fact, it is an infinite loop of paradoxes, in which a fiction-maker tells a story of a man infected with the fiction-making germ who tells the story which ends with the beginning of yet another story. The reader may want to find a way out of this plague of fictions. We recall Max's fantasy of the plucky envelope, escaping from the letter-board and skimming freely over the waves, avoiding all pursuers in the spunky magnificence of its unconstrainable communication. In fact, however, that otherwise dead letter was revived by an infected reader, Laider himself. The envelope is another figure, like influenza, which Beerbohm's self-regarding story suggests for itself. So is palmistry, the questionable practice of reading the uncreated future inscribed in the flesh of the living past.

The story's formal intricacy is not just an exercise in the bizarre, like a drawing by M. C. Escher. It mirrors a question about the status of art and artists. Like the genteel seventh man, the nondescript A. V. Laider creates fictions that unsettle reality, partly because they may *be* reality—but a reality already tainted by mediation from its origin. Lying or truth-telling, his narratives question the priority of reality to representation, or of original to copy: like the parodist, this fictive liar smudges the distinction and thereby poses a moral problem. Laider is guilty of *something*: either he can know the future but is too 'weak' to prevent its disasters, or he is too 'weak' to prevent himself from falsifying the past and present. Influenza, palmistry, and undelivered

letters are among the story's self-images. Another is the 'communication-cord' Laider didn't pull to stop the train on which he may or may
not have been riding. The story was published in 1916. Could anyone
in the preceding years have pulled the 'communication-cord' or was
the European train bound for destruction? The story wanders comically, as Milton's fallen angels did damnably, through mazes 'Of
providence, foreknowledge, will, and fate, | Fixed fate, free will,
foreknowledge absolute | And [finds] no end' (Paradise Lost, ii.
559–61). Like the debate on Faith and Reason in the letters column
of Max's weekly review, such questions go on being asked until 'even
the Editor suddenly loses patience and says "This correspondence
must now cease—Ed"' (Seven Men, p. 144). Beerbohm's pose of
ironic bemusement, which he found harder to maintain at this time
than at any other, lightens this dark fable into a social comedy about
an Englishman who only wanted to be left alone.

Great poets are strong misreaders of their giant precursors. They
wrestle art out of the anxiety of influence. This is Harold Bloom's
vision of the artist's sublimely parodic reaction to inevitable belatedness.[14] But it is a vision that holds only for the minority of writers.
The majority lead lives of a quieter desperation. Not the anxiety of
influence but the itch of envy is what most writers suffer. The
heartbreaking knowledge that the other guy is getting the attention
you deserve is an unspeakable affliction. Parody, however, like criticism, gives artistic envy a socially acceptable expression. Beerbohm is
the artist of envy not only in his specific parodies but in the stories
and essays which chronicle the envy of others. 'Hilary Maltby and
Stephen Braxton' and 'Enoch Soames' are the appropriately small
masterpieces in this marginal genre.

Authorial envy may be dignified by claiming for it a metaphysical
basis. Anyone can covet a neighbour's spouse. Everyone at some time
curses his fate, wishing himself 'like to one more rich in hope, |
Featured like him, like him with friends possessed'—to quote a
greater anatomist of envy, Shakespeare. But a writer's envy is not
driven by crass covetousness. It is driven by the writer's need to be
perceived in order to be. An unread writer might 'literally die for want

[14] Harold Bloom, The Anxiety of Influence (London: Oxford Univ. Press, 1973).

of recognition', as Max diagnoses Enoch Soames's tragic fate. To be published, read, and praised is to be a 'personality'; but to write and have one's writing go unread is to grow terminally 'dim'. Writers invest their substance in their writing, and they envy the advantage gained by anyone who is more read (hence more real) than they are.

There is only so much writerly substance to go round—at least, that seems to be the case in the stories about writers in *Seven Men*. The haves condemn the have-nots to their precarious existence; the more-perceived are responsible for the tormenting envy of the less-perceived. So writerly guilt is the alternative to writerly envy. But the parodist has a unique way of slaking envy while also avoiding guilt: he keeps both himself and his parodee before the substance-confirming public. He manages both to get and give. That is one of the odd adaptations to the writer's syndrome of envy and guilt explored in *Seven Men*.

Hilary Maltby and Stephen Braxton are the pair most openly locked in struggle. The envy of the one and the guilt of the other create an uncanny farce. Maltby was the author of *Ariel in Mayfair* and Braxton of *A Faun in the Cotswolds*. The 'reasoned and seasoned judgment of [Max's] middle age' is that 'Maltby's "Ariel" was a delicate, brilliant work; and that Braxton's "Faun", crude though it was in many ways, had yet a genuine power and beauty' (*Seven Men*, p. 57). Their one joint summer of success was in 1895, but 'anything that happened in the bland old days before the war does seem to be a hundred more years ago than actually it is' (p. 55). Both novels were 'firstlings'. The 'secondlings' appeared the following year. Both were failures. Maltby and Braxton were forgotten.

Max remembers them, however. They were antitheses: 'Dapper little Maltby—blond, bland, diminutive Maltby, with his monocle and his gardenia; big black Braxton, with his lanky hair and his square blue jaw and his square sallow forehead' (p. 59). They were alike only in 'one simple and obvious point ... Wherever they were invited, there certainly, there punctually, they would be. They were both of them gluttons for the fruits and signs of their success' (p. 59). As rivals they were perfectly matched:

Week in, week out, you saw cancelled either's every momentary advantage. A neck-and-neck race. As thus:—Maltby appears as a Celebrity at Home in the *World* (Tuesday). Ha! No, *Vanity Fair* (Wednesday) has a perfect presentment of Braxton by 'Spy'. Neck-and-neck! No! *Vanity Fair* says 'The subject of next week's cartoon will be Mr Hilary Maltby'. Maltby wins! No, next week Braxton's in the *World*. (p. 62)

Then came a sign that Maltby had taken the lead. The Monday morning paper always carried a list of the guests who had been entertained by the Duchess of Hertfordshire at Keeb Hall. 'The list published on that first Monday in June began ordinarily enough, began with the Austro-Hungarian Ambassador and the Portuguese Minister.' Dukes and Duchesses, Peers with their Peeresses followed. 'The rear was brought up by "Mr A. J. Balfour, Mr Henry Chaplin, and Mr Hilary Maltby"' (p. 63).

Max thought that the absence of Braxton's name might have been a typographical error. He wrote to Maltby, but there was no reply. He learned that Braxton had left town, had taken a bungalow on the east coast. He heard that Maltby too had left town. His own theory was that Maltby had taken a bungalow on the west coast to balance Braxton. 'Anyhow, the parity of the two strivers was now somehow re-established':

In point of fact [Max says in conclusion of the story's first section] the disparity had been less than I supposed. While Maltby was at Keeb, there Braxton was also—in a sense . . . It was a strange story. I did not hear it at the time. Nobody did. I heard it seventeen years later. I heard it in Lucca. (p. 64)

And to Lucca the narration shifts.

There Max comes upon Maltby, who was now 'a very stout little gentleman, with gleaming spectacles and a full blond beard, [who] seemed to radiate cheerfulness' (p. 65). He was pushing the wheel-chair of an old Italian lady. The rest of the story is Maltby's first-person account of the events at Keeb Hall:

At the Annual Soiree of the Inkwomen's Club, in the spring of '95, Maltby met the Duchess of Hertfordshire, who hoped he wouldn't 'think her *very* bold if she said how *perfectly* divine she thought his book' (p. 68). She asked Maltby down to Keeb. She admired Braxton too. Did he think Braxton would also care to come to Keeb?

I hesitated [Maltby says]. It would be easy to say that Satan answered *for* me; easy but untrue; it was I that babbled: 'Well—as a matter of fact—since you ask me—if I were you—really I think you'd better not. He's very odd in some ways. He has an extraordinary hatred of sleeping out of London. He has the real Gloucestershire *love* of London. . . . I think it would be *kinder* not to ask him.' (p. 69)

Rapture overcame remorse in the week that followed: 'I hadn't realised how good my book was—not till it got me this guerdon; not till it got this huge advertisement' (p. 70). He describes his awkwardness travelling by train to Keeb with 'A selection of the tall, the cool, the ornate, the intimately acquainted with one another . . .' (p. 71). He was more overwhelmed as he passed through Keeb's 'Palladio-Gargantuan hall' out to the lawn where the Duchess was pouring tea. And there was Braxton! And then Braxton was gone.

Braxton materializes repeatedly to the increasingly demoralized Maltby. The ordinary embarrassments of social climbing take on a supernatural awfulness. Braxton appears in the mirror while Maltby shaves, and he cuts himself. He appears while Maltby is eating borscht, and he spills the red soup on his shirtfront. Maltby is 'nothing but a small, dull, soup-stained, sticking-plastered, nerve-racked recluse' (p. 82) when he retreats to his bedroom for the night—only to find Braxton already in the bed. His description of Braxton's ghostly properties sounds like a theoretical analysis of character in fiction: 'He wasn't tangible. He was realistic. He wasn't real. He was opaque. He wasn't solid' (p. 85). His explanation for the apparition is a tribute to the twin powers of authorial envy and guilt: 'He was merely envious of me. And—wanly I puzzled it out in the dawn—by very force of the envy, hatred, and malice in him he had projected hither into my presence this simulacrum of himself' (p. 86).

Disaster follows disaster next day. Braxton lounges in the bathtub where Maltby hoped to soothe the fatigue of his sleepless night. Braxton looms in his way when he is bicycling around the terrace with Lady Rodfitten: he swerves, knocking over the lady to whom he had, in imagination, already been dedicating his next novel. (Arthur Balfour graciously helped the old lady up and tried to alleviate Maltby's misery.) Alone of the 'pagan' men at Keeb, Maltby offers to accompany the Duchess to church. Braxton trips him on the way. And when Maltby takes his place in the pew, Braxton is there. Braxton sits 'slowly and fully down on [him]': 'No, not down *on* me. Down *through* me. What befell me was not merely ghastly contact with the intangible.

It was inclusion, envelopment, eclipse' (p. 96). He flees to the railway station, where Braxton sees him off by the 4:03 to Victoria. He crosses the Channel next morning.

Eventually Maltby found peace. From Keeb Hall he wandered until he came to Lucca where he rented the ground floor of 'a noble and ancient house' (p. 103). The *padrona* 'was the Contessa Adriano-Rizzoli, the last of her line. She is the Contessa Adriano-Rizzoli-Maltby. We have been married fifteen years' (p. 103). Maltby's narrative, and the story, ends with his further explanation, 'She is a lineal descendant . . . of the Emperor Hadrian.'

The concluding joke about Maltby's unexorcised snobbery is typical of the anticlimactic endings of the stories in *Seven Men*. Snobbery, whether of Maltby's effete or Braxton's surly sort, is only a side issue. But the joke focuses attention on Maltby's present state—a dapper little Englishman in Italy, complaisantly enjoying his exile from the centre of English arts and letters. By the same token, it calls attention to the similarity between the author of *Seven Men* and the author of *Ariel in Mayfair*, and triangulates the story's doubling relationships.[15] The original rivals are forgotten, or exist only in someone else's memory of the distant 'nineties. Max the memorialist goes on. Braxton's envy and Maltby's guilt were literally all-consuming; their rivalry is comically physicalized as 'inclusion, envelopment, eclipse'. But Beerbohm's way is the parodist's self-preserving way: 'Hilary Maltby and Stephen Braxton' is a metafiction that includes, envelopes, and eclipses the fictions of its authorial characters. *Ariel in Mayfair* is parodied in the story of 'Braxton at Keeb Hall', and *A Faun in the Cotswolds* becomes 'Maltby in Italy'. Beerbohm does without the parodist's usual middleman: he creates his own originals.

He is similarly thrifty in 'Enoch Soames', his other story about the literary wars of the eighteen-nineties. But where Maltby's and Braxton's novels are known to us only by title and brief parodic summaries, Soames's poetry is quoted and analysed. Maltby and Braxton tried to

---

[15] See Grushow, *Imaginary Reminiscences*, pp. 141–5, and 'The Chastened Dandy: Beerbohm's "Hilary Maltby and Stephen Braxton"', *Papers on Language and Literature*, 8, supp. (Fall 1972), 149–64. Grushow analyses 'the biographical and thematic implications of this story and how the archetype of the "double" may lurk behind the hallucinatory presences conjured up by Maltby's guilty conscience' (*Imaginary Reminiscences*, p. 141).

occupy the upper reaches of the literary world; Enoch Soames plumbs
the lower depths. He is the cartoon epitome of the *fin de siècle* would-
be Bohemian, 'a plain, unvarnished, Preston man' transformed into a
seedier English Baudelaire—the caricatured representative of a generation of artists destroyed by alcoholism, poverty, madness, and
suicide. But Soames's most self-destructive vice is not his absinth-
drinking or his 'Catholic diabolism'; it is his lust for literary fame.
Soames writes in order to exist; without readers he will 'literally die
for want of recognition' (*Seven Men*, p. 26). In Beerbohm's story
Soames finally gets his readers, but the fulfilment of his wish turns
out to be a writer's nightmare; he becomes *only* that which is read, a
prisoner of language. 'Enoch Soames' is the story of a writer who sold
his soul to the devil for a glimpse at his place in history, and found
that he was remembered as a character in a story by Max Beerbohm.

It is Beerbohm's wittiest exercise in parodic imperialism. It not only
sends its parodee to the devil. It seems to triumph over the conditions
of its own being, as Beerbohm, more agile than Soames, plays across
the planes of representation, apparently freeing himself from the law
of literary gravity that anchors a character to the page. The reader,
too, feels the effect of this comic liberation. Beerbohm's conflation of
fictive with real satisfies our primitive desire to have a story come
magically to life. At the same time it flatters our sophisticated belief
that a living fiction is only a literary joke. But precisely that sophisticated self-consciousness gives the comedy a desperate edge. Soames's
memory is preserved by a writer whose own literary identity seemed
precarious as he prepared to leave Rapallo for a wartime retreat in
rural Gloucestershire. Soames is all that Max is not, a 'ridiculous',
forgotten failure. But they are both writers who, in the course of the
story, look to books for traces of themselves, and find no self except
the trace. Each lives a life in art. As in the other stories in *Seven Men*,
Max's apparent opposite becomes his threatening double. Each is the
other's *hypocrite lecteur*, his *semblable* and *frère*.

The critic will find his own unlovely *semblable* in T. K. Nupton, the
humorless literary historian within the tale.[16] But Nupton is indispens-

---

[16] Nupton's name sounds as though it ought to yield hidden significance, but all I
can make out is that it's not a pun. Soames may owe part of his name to the critic
George Somes Layard, whose generally respectful review of *A Christmas Garland*, in
The Bookman December 1912, took exception to the 'fun poked at George Meredith,
Mr Thomas Hardy and Mr Henry James. It may be that I am old fashioned, but I

able: his chapter on 'Inglish Littracher 1890–1900' (published in phonetic spelling 'bi th Stait, 1992' [*Seven Men*, p. 43]) confirms Soames in his status as fiction. The (parodic) work of literary critical fact completes the logic of the (parodic) fiction. When fact and fiction become this hard to distinguish we approach the realm of the hoax. But from the artist's point of view, anyone who labours to untwine the strands of a carefully plaited hoax is a morbid pedant, prig, and fool. Beerbohm's invitation to enter into 'Enoch Soames' carries the threat that one will either be the victim of his hoax or (what amounts to the same thing) a pedantic unweaver of it, like T. K. Nupton.

Mindful of the risk, I will nonetheless notice that Beerbohm's hoaxing brings together some usually separate ways of *existing*. Take, for instance, this exchange between Max and Will Rothenstein about Rothenstein's refusal to draw a picture of Enoch Soames:

'Why were you so determined not to draw him?' I asked.

'Draw him? Him? How can one draw a man who doesn't exist?'

'He is dim', I admitted. But my *mot juste* fell flat. Rothenstein repeated that Soames was non-existent.

Still, Soames had written a book. (*Seven Men*, p. 15)

To Rothenstein Soames doesn't exist in a qualitative sense: he is too insignificant. To the reader Soames doesn't exist because he's a character in a story. Rothenstein says one can't draw a man who doesn't exist. In either sense of 'exist', Rothenstein is demonstrably wrong. Rothenstein's mistake shows how he himself has become a character in the story; one of his roles is to be a speaker of dramatic ironies, investing such words as 'determined' and 'exist' with meanings of which he is unaware. The quality of his own existence is therefore called into question by his questioning of Soames's existence. Yet Rothenstein the character is also the artist who actually drew the picture of Max Beerbohm. By including him in his collection of *Oxford Characters*, Rothenstein helped make Max 'a—slight but definite— "personality"' (*Seven Men*, p. 27) and gave him the edge over the dim, undrawn Soames. Now Beerbohm makes Rothenstein a character in

---

prefer not to laugh at sacred subjects.' With that qualification, Layard went on to 'recommend to those who like this sort of thing Mr Max Beerbohm in his assumption of the character of "the sedulous ape"' (*Bookman*, 43 [December 1912], 183). Unwittingly, perhaps, George Somes Layard was aping *Zuleika Dobson*'s 'For those who like this sort of thing, this is the sort of thing they like'.

Seven Men. Where is the solid ground in all this? Max thinks he can clinch the matter: Soames must exist because 'Soames had written a book'. But who hadn't?

Indeed the immediate occasion for the story is the publication of another book, one dedicated (literally) 'To Max Beerbohm'. Holbrook Jackson's *The Eighteen-Nineties* (1913) is a work of popular literary history; a work of non-fiction. It is more trustworthy than Nupton's later work but still not the stuff of real life. 'The past', as Beerbohm says, 'is a work of art', and Jackson's history necessarily recreates Max Beerbohm (along with Beerbohm's own stock company, from Wilde through G.B.S.) as a character in that work. In a chapter called, inevitably, 'The Incomparable Max', Jackson says that 'The New Urbanity [of the 1890s] had no finer expression than that which was summed up and set forth in the personality and art of Max Beerbohm.' According to Jackson, 'Max was the comic spirit of the Nineties. . . .'[17] In *The Eighteen-Nineties*, the living author of 1913 has become the 'expression' and 'spirit' of a vanished age. His apotheosis by Holbrook Jackson seems opposite to the fate of Enoch Soames, for Max begins by telling us that he 'looked eagerly in the index for SOAMES, ENOCH' and, as he feared, could not find him there. Max successfully exists because he is a character in someone else's book. But so, now, is Enoch Soames.

Because Holbrook Jackson had not written about Soames, Beerbohm will. He is as determined to memorialize him as Rothenstein is determined not to. He is determined to write about him though he will have to make him ridiculous. For Soames's sake, Max 'should be inclined to keep [his] pen out of the ink' (*Seven Men*, p. 10). But Max and Soames share a story, which is the story of Max writing about Enoch Soames. 'You will see, in due course, that I have no option' (p. 10). Freedom to choose, as we may or may not learn from A. V. Laider, is reserved for the uninscribed; and in the world of *Seven Men*, where 'to be' is 'to be perceived', only the already-written exists. Max has no option but to write 'Enoch Soames', so that T. K. Nupton can read it and write the literary history in which Soames will read about himself. Not Max's free will but literary history impels this story. Not Soames's existence only, but Max's, depends on it.

[17] Holbrook Jackson, *The Eighteen-Nineties* (London: Grant Richards, 1913; rpt. London: The Harvester Press, 1976), 117.

From Holbrook Jackson, the latest inscriber of Max's image, the story moves back to Rothenstein, one of the early inscribers: 'In the Summer Term of '93 a bolt from the blue flashed down on Oxford. It drove deep, it hurtlingly embedded itself in the soil. Dons and undergraduates stood around, rather pale, discussing nothing but it' (p. 10). The exuberant paragraphs that introduce Rothenstein, and in which Rothenstein introduces the undergraduate Max to the London art world, are dense with fact. They give an indelible illusion of reality, which is complicated (not contradicted) by the fact that they are *about* illusion—about artistic representation—itself. In Max's caricatures Rothenstein usually appears as an enormous, upthrusting head, with huge spectacles and thick lips, perched on a dwarfish body (Plate 21). The verbal caricature in 'Enoch Soames' is less grotesque—invariably the case in comparisons between Beerbohm's written and drawn figures. There is only a single physical detail, and that is of a comically mythic sort: 'He wore spectacles that flashed more than any pair ever seen.' The idea of a small, self-important man is conveyed in the rhythm of short sentences and the vocabulary of absolutes: 'The matter was urgent. . . . He did not sue: he invited; he did not invite: he commanded. . . . He knew every one in Paris. He knew them all by heart. He was Paris in Oxford' (p. 10).

The artistic Rothenstein is all business, all realism. And he trails with him, 'meteoritically', a wealth of historical associations—Whistler and Edmond de Goncourt; Walter Sickert and Aubrey Beardsley; Chelsea, Pimlico, the Bodley Head, the Café Royal—which make him the epitome of a time and place, a shorthand gesture toward a reality beyond the plane of the page. He also brings with him a history which extends into the story's already known future, guaranteeing a continuity between the story and the unrepresented life of the real Max Beerbohm: 'I liked Rothenstein not less than I feared him; and there arose between us a friendship that has grown ever warmer, and been more and more valued by me, with every passing year' (p. 11). Rothenstein is the story's solid ground, but he is also a product of its language as surely as 'the Warden of A, and the Master of B, and the Regius Professor of C' will be products of paint when they have 'sat' for him. Beerbohm caps this sophisticated exercise in illusory realism when, in London, Rothenstein inducts him into that 'haunt of intellect and daring, the domino room of the Café Royal'. There, 'amidst all those opposing mirrors and upholding caryatids, with fumes of tobacco ever rising to the painted and pagan ceiling', Max draws a deep breath, 'and "This indeed", said I to myself, "is life!"' (p. 11).

And in the midst of that life, while Rothenstein discourses on Puvis de Chavannes, they meet Enoch Soames, whose first words ('in a toneless voice') are 'You don't remember me' (p. 12). Against Rothenstein's positive, Soames is sheer negative—indeed the book he has written, which confirms his existence in Max's eyes, is called 'Negations'. He has another book coming out: '. . . he rather thought of giving the book no title at all. "If a book is good in itself—" he murmured, waving his cigarette.' Rothenstein counters Soames's pretentiousness with his realistic commonsense: '"If", he urged, "I went into a bookseller's and said simply "Have you got?" or "Have you a copy of?" how would they know what I wanted?"' (p. 15). Soames answers that the book will have his name on the cover, and he rather wants (looking hard at Rothenstein) a drawing of himself as frontispiece. But Rothenstein is determined not to draw what doesn't exist.

It would take a T. K. Nupton to explain all the jokes on the subject of non-entities. Soames's writing is unwittingly full of them. The preface to 'Negations' begins:

> Lean near to life. Lean very near—nearer.
> Life is a web, and therein nor warp nor woof is, but web only . . .
> (Seven Men, p.16)

'Stark: A Conte', is 'about a midinette who, as far as [Max] could gather, murdered, or was about to murder, a mannequin. It was rather like a story by Catulle Mendès in which the translator had either skipped or cut out every alternate sentence' (p. 17). Throughout 'Negations' 'there was a great variety of form; and the forms had evidently been wrought with much care. It was rather the substance that eluded me. Was there, I wondered, any substance at all?' Max meets Soames a second time in the domino room. Soames is reading; Max apologizes for interrupting; 'but "I prefer", Soames replied in his toneless voice, "to be interrupted" . . .' (p. 18). He tells Max that he goes every day to the British Museum reading room. Max had been there once but found it depressing: 'It—it seemed to sap one's vitality.' 'It does', Soames replies; 'That's why I go there' (p. 19). He goes there to read Milton: '"It was Milton", he certificatively added, "who converted me to Diabolism"' (p.19). And it is in the reading room of the British Museum, on the afternoon of June 3, 1997, that Soames will read Nupton's description of how

a riter ov th time, naimd Max Beerbohm, hoo woz stil alive in th twentieth senchri, rote a stauri in wich e pautraid an immajnari karrakter kauld 'Enoch Soames'—a thurd-rait poit hoo beleevz imself a grate jeneus an maix a bargin with th Devvl in auder ter no wot posterriti thinx ov im! It iz a somwot labud sattire but not without vallu az showing hou seriusli the yung men ov th aiteen-ninetiz took themselvs. . . . Thank hevvn we hav no Enoch Soameses amung us to-dai! (p. 43)

So the reading room that saps the writer of vitality also gives him his existence; it is where he exists as the thing which is read. But Soames is very little read. His second book, 'Fungoids', sells only three copies. His moroseness, Beerbohm writes, 'might have alienated me if I had regarded myself as a nobody. But ah! hadn't both John Lane and Aubrey Beardsley suggested that I should write an essay for the great new venture that was afoot—"The Yellow Book"? And hadn't Henry Harland, as editor, accepted my essay? And wasn't it to be in the very first number?' (p. 24). As Max becomes increasingly distinct in his success, Soames fades in failure. They are connected by the reciprocity of writer's envy and writer's guilt; and Soames, by virtue of the absoluteness of his failure, even has an advantage over Max:

Failure, if it be a plain, unvarnished, complete failure, and even though it be a squalid failure, has always a certain dignity. I avoided Soames because he made me feel rather vulgar. John Lane had published, by this time, two little books of mine, and they had had a pleasant little success of esteem. I was a—slight but definite—'personality'. Frank Harris had engaged me to kick up my heels in *The Saturday Review*, Alfred Harmsworth was letting me do likewise in *The Daily Mail*. I was just what Soames wasn't. And he shamed my gloss. (*Seven Men*, p. 27)

'I was just what Soames wasn't': that odd negative state includes being the parodic inventor of the poems that create Soames's identity as a writer. Beerbohm had a wealth of models; we can think of Soames as a caricatured composite of the Rhymers' Club, whose members included Lionel Johnson, Ernest Dowson, Arthur Symons, Richard LeGallienne, and the Yeats of *The Celtic Twilight*. Beerbohm decorated his own copy of *The Book of the Rhymers' Club* (1892) with jolly Bab-ballad figures that emphasize the suburban quality of their anglicized decadence.[18] Soames's character is similarly softened from the desperate originals. His comic dedication to absinth, for instance, recalls Lionel Johnson's suicidal alcoholism; and his 'Catholic diabolism' makes a joke out of Johnson's attempt to give ritual dignity to personal guilt. But the parodies could almost pass for the real things. Indeed, Soames's poetry is more restrained than some actual Rhymers' Club poems about 'palpitating passion's ecstasy', or about 'strange desire ... uncouth love ... oozy lips ... [and] creatures of the mire'.[19] From 'Fungoids' we have two poems:

To a Young Woman

Thou art, who hast not been!
　Pale tunes irresolute
　And traceries of old sounds
　Blown from a rotted flute
Mingle with noise of cymbals rouged with rust,
Nor not strange forms and epicene
　Lie bleeding in the dust,
　　Being wounded with wounds.

　For this it is
That in thy counterpart
　Of age-long mockeries
Thou has not been nor art.

(*Seven Men*, p. 21)

Beerbohm, as parodist-turned-critic, comments '. . . even now, if one doesn't try to make any sense at all of the poem, and reads it just for the sound, there is a certain grace of cadence. Soames was [Max concludes] an artist—in so far as he was anything, poor fellow!' (p. 22). The comment fits Ernest Dowson, but the poem itself sounds like several by Arthur Symons; for instance:

Enigmatical, tremulous,
Voice of the troubled wires.
What remembering desires
Wail to me, wandering thus
Up through the night with a cry,
Inarticulate, insane,
Out of the night of the street and the rain
Into the rain and the night of the sky?

---

[18] Copy in the Houghton Library, Harvard University.
[19] The first quotation is from 'The Sonnet' by G. A. Greene, and the second from 'Beauty Accurst' by Richard Le Gallienne, both in *The Book of the Rhymers' Club* (London: Elkin Matthews, 1892), 32, 28–9.

Inarticulate voice of my heart,
Rusty, a worn-out thing,
Harsh with a broken string,
Mended, and pulled apart,
All the old tunes played through,
Fretted by hands that have played,
Tremulous voice that cries to me out of the shade,
The voice of my heart is crying in you.[20]

Soames's other poem is from his diabolistic side. Max prefers it: 'Diabolism seemed to be a cheerful, even a wholesome, influence in his life':

Nocturne

Round and round the shutter'd Square
I stroll'd with the Devil's arm in mine.
No sound but the scrape of his hoofs was there
And the ring of his laughter and mine.
    We had drunk black wine.

I scream'd, 'I will race you, Master!'
'What matter,' he shriek'd, 'to-night
Which of us runs the faster?
There is nothing to fear to-night
    In the foul moon's light!'

Then I look'd him in the eyes,
And I laugh'd full shrill at the lie he told
And the gnawing fear he would fain disguise.
It was true, what I'd time and again been told:
    He was old—old.

                    (*Seven Men*, p. 22)

Max especially likes the third stanza: 'it was so bracingly unorthodox, even according to the tenets of Soames' peculiar sect in the faith' (p. 23).[21]

---

[20] 'The Barrel-Organ', in *Amoris Victima* (London: Leonard Smithers, 1897; rpt. New York and London: Garland Press, 1984), 44.

[21] *Seven Men*, like *A Christmas Garland*, has a life of its own. So it isn't surprising that a third poem by Soames should have surfaced elsewhere. From *The Winter Owl*, ed. Robert Graves and William Nicholson (London: Cecil Palmer, 1923), 20, here is

Max and Soames meet the Devil in the Restaurant du Vingtième
Siècle in Soho, 'almost opposite to that house where, in the first years
of the century, a little girl, and with her a boy named De Quincey,
made nightly encampment in darkness and hunger among dust and
rats and old legal parchments' (p. 28). The reference to De Quincey
indirectly raises a question about originality that haunts Soames's
story throughout. Soames claims that he owes nothing to France:
Baudelaire was a *bourgeois malgré lui*, Verlaine an *épicier malgré lui*, 'and
two-thirds of Villon were sheer journalism' (p. 20). But Soames
himself derives from such originals as Lionel Johnson and Arthur
Symons—who derived their artistic personalities from Baudelaire and
Mallarmé, as well as from Keats, Swinburne, and Wilde, and also
from the De Quincey who wrote about opium-eating and murder as a
fine art. English symbolist poetry of the 1890s was a movement
doomed to derivativeness yet struggling mightily for originality. It was,
in Soamesian phrase, 'rouged with rust' from its start. Beerbohm
recreates this decadent aestheticism in a parody which creates its own
version of the problem. It sends us in search of Enoch Soames's
original; but wherever we look—in Holbrook Jackson's book or in
Nupton's book-within-the-story or in such allusions as the one to De
Quincey—we find that each supposed original leads to some prior
representation.

No one in the story, including its author, is immune to the taint.
Max acknowledges and tried to deflect one of his own originals at the
very moment Soames vanishes into the future: 'A shudder shook me.

Soames's 'Tracked':

> He raked the ashes from the rusty grate,
> Coaxed the dull embers to a tremulous flame,
> And laid thereon the ashes of his shame.
> They burned in wreathes and spirals delicate,
> They vanished. That was done at any rate.
> Still, 'twixt the curtain and the window-frame,
> Lurked that soft other thing of evil name
> Which was less easy to annihilate.
> And what if—Hark! He stood erect and still,
> Then tip-toed noiselessly across the floor
> And listened. What if long-lipped Radziwill
> Knew? He knelt down, a man most loth to die,
> And, peering through the key-hole of the door,
> Saw there the pupil of another eye.
>   (Reprinted in *Max in Verse*, p. 119.)

With an effort I controlled myself and rose from my chair. "Very clever", I said condescendingly. "But—'The Time Machine' is a delightful book, don't you think. So entirely original!"' (p. 35). Beerbohm had parodied Wells in the first *Christmas Garland*, in 1896, and again in revised form in the volume of 1912. In caricatures too, as in the later parody, he treats Wells as a 'prophet and idealist, conjuring up his darling future'—to quote the caption of a caricature of 1907 (Hart-Davis, *Catalogue*, no. 1756). He treats him, that is to say, as a socialist, a Utopian, a thinker, like Shaw, and by those tokens not an artist. And he is, of course, unfair to Wells. A caricature from 1903 shows 'Mr H. G. Wells and his patent mechanical New Republic; and the Spirit of Pure Reason crowning him President. (View of Presidential Palace in background)' (Plate 22). The Presidential Palace is a nondescript modern apartment block. The Spirit of Pure Reason is a skinny, unsmiling man in a toga, operating an elaborate contraption to place a bowler hat on the head of H. G. Wells—who, eyes closed, and looking very much the grocer's son, awaits his democratic crowning. The social engineer in Wells did sometimes defeat the story-teller. But that is not the case in *The Time Machine*.

Wells's short novel was published in 1895, two years before Soames's disappearance. Its specific influence on Beerbohm is most apparent in *The Mirror of the Past* (which I discuss in the next chapter); but there is more of it in 'Enoch Soames' than Max's breezy remark to the Devil. In it Wells is far from being an optimistic spokesman for 'pure reason': in the year 802,701 AD the Time Traveller finds that 'the human intellect . . . had committed suicide' (Chapter 10). But *The Time Machine* is also intermittently humorous; at one point the Time Traveller even sounds closer to my idea of Beerbohm than to Beerbohm's caricatures of Wells: 'The fact is, the Time Traveller was one of those men who are too clever to be believed: you never felt that you saw all round him; you always suspected some subtle reserve, some ingenuity in ambush, behind his lucid frankness' (Chapter 2). His description of the Palace of Green Porcelain, a vast museum which links the upper and lower worlds, has an almost Beerbohmian ingenuity. The Time Traveller calls it 'the ruins of some latter-day South Kensington!' Books, rotted and entirely illegible, are among its exhibits: 'Had I been a literary man [the Time Traveller says] I might, perhaps, have moralized upon the futility of all ambition. But as it was, the thing that struck me with keenest force was the enormous waste of labour to which this sombre wilderness of rotting paper testified' (Chapter 8). The British Museum in 1997 and the Palace of Green Porcelain in 802,701 are, for an instant, surprisingly alike.

Like 'Enoch Soames', *The Time Machine* implies a satire on the aesthetes of the 1890s. The indolent, epicene Eloi 'had decayed to mere beautiful futility'; the 'delicate ones' represent the 'last feeble rill from the great flood of humanity' (Chapter 7). Beerbohm did not need Wells's example in order to write his own stories about two classes of mankind. But Wells was *there*, an unelected original. Beerbohm's artistic relation to Wells recapitulates the relations enacted within the stories of *Seven Men*. In parody and caricature, and in such ironic touches as Max's remark to the Devil about Wells's originality, Beerbohm puts as much distance as possible between himself (small, agile, ironic) and Wells (heavy, slow, serious). But each gesture of evasion is also one of recognition. Beerbohm *c.*1915 looks back to 1897 and sees himself mirrored, not only in Enoch Soames, but in a more durable literary double, H. G. Wells.

The story recognizes other figures from Beerbohm's literary land- scape as well. Shaw is there in the phonetic alphabet and Jaeger clothes glimpsed by Soames in the (future) British Museum. But Wilde is conspicuous by his absence: in 1897, the year of Soames's disappearance, Wilde was in Reading Gaol. Wilde's history gives point to the discussion in Beerbohm's story about the relation of the laws of art to the laws of life. Soames has returned from the future with Nupton's 'screed', which reveals how Beerbohm has sentenced him to spend eternity as an imaginary character. Max tries to exonerate himself: 'the name "Max Beerbohm" is not at all an uncommon one, and there must be several Enoch Soameses running around—or, rather "Enoch Soames" is a name that might to occur to any one writing a story.' And anyway, says Max,

'. . . I don't write stories: I'm an essayist, an observer, a recorder . . . I admit that it's an extraordinary coincidence. But you must see—'

'I see the whole thing', said Soames quietly. And he added, with a touch of his old manner, but with more dignity than I had ever known in him, '*Parlons d'autre chose*'. (*Seven Men*, p. 44)

In the evening that follows, Max repeatedly urges Soames 'to slip away and seek refuge somewhere' (p. 44)—as Wilde's friends had

urged him to do between the first and second trials. Like Wilde's
friends, Max advises Soames to give his story 'a happy ending'. And
like Wilde, Soames remains true to his aesthetic creed: '"In Life and
Art", [Soames] said, "all that matters is an *inevitable* ending"' (p. 45).
Max insists that 'an ending that can be avoided *isn't* inevitable'.
Soames's reply comes from the wounded heart of the parodee, angrily
confronting his parodist:

'You aren't an artist', he rasped. 'And you're so hopelessly not an artist
that, so far from being able to imagine a thing and make it seem true, you're
going to make even a true thing seem as if you'd made it up. You're a
miserable bungler. And it's like my luck.' (p. 45)

A new edition of *Seven Men* was published in 1950, long after Max
had slipped into his role as what *Life* magazine called 'beloved old Sir
Max Beerbohm'.[22] A reviewer in *The Scotsman* wrote that he was 'one
of the few modern writers who has become the object of a cult'. But
the same reviewer also entered a dissent: 'Masterly as [the stories in
Seven Men] are ... in tone, construction, and style, they are minor
works in the sense that they do not really have anything of vital
importance to say about life.'[23] This was written in the heyday of
the Leavises in England; the phrase 'vital importance ... about life'
may now sound very dated. But the implied questions—what is a
'minor' work? what are the important things a 'major' work says about
life—are inescapable in a consideration of *Seven Men*. And this is so
in part because Beerbohm himself raises them. The stories are, of
course, all mirror-like surface: they withhold the depths they seem to
disclose. The raw stuff is filtered by parody and caricature. Such a
pervasively self-referential art, when it happens also to be very funny,
invites the judgment that it is trivial—and by the same token disarms
the judgment, which it has already passed on itself.

Seven Men seems to have nothing of vital importance to say about
life partly because it is so resolutely about art. But 'art' thus becomes
the binary term with 'life', so that to think of one is to define the
other; and in *Seven Men* the axis keeps turning. In '"Savonarola"
Brown' the amateur playwright wants his characters to live with a will
of their own, unbounded by any laws of art. Max insists that the

<hr />

[22] *Life*, 20 September 1943.   [23] *The Scotsman*, 16 February 1950.

playwright must impose a form on their life. Centuries of theory about
the mimetic relation of art and life are summed up in their fatally
absurd debate:

'. . . in a tragedy', I insisted, 'the catastrophe *must* be led up to, step by step.
My dear Brown, the end of the hero *must* be logical and rational.'

'I don't see that', he said, as we crossed Piccadilly Circus. 'In actual life it
isn't so. What is there to prevent a motor-omnibus from knocking me over
and killing me at this moment?'

At that moment, by what has always seemed to me the strangest of
coincidences, and just the sort of thing that playwrights ought to avoid, a
motor-omnibus knocked Brown over and killed him. (*Seven Men*, p. 178)

Brown's death strikes a little blow for human freedom by breaking the
laws of art. His art—*Savonarola: A Tragedy*—tries to do the same.

With this story, strict parody engulfs the fable: Brown's play does
not merely illustrate his character, the way Soames's poems do; the
larger part of the story literally is his 'tragedy'. In 'A. V. Laider',
influenza caused fiction, which in turn contaminated truth. In
'"Savonarola" Brown', too, the amateur playwright is 'not immune
from influences' (p. 179). Everything flows indiscriminately into his
art, which (as his nickname suggests) virtually usurps his inartistic life
and death. Brown is hopelessly belated: even as a theatre-goer, he is
'a confirmed second-nighter' (p. 173). At his death, his uncompleted
play passes into the keeping of Max Beerbohm, who passes judgment
on it in his best *Saturday Review* style: 'Here is a play that abounds in
striking situations, and I have searched it vainly for one line that does
not scan. What I nowhere feel is that I have not elsewhere been
thrilled or lulled by the same kind of thing' (p. 179). Brown's
unfinished creation wallows in history. There is the 'history' it is
supposedly about, in fact a wildly bookish fantasy. The directions for
the third act curtain give the flavour of the thing:

Re-enter Guelfs and Ghibellines fighting. SAV. *and* LUC. *are arrested by Papal
officers. Enter* MICHAEL ANGELO. ANDREA DEL SARTO *appears for a moment at
a window.* PIPPA *passes. Brothers of the Misericordia go by, singing a Requiem for
Francesca da Rimini. Enter* BOCCACCIO, BENVENUTO CELLINI, *and many
others, making remarks highly characteristic of themselves but scarcely audible through
the terrific thunderstorm which now bursts over Florence and is at its loudest and
darkest crisis as the Curtain falls.*

And there is the history of the theatre: 'Savonarola' is a parody of
Stephen Phillips's verse dramas, which were themselves pastiches of

Shakespearean drama. Brown expects this mishmash of influences to take on a life of its own. As the story ends, Max is still waiting to record the skeleton's slightest movement.

The two 'other' men added to the later edition of *Seven Men*— Walter Ledgett and Felix Argallo—also become enmeshed with Max in a fatally collaborative literary creation. Their story was written in 1927 and published in *A Variety of Things* as 'Not that I Would Boast'. Except for its late date, it justifies Leo Braudy's comment that 'with the exception of Hazlitt's intricate ramblings, Beerbohm probably has more to say about the ontology of fame than any other writer before World War One'.[24] But 'Not that I Would Boast' is also significantly different from the earlier stories. It contains not even a hint of the uncanny: the mechanisms of literary fame are demystified; the production of books is seen as a branch of squalid commerce; and the liberal inventiveness of parody degenerates into literal hoax and forgery. It is not merely anxious about the status of art and artists, like the stories in the original edition, but openly angry. And it is unusual in that its anger is directed as much at the reader as at its rival authors. It reveals some of the stronger emotions that underlie the otherwise fastidious disdain Beerbohm mimed toward the vagaries of a literary reputation.[25]

Walter Ledgett is a clubbable little literary hack whose unpretentious good humour is eventually dampened by some volumes of collected letters. In the posthumous publications of Stevenson, Coventry Patmore, Henry Irving, and Meredith, Walter Ledgett is written down an ass. Supposedly out of pity, Max cooks up a scheme to rescue Ledgett's reputation and good humour. His scheme depends on the help of Felix Argallo, the dark, withdrawn, infinitely pitying Anglo-Spanish author whom Max had once sought out in his sad obscurity at Penge. Max puffed Argallo's work over the years; his reputation

[24] Leo Braudy, *The Frenzy of Renown: Fame and its History* (New York: Oxford Univ. Press, 1986), 524. Braudy also writes, 'In the comic mockery of Max Beerbohm . . . the grand and ghastly battles with the double that image the turmoil of artistic ambition for Poe or Stevenson or even Wilde are represented as by-products of the rage for publicity' (p. 523).

[25] Beerbohm's one universally acknowledged failure, the long parable called *The Dreadful Dragon of Hay Hill* (London: Heinemann, 1928; and included in *A Variety of Things*), is ostensibly about the aftermath of the War, and the way heroes are forgotten when danger is passed. But it is connected more than chronologically to 'Not that I Would Boast': they are both parables about the dependence of the performer on a fickle audience, and about the artist's need to go on producing illusions of creative heroism.

had risen; but his capacity for pity and self-effacement was undiminished. Max dictates several letters for Argallo to write: dated over the space of many years, they record Argallo's admiration for that great artist, Walter Ledgett. Argallo plays his part in the hoax to perfection: he commits suicide so that his *Life and Letters* can appear (edited by his semi-literate nephew) in time to do Ledgett some good. The forgeries are accepted, and soon, though Felix Argallo's own reputation once again fades, Walter Ledgett emerges as one of the great—if now no longer good humoured—writers of his day.

So far, 'Not that I Would Boast' could almost be an optimistic inversion of 'Maltby and Braxton': instead of destroying a rival, Argallo promotes his authorial double. There is some sting in the fact that the promotion requires Argallo's suicide, and that success only brings Ledgett unhappiness. But the real sting is in the story's end: Max now reveals that he has all along been buying Ledgett first editions in expectation of the time when their stock will rise in response to the fictitious revelations in Argallo's *Life and Letters*. The payoff is delayed by the War and Ledgett's longevity. But finally, on the very day of Ledgett's memorial service in Westminster Abbey, Max displays his wares to the American 'magnoperator' Nat Heinz. Along with the 'firsts' is a collection of 'relative matter' including letters from Ledgett, '*menus* that had been handed round after convivial dinners and signed by the diners of whom Ledgett was one . . . [and] several sketches of Ledgett made by Phil May'.[26] And there are the forged letters from Argallo to Beerbohm. The Argallos have 'greatly dee-preciated', according to Mr Heinz, but the Ledgetts draw from him a gratifyingly large cheque. The story ends with Max and a friend discussing the transaction. The friend protests that Max has sold cheap: 'My dear good fool, you've put nine hundred pounds into Nat Heinz's pocket!':

'Well, after all', I reasoned with him, 'that's exactly the sum he put into *my* pocket. So we're quits. I never want to get the better of anybody. Enough that for once Europe has held her own!'
'But she hasn't!' my friend retorted. 'America has got the books!'
This, I confessed, was a point I hadn't thought of. But perhaps also (not that I would boast) it is a point which Mr Heinz's clients, when these pages shall have appeared, won't think very much of.

[26] *A Variety of Things* (New York: Knopf, 1928), 267.

(The manuscript of 'Not that I Would Boast' was sold by Sotheby's in 1960 with other items from the library of Sir Max Beerbohm. The 388 manuscripts, hoaxes, forgeries, 'improvements', and other original work fetched a total of £26,654, much of it provided by Americans.)

Beerbohm had been proclaiming his belatedness since the publication of *The Works of Max Beerbohm*. There, the joke was to make the author posthumous at the moment of his literary inception. In 'Not that I Would Boast' the joke has become bitter; the turn against his own bibliophilic 'clients' is a symptom of disabling estrangement. In fact, Beerbohm's active career as a writer and caricaturist was virtually over in 1927. What followed was a careful, slow mining of work that had been started earlier. There was a surprising amount of it. In my next chapter I will do some mining of my own in order to present one of the most fascinating products of his active years, the unfinished novel he called *The Mirror of the Past*.

8.

The Mirror of the Past

JULIUS BEERBOHM, who had been known in his young manhood as 'Monsieur Superbe Homme', was sixty-two years old when Max, the last of his nine children, was born. I imagine he was built more on the scale of his son Herbert than of Max. Max wrote virtually nothing about him, and though he often caricatured his school masters, I have never seen a drawing of his father. But repeatedly he wrote about and drew the men of the generations between his father's and his own. His fascination with 'the period that one *didn't* quite know, the period just before oneself, the period of which in earliest days one knew the actual survivors'[1] is related to his distance from his father. It is compounded of nostalgic yearning to bridge the distance and dwell lovingly in a past he never had; and—because it is satiric and caricatural—of revenge, a grown boy's way of cutting the old man down to size. The motives are reciprocal. Love's insatiability feeds the satire; and the satire emphasizes the distance and increases the longing for an object always recreated as unattainable. Beerbohm's early retirement may have been motivated partly by a reasonable disgust with the modern world. But it also suggests his exhaustion with the task of engaging the endless series of intermediaries who stood between him and the unreachable object of his desire.

It was a version of an emotional double bind out of which have been created, along with much ordinary unhappiness, the utopias and dreamscapes of art. But Beerbohm found his utopia not only in the past. Books, like time itself, have the teasingly dual aspect of permeability and inviolability; the reader enters the text, as memory does the past, without possessing it—except, perhaps, when parody tears open the seamless text. Max burrows into the secret margins and unsuspected interlinear spaces. He reads 'Books within Books' and

---

[1] Letter to Holbrook Jackson, 30 Oct. 1913, in the Taylor Collection, Princeton University.

appraises the uncreated work of James's Hugh Vereker or Neil Paraday.[2] He creates a living clergyman from the silence that follows Dr Johnson's judgment that Dodd's sermons 'were nothing, Sir, be they addressed to what they may', and in the process raises the literary footnote to the status of primary text.[3] His imagination dwells on unfinished books ('Mr Pickwick and the Ancient Mariner are valued friends of ours, but they do not preoccupy us like Edwin Drood or Khubla Kahn'[4]) and vanished works of art, like Rossetti's faded fresco in the Oxford Union.

In the essay 'No. 2. The Pines' (1914) he actually visits one of the places where time and text lay themselves open, and where the old fathers become playmates. It is a perfect combination of nostalgia and satire. 'The Pines' in suburban Putney is where the elderly Swinburne lived with his friendly keeper Theodore Watts-Dunton. Young Max's sense of the ridiculous is not excited by the address nor his wonder by the simple fact of Swinburne's longevity; rather it is the discovery of a place entirely out of time that makes his first and subsequent visits to Putney so wonderful: 'The essential Swinburne ... was and would always be the flammiferous boy of the dim past—a legendary creature, sole kin to the phoenix' (*And Even Now*, p. 58). The discrepancy between the boy 'who had erst clashed cymbals in Naxos' and the little old man who 'smiled only to himself, and to his plateful of meat, and to the small bottle of Bass's pale ale that stood before him' (p. 66) is an obvious point of satire, but redeemed from the obvious by ironic affection: 'I loved those sessions in that Tupperrossettine dining-room, lair of solid old comfort and fervid old romanticism' (p. 79), where Swinburne talked excitedly about obscure Jacobean playwrights and where 'loomed vivid and vital on the walls those women of Rossetti whom I had known but as shades' (p. 62) (Plate 23).

Swinburne and Watts-Dunton are a pair like the characters in *Seven Men*, physically and spiritually opposite but bound in a relationship that is ambiguously symbiotic or parasitic. The poet and the proser have become parodies of one another in a place, No. 2 The Pines, that is itself a parody of domesticity. Max is as ambiguously related to

---

[2] 'Books within Books' (1914) in *And Even Now* (New York: E. P. Dutton, 1921), 110. Neil Paraday appears in James's 'The Death of the Lion', Hugh Vereker in 'The Figure in the Carpet'.
[3] 'A Clergyman' (1918), in *And Even Now*, p. 234.
[4] 'Quia Imperfectum' (1918), in *And Even Now*, p. 197.

both men as they are to each another. He is Watts-Dunton's sensible partner, like him a sober representative of the responsible world, unlikely to lose his head in rapture or humiliation; yet Swinburne draws him to Putney, and with Swinburne he shares his deeper affinities. Typically, Beerbohm softens certain facts. Swinburne's sexual kink about whipping and dominant women is transformed into a symptom of essential innocence. It becomes literally infantile: 'For babies, as some of his later volumes testify, he had a sort of idolatry . . . babies were what among live creatures most evoked Swinburne's genius for self-abasement' (p. 69). Like Max, Swinburne dwells in a fantasy of the past where he is forever the wise child and infantile father: 'In life, as in (that for him more truly actual thing) literature, it was always the preterit that enthralled him . . . he revelled as wistfully in the days just before his own as I in the days just before mine' (pp. 72–3).

The essay is caricature in the guise of memory, memory recognized as a parody of the real. Its sentimentality is shaded by its sense of the ridiculous yet never entirely extinguished. Its utopianism is figured in the comfortable womb-like interior of The Pines, which remains, however, anomalously suburban. Specifically Max sees it as Wonderland, with himself as a wide-eyed Alice, Watts-Dunton as the dormouse, 'And, had the hare been a great poet, and the hatter a great gentleman, and neither of them mad but each only very odd and vivacious, I might see Swinburne as a glorified blend of those two' (p. 74). Originally he was drawn to The Pines as a place of living memories. Now his own memory of that utopia is fading. He ends the essay with a comic reverie of some day meeting the old men in Elysium. Watts-Dunton will be as he had been at The Pines:

He will still be shaggy and old and chubby, and will wear the same frock-coat, with the same creases in it. Swinburne, on the other hand, will be quite, quite young, with a full mane of flaming auburn locks, and no clothes to hinder him from plunging back at any moment into the shining Elysian waters from which he will have just emerged. (p. 87)

Mazzini will be there, and Rossetti and Dante himself. Watts-Dunton will still be clucking over Swinburne: 'Look!—there's Algernon going into the water again! He'll tire himself out, he'll catch cold, he'll—'; only to break off with a guffaw, 'remembering that his friend is not deaf now nor old, and that here in Elysium, where no ills are, good advice is not needed' (p. 88).

'No. 2. The Pines' was written in 1914, the same year as 'James Pethel' and 'Enoch Soames'. Concurrently, Beerbohm was working on the potentially novel-length project called *The Mirror of the Past*. Like 'No. 2. The Pines', *The Mirror of the Past* is parody in the service of utopian nostalgia. Like the stories in *Seven Men* it blurs the lines between fact and fiction. As in the stories and the essay, its characters are spectral artists whose images exist insofar as they are perceived to exist. Swinburne himself is one of the characters in *The Mirror of the Past*. So are Rossetti, William Morris, Thomas Carlyle, and—incredibly—Max Beerbohm. With the exception of the last, these are the same characters who appear in the drawings published in 1922 as *Rossetti and his Circle*. Indeed, the drawings in *Rossetti and his Circle* and a few passages used in the 1955 radio broadcast called 'Hethway Speaking' were all that Beerbohm published of what would have been his most ambitious work.

The Mirror of the Past is unfinished in a peculiar way—more like a painting for which we have a partially coloured canvas and some preliminary sketches than like a novel which simply didn't reach its last chapter. Beerbohm saw his work-in-progress with a visual artist's eye as much as with a writer's feeling for the syntax of beginning, middle, and end. Thus on one page of the manuscript he puts a quick verbal sketch, sometimes the merest notes, for an entire scene or episode; on another page (which may appear anywhere in the manuscript's present order) he sketches part of the scene in greater detail; and on another page he breaks that detail into constituent parts and further elaborates it. To read the scene one has to refer to all three stages of composition and sometimes more. To make matters worse, the story that emerges from this palimpsest moves simultaneously forward and backward in narrative time; and because Beerbohm did not compose it sequentially, the reader of the manuscript (like its author) has to make frequent use of its several calendars and schemes. The page numbered 18 is headed 'Ending' while page 25 is headed 'His story'; page 19 is 'His death' and page 28 'First sight of him'; but none of those pages contains all the details that make up even the designated parts of the narrative.

I have tried to do something unusual with this fascinating hodge-podge. What follows is not an edition (which would be unreadable) but a reconstruction of a story that was never fully constructed in the first place.[5] As much as possible I have used the words of the manuscript itself; occasionally I have provided narrative links, and in this I have been helped by a letter Beerbohm wrote to the editor of the *Century* magazine with 'a very brief and arbitrary account of a book I am writing, entitled *The Mirror of the Past*'.[6] And I have taken the opportunity to interpolate my own observations. For his radio broadcast in 1955 Beerbohm stitched together several paragraphs from the manuscript. Ostensibly quoting from his deceased friend Sylvester Hethway (called in the manuscript, as I will call him here, Sylvester Herringham), Beerbohm gave first-person accounts of how Carlyle sat for his portrait to Whistler, of the sedentary Rossetti's troubles with the indefatigable walker George Meredith, of William Morris's manic plan to redecorate Sylvester's gracious sitting-room, of Meredith's opinions about Swinburne, and of Sylvester's teasing of Walter Pater. Because they are already available I have concentrated instead on Sylvester's own story and the story of how Beerbohm came to share with him the sight of the writers and artists of the 1860s through the 1880s.

[5] A version of my reconstruction was published in 1982 in *The Princeton University Library Chronicle* simultaneously with a limited edition volume called *Max Beerbohm and 'The Mirror of the Past'*. Ira Grushow discusses *The Mirror of the Past* in his book, *The Imaginary Reminiscences of Sir Max Beerbohm* (Athens: University of Ohio Press, 1984).

[6] Like the rest of *The Mirror of the Past*, the holograph letter to the Editor of the *Century* is in the Taylor Collection, Princeton University. Apparently the letter was never sent. It is written on the same paper as the rest of the manuscript, which consists of approximately 100 unbound leaves of very heavy, cream-coloured paper measuring 13 by 8 inches. Following the letter in the manuscript's present order come three pages from the work-in-progress, reasonably clear and with Beerbohm's instructions to a printer, but also bearing revisions and deletions, the latter made in heavy black India ink. After those pages the going gets rough. There is a group of pages numbered consecutively 1 to 64, but with pages 7 to 15 and page 52 missing. (Page 52 is owned by Virginia Surtees, to whom it was given by Beerbohm in 1954. It contains a copy of a drawing of Miss Surtees's great grandmother, Ruth Herbert. [Information from N. John Hall.]) Some of these pages are marked on both sides or have annexes; some contain drawings; some contain calendars or other schematic designs for the book's elaborate chronology; some contain only a few words while others are crowded with tiny notes linked by cross-referencing marks and criss-crossing arrows. Next come eighteen more pages, variously numbered. This group seems to come from the earliest stage of composition, but while some of its contents are found in revised form in the previous group of pages, other parts exist only here. Finally there are two typescript pages transcribing passages from the manuscript, with corrections in Beerbohm's hand. The manuscript's difficulty for the reader begins in trying to decide what ought to come where in this jumble of words, pictures, dates, quotations, lists of facts and names, dialogue, and narration.

At the conclusion of 'Hethway Speaking' Beerbohm plays on the opposition between a fictitiously 'real person' and his own less substantial reality as a 'fabricator'. He confesses that his memoirist existed

only in my imagination and in the intention I had many years ago to write a book about him—a book to be entitled *The Mirror of the Past*, a mirror which, hanging in his drawing-room, gradually ceased to reflect present things and began to reflect things long past. I had made many notes for such a book; and among them were those notes of Hethway's conversation which I have just been reading to you. Please don't be vexed with me for having let you suppose that Sylvester was a real person. I thought that he as a real person would be likelier than I as a fabricator to impress and please you. (*Mainly on the Air*, p. 130)

In his unpublished letter to the Editor of the *Century* he also confesses, 'Purely apocryphal these memoirs are—founded only on my rather full knowledge of the *actual* memoirs of the period, on my instinct for character, and on my rather dreadful little talent for "parody"'. In that letter he reverses but doesn't unperplex the relation of fabricator and fabrication:

The book is written in the first person; and the 'I' is not a fictitious I, but I myself.

The principal character in the book is a (fictitious) friend of mine, Mr Sylvester Herringham, now deceased.

We cannot fault either assertion nor entirely believe them, since a real person who converses with fictitious friends (now deceased) must either be crazy or be himself a kind of fiction. The first alternative is impossible in this case, but the second is not. It reminds us that Beerbohm's artistic affinities stretch forward to writers like Borges and Nabokov who similarly submit themselves to the secret spaces behind the plane of the page.

My reconstruction of *The Mirror of the Past* should demonstrate this. Incidentally it may demonstrate how a critic can make himself into a 'Savonarola' Brown or Enoch Soames—a ghost caught in a fiction solemnly protesting reality: Kinbote to Nabokov's John Shade, or Borges's Pierre Menard, author of the *Quixote*. I risk entering the world of spectral artists and imaginary memoirists because *The Mirror of the Past* is quintessential Beerbohm and therefore worth recovering. It plays with several genres and narrative forms, simultaneously exploiting them and commenting satirically on them. It is a mystery story and a historical novel, the two forms linked by their participation in the time-travel variety of science-fantasy. It is a *doppelgänger* tale: Max the narrator finds his double—both complement and opposite—in Sylvester Herringham, 'an interesting link with the past', as years later Beerbohm called himself.[7] It explores the narrative possibilities of limited perspectives. Herringham, who participated in the story-within-the-story, is a scientist among artists, a man of self-restraint in the midst of raging eccentrics. Max, who inherits the tale, is an ostensible *naïf*. And the mirror into which both are looking is silent. Like Henry James's *doppelgänger* tales it merges with 'the lesson of the master' form, the story, that is, of art's disturbing interventions in life. Like parody it pursues an originating occasion which at the moment of capture reveals more distant originals.

He worked on *The Mirror of the Past* from 1913 to 1916. The War may in part account for its incompleteness and the various layers of its composition. Its nostalgic irony—the product of Beerbohm's filtering of Sylvester Herringham's sentimental vision—may also reflect the unsettled times. In the preface to *Rossetti and his Circle* in 1922, explaining the sources of his knowledge of the Pre-Raphaelites, he writes that, in addition to old drawings and photographs, 'I have had another and surer aid, of the most curious kind imaginable. And someday I will tell you all about it, if you would care to hear.' That aid was, of course, Sylvester Herringham's mirror, so that he would seem still to have intended it for publication as late as 1922.[8]

Here is the manuscript's revised opening: three pages of reasonably clear copy, marked for the printer:

I.

In the Spring of 1896 appeared a little book of which I was author and (for it was my first book) proud. It contained seven essays. One of these was a mock-archaeological discourse on 1880—the year in which, with results amusing and touching, the Aesthetic Movement was made known to Mayfair. By

[7] 'A Small Boy Seeing Giants', in *Mainly on the Air* (New York: Knopf, 1958), 34.
[8] An undated prospectus for *The Collected Edition of the Works of Max Beerbohm* lists two otherwise unknown books, *Sylvestre* and *Memories*. Seven volumes of this edition were published in 1922, two others in 1924, and the final volume in 1928. The ghostly *Sylvestre*, possibly also *Memories*, refers to *The Mirror of the Past*. (See John O. Kirkpatrick, *Max on View* [Austin: Univ. of Texas Humanities Research Center, 1978], 48, item 79.)

reason of that essay I was, in the hallowed phrase of the publicist, 'inundated with correspondence'. In other words, I received one letter.

Bell House, Cheyne Walk, S.W.   July 22, 1896

Sir,—I am an old man, & you are a very young one. I have moreover had the pleasure of knowing several members of your family. I trust you will take these three facts as sufficient excuse for my informality in addressing you.

I have read with no small amusement your whimsical paper '1880'. That is a period which may well seem remote to yourself. Not so to me who celebrated in 1880 my 51st birthday[9] & had thus already reached an age when (as you yourself will find later on) time flies with ever-increasing celerity. To me the 'Aesthetes' & 'Professional Beauties' & other folk of whom you write with not unkindly malice seem no more remote than the persons of today—indeed considerably less so, for during the past years I have become something of a recluse. I am the more amused therefore to find that these persons have as it were 'passed into history'!

Perhaps 1880 & the two or three years subsequent really were, as you seem to think, a definite & important era in our social history. I am too near to them to give them their due. But it has occurred to me that as you are so much interested in them, you might care to come in contact with one of the poor old survivors. If ever you are in this quarter of the town you might possibly care to come in and see me. I go out (in fine weather) between 11 & 12 in the morning and 3 & 4 in the afternoon. At all other hours I am at home.

Believe me to be
Yours faithfully
Sylvester Herringham.

To how many people in 1913 is that signature significant of anything, I wonder? It would not have meant much to many people even in 1896. But to me it meant rather much.

In 1880 I had been eight years old. Every child needs and must somehow have some sort of imaginary life. I was not a strongly imaginative child. I could not create out of my own heart a world for my habitation. I disbelieved in fairies. I was not at all sure about knights errant. I was glad to hear that the sea had been swept clear of pirates, and that Red Indians were dying out; for I was a timid child, always on the side of law and order—a predilection which perhaps accounts for my having chosen to imagine myself a policeman, usually. Night-beats, as tending to the possibility of conflict with ferocious burglars, I eschewed. After dark I was simply a man of the world. I was a very

---

[9] Sylvester mistakes his age. He was born in 1838, and should therefore have reached his forty-second birthday in 1880. When Beerbohm met him he was fifty-eight.

tall man of the world, with a large blond moustache and a pair of those small side-whiskers which lingered as a relic of the so very hirsute 'sixties. In my eye was a monocle, in my buttonhole a gardenia, in my shirt-front a jewelled solitaire. I dined at my Club, on chicken and cherry tart, and then went to a Party. I had a great contempt for the Professional Beauties and for the Aesthetes; and also for the Mashers, because, although I looked like one of them, I was tremendously clever. Indeed, I hardly know why I went to the Party: I suppose I had nothing better to do. As I have said, I was not a very imaginative child . . . Unequal to the task of inventing anything for myself to do after the Party, I always stayed late there—was still there when I fell asleep in my crib. I never invented even the name of my host or hostess. Always I was the guest of some one about whom I had fragmentary knowledge from the talk of my grown-up brothers and sisters. Sometimes the Party was at Mr Hamilton Aïdé's, sometimes at Mr Ionides' or at Lady Freke's; and on Mondays it was always at Mr Sylvester Herringham's. 'Herringham's Mondays' were famous in the London of that era. They were almost as famous as Ste. Beuve's had been elsewhere.

II.

And I had forgotten to bring them into my essay! This was my first thought when I read that letter.

And Herringham was still alive! This was my second thought.

And it really was very nice of him to write to me. That was the third of my thoughts, and the only one, of course, expressed in my reply to him.

I was leaving London within a few days, and was going to be away for two months. I wrote that I looked keenly forward to the privilege of visiting him as soon as I came back.

The receding dates—a narration set in 1913 or thereabouts, looking back to 1896 and the publication of the essay '1880'—begins the movement into the past that the novel will fulfil in its surprisingly literal way. The heading 'Charm of the Past' occurs several times in the manuscript. But one entry under the heading records 'the inferiority of the *remote* past'. Quoting Rossetti's poem 'The Burden of Ninevah' ('One of his most "amusing" ', Herringham calls it), the speaker says, 'One gets more thrill out of ["Sighing I turned at last to win | Once more the London dirt and din"] than out of Semiramis-One is real to us, the other not- Had you your choice you would choose Rossetti or even Sir Henry Layard' rather than ancient Ninevah with its 'grossness- drink- smells- cruelty to animals'.[10] In

[10] The occasion of Rossetti's poem (1870) was the installation in the British Museum of ancient Assyrian monuments excavated by Sir Henry Layard (1817–94).

'No. 2. The Pines' Beerbohm's nostalgia for the prenatal 'period of which in earliest days one knew the actual survivors' makes him, in his visits to the warm Victorian interior at Putney, *like* an Alice behind the looking-glass. In this unfinished novel the looking-glass really opens.

In its present order the manuscript continues with an anticipatory biographical account of Sylvester Herringham:

He was the only son of that Alfred Herringham of whom, when he was appointed Painter Extraordinary to William IV, it was said by Charles Lamb that 'he would be a very extraordinary painter to any one'. But Charles Lamb was a rather fastidious critic; and Sir Alfred (he was knighted in 1834) was much admired by the simple many as well as by the simple Sailor King. His colossal 'Ajax Defying Lightning' drew crowds to Brandon's Hall of Wonder, Regent Street, throughout the winter of 1831. His vast 'Re-union of Ulysses and Penelope' and 'Hector Taking Farewell-Leave of His Wife Andromache and the Child Astyanax' were displaced from their wall in Windsor Castle only when the royal collections were re-arranged after the death of Queen Victoria. They exist, I suppose, as dishonoured rolls of canvas in one of the royal attics or cellars; but this is better for them, poor things, than being thrown on the market. Two years ago I saw with my own eyes their creator's almost infinite 'Juno Upbraiding Jupiter in the Presence of Mars, Neptune, and Minerva' in the sale-room of Christie's. It fetched seventeen guineas. Though I am no expert I am bound to say that the price seemed to me rather excessive. Luckily for his son and heir, Sir Alfred did not invest in the purchase of his own paintings the money he made out of selling them. With that money, instead, he bought railway stock, right and left, in the early 'forties, and in the seventh year of that decade died, leaving in trust a comfortable fortune for Sylvester, who had just been transferred from Harrow to Oxford. Lady Herringham was no more—had lived, indeed, only long enough not to die Mrs. It might have been feared that the orphan would misuse the wealth in store for him. But he was not as other orphans. He celebrated his majority by selling the bequeathed house in Cavendish Square and buying Bell House, a place more suited to the life of a student. His bent was to Chemistry, and he caused a room at the top of the house to be fitted up as a laboratory. There he spent most of his time; and it was said of him by Faraday, whom he delighted to entertain, that were he not rich he might rise to high eminence. He was also a lover of music and (rather a blow, this, to believers in heredity) a shrewd connoisseur in the graphic arts: He bought and treasured Blake's drawings at a time when it was generally regretted that Blake could not draw. He was one of the earliest patrons of Rossetti, and one of the stoutest abstainers from Holman Hunt. Some time in the 'sixties he had married, and some time later, but still in the 'sixties, his wife had left him. She was said to have been beautiful, and to have become famous, under a pseudonym, in Paris, during the last two or three years of the Empire. It was not known what became of her after Sedan. Frederick Sandys had painted her in the first year of her marriage, but the portrait had disappeared from its place in the drawing-room at about the time of her disappearance. It was certainly not there in [1896].

Beerbohm's account of his first meeting with Herringham appears on one of the manuscript's unrevised pages. It is more fully written out than the sketchy notes that make up many of the pages, but it still contains queries to himself and directions for future elaboration. At this stage Beerbohm tends to punctuate with a delicate little stroke somewhere between a dash and a period. It is impossible to duplicate that mark in printing, so I have chosen a hyphen followed by a space as the closest approximation, except where the manuscript clearly intends something else. These little marks, along with the author's queries and sets of alternative readings (indicated here by braces { }) give the feeling of a diary, written in haste and catching the flow of thought. In this unrevised stage, the manuscript, with its occasional disregard for the rules of ordinary prose, its directness and quirky immediacy, brings to mind Lamb's essays and letters. The idiosyncratic punctuation, in Beerbohm as in Lamb, should become part of the reader's pleasure. Only the briefest pause is intended by the hyphen:

Describe room- Shown into a large drawing-room- panelled all around to ceiling- with 4 tall square-paned windows looking to river- This was the scene of the famous, forgotten Mondays!

Between second and third window- small writing-table- And now, after a gaze at the river, I leaned back against the table and surveyed the room—the great, low-ceilinged room that was to become so familiar to me and (though I haven't been in it for — years, {and know not what havoc the present tenants may have made of it}) still is, in a queer way, {always open to my inspection seen by me daily very often surveyed by me}. It seemed to me—it seems to me now—one of the loveliest of rooms; restful, as only a low-ceilinged room can be; noble, and yet homely; austere, without pedantry. The dark unpolished oak of the panelling might, by itself, have cast a gloom, but was prevented by the expanse of well-polished and highly reflecting parquet, and by the flood of light from the four windows. It was a double room. The back part was just half the width of the front, and the front was square. As I stood surveying it from between the two middle windows, the point at which the two rooms joined each other was therefore exactly opposite me. The back room was to the left of my vision. To the right, in the middle of the short wall facing me, was the door by which I had entered—a double door delightfully low in proportion to its width, and with a carved arch above it . . . These details are arid and tiresome? Bear with me. I want you to see the room just as I saw it—just as I am still privileged to see it. It is the background and setting of nearly all that I have to {record tell you} in these pages, and (assuming you will do me the honour to read on) I {think you will need want you} to visualise {the scene it}. With this apology, and prom-ising to write as little like a house-agent as may be, I proceed to say that the fire-place was in the middle of the wall to my left. At right angles to the fire-place stood a slim-legged sofa, facing me—a formal and elegant thing of satin-wood. It and the chairs that stood about were, I judged, of Queen Ann's day; so too the narrow table against the side-walls, and the very many candelabra ranged along these tables. I conjectured—rightly—that by plent-eous candle-light, with the very dark-red silk window-curtains drawn, the room would {look even finer than by day. positively excel the distinction it had by daylight.} On the short wall opposite to me hung an oval mirror that reflected one of the windows and the river beyond. The back-room had two windows, through which the trees of a garden were visible.

He came in, apologising-

Describe him- Light, quick step- smaller than I expected- below medium height (whatever that may be) such words as ask- glass- past he pronounced with a narrow a- Scotch-American- finicking and chilling- Silver hair parted in the middle and brushed down toward ears- Very fine in texture- thin white silk cap- Ivory skin- large thin high-bridged nose- deep-set grey eyes- sunken but very clear- hollowed temples- jutting pointed beard- John Bellini, Proces-sion of Holy Cross- looked as if he took great care of himself and caused great care to be taken of himself by others- absence of magnetism-

'To you seems a long time ago- Fourteen years- Nothing at my age- You will find that out- You are 24- Does not time seem to pass quicker already?' (Yes- term-time)- 'It will pass quicker and quicker- Fewer and less deep impressions, I suppose- For me it rushes- And I am glad of it-' (This seemed to me odd- Many years later I knew-) 'Only yesterday—hardly yesterday—more today-' (He paused) 'Especially natural in me- You see, I have no to-day- Solitary- People have changed- manners- everything. Bound to be so- But I only see a few old friends- I take in The Times newspaper' (so he called it)- 'Hardly look at it- Never did- art and science- New books, yes- Mudie sends me them- I read when I go to bed-' (Rather *froissé*-) 'I read "1880" with much amusement- Seemed to me very droll- *Past*! 1880!' (I explain '79–83 or so) 'Ah, you go so far back as '79-' (Oh, yes!) 'To me these people have no fascination- But I understand your feeling- What one has *just* missed-'

Beerbohm returns for the first of many luncheons. They dine on 'oyster broth- of great purity and strength- or clear turtle- steamed "fowl"'. Max drinks claret, Herringham nothing except 'a glass of port-wine- Doctor's orders- sustaining'. He is fastidiously concerned with his health ('You will consult the barummeter, Peltham- '): 'A man whom it was as hard to imagine married as it would have been to imagine him without private means- '. And they talk of the past, of Rossetti and the Pre-Raphaelites ('Says they owed much to Philistinism- Spencer and Mill- Utilitarianism- driven in on themselves- not spoilt-') but still mainly of 1880.

Then, 'one morning at 10.30- Dec. '96' a letter arrives from Herringham inviting Beerbohm to come see 'something that may interest you as an historian- a sort of document- discretion-' Upstairs in a locked room that used to be his laboratory, Herringham takes from a cupboard a large, padlocked, circular leather box, its interior quilted with black silk:

Carefully drew out a round guilt frame- with a round black space in the middle- He carried it by frame (deeply bevelled) to a wall and hung it by a chain that was on the back to a nail- about 2 ft. from floor. Low leather arm-chair- bade me be seated- he took small chair- My face came to about middle of framed black space- apparently a convex mirror- gilt wood- key-pattern-and black wood except that where the mirror itself would be there was blackness-

'What do you make of it?'

'Like a mirror—only with black felt stretched over the glass.'

'Black felt? No. Lay your hand on it.' A moment's hesitation- Hard and cold to my palm, which I quickly withdrew. 'What do you make of it?'

'*Feels* like glass.'

'Quite right. It *is* glass.'

'But it has no highlight on it.'

'No; no highlight, just now. Glass, nevertheless—ordinary transparent glass. What would you say is behind it?'

I looked. 'Black felt?' I hazarded.

He laughed. 'You must get rid of the black felt theory. Hark back to your first impression—a convex mirror. What is behind this glass is ordinary quicksilver. It is just a looking-glass.'

I accordingly looked at it. Was he mad? I wished I had not come. 'Well, why isn't it reflecting anything?'

'It is reflecting something. What do you see?'

'I see darkness.'

'Exactly. Darkness is what it is reflecting.'

I looked around with a smile. 'I don't see the darkness.'

'No. It passed away more than 14 years ago- Bygone darkness- and not very interesting, is it? However, I didn't bring you merely to see that. Have patience.' He looked at his watch. 'You'll be seeing something very soon. At almost any moment now.'

I was sure he was mad. But I was in no danger. I humoured him. I sat comfortably back in my chair silently watching the large dull black disc. The minutes passed. I don't know how long I had sat motionless when I became aware of a change in the disc- a sudden faint suffusion of its surface. There was a tiny point of light on the glass, and now—I had sat forward—there were two such points, three. And something was moving—moving and *growing*. It was a little human figure, moving backward and growing bigger. It paused, it nodded its head thrice, three other points of light appeared. And they were candle-flames: I saw the candles, the silver sconces that held them, standing on a long table adown one side of the mirror—of the room that now discernibly filled the mirror. And the man in the room- still stepping backwards into the foreground of the mirror- a growing silhouette in the candle-light. Three more nods, three more lit candles. Ah!—I had pushed back my chair violently, I stared vacantly aside at him whose own semblance I had just beheld. I was aware of his hand laid quickly on my arm, and of his voice:

'It's all right. No witch-craft- I'll explain later- It *is* rather novel and curious- But nothing to fear.'

In the mirror Beerbohm now watches (as he describes the scene in his letter to the Editor of the *Century*):

A younger Herringham, in evening dress, mysteriously walking backward around the room, lighting innumerable candles by merely puffing his cheeks at them. He walks backwards to a sofa, he reclines on it, a little white thing springs from the hearth and lodges between his fingers: he is smoking the end of a cigarette. The cigarette gradually lengthens. He rises, at length, from the sofa, walks backwards to a candle, bends over it, and then places the cigarette in a case which he draws from his pocket ... !! I now grasp the fact that everything in the mirror is reversed—not merely, as in other mirrors, reversed in point of space, but in point of *time* also. But how—what—why? Herringham promises to explain later, bids me watch the mirror: 'it will be more interesting directly.' In at the open door of the drawing-room comes backwards a small figure, somehow familiar. It turns—I recognize the profile of Whistler—a younger Whistler gesticulating to this younger Herringham. In come others— some of whom I recognize—Walter Sickert, Lady Archibald Campbell, Oscar Wilde, Lord Lytton ('Owen Meredith'), Sir Frederic Leighton, Cecil Lawson, etc., etc. The room is gradually full of 1880 figures. I am evidently present, as it were, at one of the famous Mondays . . .

After luncheon, sitting in the drawing-room that was the background to the unimaginable scene that I have beheld, Herringham explains—

It all began with a platitude uttered in 1877 by 'poor Alfred Tennyson'—'Friend of my father—Sometimes saw him in London'. He had come to consult Herringham about a current scientific theory 'that he wanted to seem to know all about in a poem he was writing'. Herringham entered the room and found Tennyson looking at himself in a mirror; to excuse himself, Tennyson said 'I was thinking how many things that mirror must have reflected':

It was like him to be looking at himself, it was like him to be anxious not to be supposed to be looking at himself, and it was like him to say what he said. He had a great command of platitudes—greater even, I always thought, in his conversation than in his poems. But he had a splendid sonorous voice, a noble utterance, a noble head and bearing. He was kingly. One was apt to remember his platitudes. I remembered this one. When Tennyson was gone, I thought how many things, even in my time, this mirror had reflected . . . how many people . . .

Tennyson's remark eventually led Herringham to undertake the experiment whose amazing results Max has just seen. Herringham learned from a French scientific book that an image 'is not an illusion- That is certain- It is something- In other words it has substance- That was the Frenchman's great discovery- Infinitely tenuous perhaps- but substantial—while it lasts'. A mirror, Herringham explains, 'is just the receiver- You are the source—the headquarters—from which the images of yourself come- In fact you are *all the time* giving out images of yourself, Mr Beerbohm- innumerable images- You are diffusing them all the time as a flower diffuses its scent.'

Herringham explains that the images we emit are trapped in a mirror between glass and quicksilver, and held in place by successive images. All the images the mirror has received are stacked there, waiting to ricochet once the pressure of oncoming images is removed. Herringham began experimenting in 1883 and succeeded in 1889, 'at 6.0 A.M. (after working all through the night and the small hours). Thus it is [Beerbohm explained to the Editor of the *Century*] that it is in the *morning* that I see the end of his evening party. At 7.0 A.M., July 2nd, 1889, the mirror had reached back to 5.0 A.M. of that morning.

At noon it had reached back to midnight. And so on, continuously.'
This progressively regressive mirror-time accounts for the oddness of
the mirror image: 'As thus: Whistler said good-night to his host and
walked out of the room in the usual manner. But in the mirror the
first that you see of him is the last that the mirror reflected of him.
His receding and disappearing back-view is now an appearing and
*pro*ceeding rear-view. And so on. It is really quite simple. There is no
cause for alarm.'

Max became a frequent guest at Bell House as the mirror continued
to unreel the stored past. At 'Herringham's Mondays' they might see
Hamilton Aïdé, the socialite and poetaster to whom Beerbohm had
attributed the epigraph to his essay '1880':

> *Say, shall these things be forgotten*
> *In the Row that men call Rotten.*
> *Beauty Clare?*

Sometimes there was music: Pablo de Sarasate playing the violin—
but, in the mirror, silently—looking as he does in Whistler's portrait
'Arrangement in Black' (1884). They see Browning, and Beerbohm is
reminded of 'A Toccata of Galuppi's'—but 'reversed: Browning
heard tune, imagined scene- I see scene, imagine tune- All the
stranger because Browning here- eupeptic and of the present- little
imagining himself romantic and past- Browning- opening mouth-
laughing- rubicund- someone says "sh" '. Herringham explains that
Browning was 'always everywhere as often as possible- always behaved
as if never been anywhere'. Beerbohm catches a glimpse of Sarasate's
accompanist:

Pale- red-bearded- marked face- quick-shifting light-grey eyes- nervous
buoyancy of gait- arms strained behind him- springy nervous step- seemed to
know few- Surely! Shaw! Herringham did not remember- People sometimes
brought friends- At that moment, looked in glass- combed beard-

'It *is!*'

'George Bernard Shaw? Oh yes, an anarchist, I heard- I remember now he
talked to me- Scotch accent- Said that Sarasate ought to play second fiddle
in a theatre orchestra for 2 years- Then he would be a good deal less
"wonderful" and a good deal better. *Non, je ne m'en souviens plus.*'[11]

[11] In Shaw's advice that Sarasate ought to play second fiddle in a theatre orchestra
Beerbohm is remembering the kind of advice Shaw had given him: 'You mut go on a
vestry at the first opportunity. . . . That is all your genius needs to sun away the north

Usually Herringham's memory and ear for accents serve them better. To help, they have Herringham's album-diary. In it, for instance, they find an exchange of letters, written in 1882, between Whistler and Herringham. Herringham seems to have commented on Whistler's notorious inability to finish commissions on time, or at all. That is what I derive from Whistler's 'first furious but amusing letter':

Fi donc, my old droll! Stick to your test-tubes, and not again let your proboscis impinge upon my palette.

Is perfection to be timed by the stop-watch, and must the painter in his wisdom compete with the perspiring fleet ones of Lily Bridge?[12]

Was it between the fish and the soup that your Darwin knew Man a Monkey? And shall I prove myself a greater savant than he because I did— *tout nettement*—in all delicacy know Herringham an Ass from the moment of my meeting him? *Hein?*

[Butterfly mark]

Then there is Herringham's reply:

Dear Mr Whistler,

Your note has reached me. In so far as I can extract any meaning from its polyglot and illiterate verbiage, I deduce (1) that you are angry and (2) that you are, at the same time, attempting to be funny. As to the reason for your anger I am as profoundly indifferent as I am depressed by your efforts to be funny.

Faithfully yours,
Sylvester Herringham

And finally, 'Whistler's rather baffled but more than spirited rejoinder':

Had it occurred to me that you had any dignity to stand on, I would have warned you to keep off it, *mon bon*. 'By your efforts' *not* 'to be funny'—just for once—in my eyes, you were foredoomed to tumble, with all hoofs in the

---

light of the studio', or 'Ten minutes on the Drainage Sub Committee of the St Pancras Borough Council . . . would shatter [your] academicism for ever' (Shaw, *Collected Letters of Bernard Shaw 1898–1910*, ed. Dan H. Laurence [London: Max Reinhardt, 1972], 43, 374).

[12] Whistler refers to the pedestrians and bicyclists at the Lillie Bridge Running-ground, which stood in the vicinity of the present Earl's Court Exhibition. These letters are of course in imitation of the letters Whistler gathered in *The Gentle Art of Making Enemies* (1890).

air, of course, rather uncouthly. '*Alors, tais-toi, pauvre bête!*' and cease to grieve with your despairing bray the ears of the humane.

[Butterfly mark]

Herringham recalls other notable men—the sociable Browning, for instance, and Tennyson whose chance remark had such strange consequences: Browning who grew smoother in person as his poetry grew more rugged and tangled, Tennyson who became more rugged and tangled as his verse became smoother.[13] But mostly Herringham talks about Rossetti: 'the best man I have ever known', Herringham calls him, 'the noblest and best'.[14]

They met first in Oxford in the summer of 1857. Herringham was an undergraduate, and Rossetti had come with his enthusiastic disciples Morris and Burne-Jones to paint Arthurian frescoes in the Debating Hall of the Oxford Union. 'Herringham, coming up for his second year, member of Union, finds work in full progress- Knew something about frescoes- "My dear father always wished"- and I thought I saw in Herringham's eyes a look of relief that fate had not {fulfilled smiled on} {his father's the} aspiration-'. With his knowledge of frescoes, seeing them all at work on 'walls newly built- mortar still damp- one coat of whitewash-' immediately Herringham pronounces 'It can't last.'

Of course he was right. The Union frescoes are 'gone as surely as speeches by undergraduates- the work [Rossetti] will be most remembered by-'. To this observation about the faded image, Beerbohm adds a note: 'Herringham does not seem to have been aware, and I have only learnt since, that a copy was made by Dunn- This a pity- A copy, however, always leaves us pleasantly free to imagine that it gives us no idea of the beauty of the original-'[15] In *Rossetti and his Circle*

[13] The anecdote is in *Mainly on the Air*, p. 127.

[14] Cf. the preface to *Rossetti and his Circle* ed. N. John Hall (New Haven, Conn.: Yale Univ. Press, 1987): 'In London, in the great days of a deep, smug, thick, rich, drab industrial complacency, Rossetti shone, for the men and women who knew him, with the ambiguous light of a red torch somewhere in a dense fog. And so he still shines for me' (p. vi).

[15] Beerbohm suppresses the fact that there are photographs of the frescoes: see W. Holman Hunt, *The Story of the Painting of the Pictures on the Walls and the Decorations on the Ceiling of the Old Debating Hall (Now the Library) in the Years 1857–9, Oxford Union Society* (Oxford: Oxford University Press; London: Henry Froude, 1906). His obliviousness to the photographic record (in favour of less stable representations) is like his failure to make the obvious comparison between the temporally reversed scenes in the mirror and a movie run backward. Beerbohm's other sources of Pre-Raphaelite images and information are described by N. John Hall in his edition of *Rossetti and his Circle*.

he provided his own copy of the fresco, its paint still wet, being examined by the Master of Balliol, Benjamin Jowett ('And what were they going to do with the Grail when they found it, Mr Rossetti?' [Plate 24]). The manuscript of *The Mirror of the Past* has sketches of the Rossetti fresco, Rossetti's portrait of Swinburne, Legros's portrait of William Michael Rossetti; sketches of Ford Madox Brown, William Bell Scott, Ruskin; and several versions of Rossetti's models Elizabeth Siddal, Ruth Herbert, and Fanny Cornforth. Missing but described is the portrait of the one Rossetti 'stunner' unknown to art historians, the one Sylvester Herringham destroyed in a jealous rage—the portrait of Mrs Herringham entitled 'Lilies that Fester'.

The fastidious Herringham was an odd companion for Rossetti, but then Rossetti made a habit of collecting oddities. He became Herringham's neighbour at 16 Cheyne Walk in 1862, after Lizzie Siddal's death. There he lived with his brother William ('like a Newfoundland dog- affectionate- trusty- a guardian'), with Swinburne, occasionally with George Meredith, and with his menagerie: 'kangaroo, laughing jackass, small Brahmin bull, zebu, owls, wombats, a deer, armadillos, a marmot, wallabies, salamanders, a raccoon' (Plate 25). But the artist and the scientist had one thing in common: 'Rossetti (unlike Morris) *loved mirror.*' Because of its convexity, Herringham's mirror was (said Rossetti) 'the only artist among mirrors- emphasising and attenuating- always a composition- *rondure*- the aim of all art'. Rossetti said 'all paintings ought to be round', and Swinburne 'used to speak of him as the dear great *cyclolatrist*'. But Morris hated mirrors: 'They lie- you can see a thing straight for yourself.' Sandys, like Rossetti, loved the mirror and often put it in his paintings:

Wanted to paint me in front of it [Herringham recalls]- back of head reflected- and room- Rossetti said 'Don't you- it won't end there- endless business- I know Sandys- he'll insist on the round mirror's reflection of the *oval* mirror's reflection of your face- And then the pupil of each of your eyes reflecting the oval mirror's reflection of the round mirror's reflection of the back of your head.'

In Herringham's mirror Beerbohm watches his host grow gradually younger while at his side he grows older. In 1905 Herringham falls ill and the mirror, for its own reasons, goes dark. It is the occasion for Herringham to confide his secret reason for gazing into the mirror of the past:

He tells me the story one day when he is convalescent from first serious illness.

'Trust to your absolute discretion. I have never spoken to you of my wife. We were together for 2 years. Then—we parted. I never saw her again. She is dead. She died many years ago. I have never spoken of her to any one. It seems strange to me that I should wish to speak to you. But I do wish to—for a certain reason. It is very difficult to me. I am, I have always been a rather reserved man. But if I speak at all, it is just as well that I should tell you all. It isn't so much that I want you to understand me, as that I want you to understand *her* . . . Perhaps you know something about her.'

I told him that I had always known he had been married—that she was beautiful—that she had been painted by Rossetti, that he and she had 'parted'.

'Yes, painted by Rossetti. It was through him that I met her. I doubt if but for him I should ever have married her—or any one. I have told you what an influence he was for all men who knew him- Consciously or unconsciously every one was affected by him- True, no interest in Science; and I continued mine- Meant to devote my life to it- My interest in art had begun at his Launcelot- and was entirely shaped by his talk—tho' here again I kept some independence- same in literature.

'Rossetti and women- Women always there- Kind of religion- Mysticism-Rossetti's very religious nature- Dead Rossettis and Polidoris telling their beads- Christian and pagan- Spiritual and sensual moved together.

'I was not romantic by nature- My Work- by nature a bachelor- But troubled vaguely- One or two light adventures- wished I could- Had had mild attractions to young ladies- daughters of families we knew.

'Rossetti scoffed at these- "Bread and butter misses- *thin* slices- swallow a dozen of them, unsatisfied- Miss Clara- playing a few *pieces*-" He said women of humble class alone could inspire passion- they were natural- they had mystery- they inspire pity- King Cophetua- "Imagine Lizzie a young lady! Or Janie!" Not that they didn't beat *ladies* at their own game- Easy thing to pick up at any moment at right age- But to teach it—that and nothing else— was to wreck charm.

'I did despise Miss Clara- At the same time no desire for a "misalliance"- no desire for any kind of matrimony- And yet, as I say, vaguely troubled- But I went on with my work- So I lived- Then came a change.'

A Pre-Raphaelite painting, Rossetti's 'Lilies that Fester', brought the change. Rossetti began work on it in 1864. It did not go well at first; the model was inadequate and the mongoose ate the lilies. But in the first week of March 1865, Rossetti, prowling in a curio shop off the Brompton Road, found a new model, a 'stunner' he calls 'the Lady Mildred'. Herringham goes to see the work in progress, then goes again. He talks to the model during rest periods:

Smell of lilies- Fifth day or so, she faints- Rossetti puts her on sofa- rushes for water- 'I believe she's hungry-' Revives- eats sandwiches- Herringham in turmoil- His big house- Why not marry?- Next day, Rossetti arranges drapery caressingly- Herringham proposes- she stares- accepts- Herringham afterwards amazed- Wants to hurry- so as not to change mind.

Thus Sylvester Herringham bought a painting and, with Dante Gabriel Rossetti as his best man, in the presence of William Rossetti and Algernon Swinburne, became for a while the husband of Mildred Crump.

Ruskin sent a present. William Bell Scott composed a limerick:

> There was a young man named Sylvester
> Who said he liked lilies that fester,
> But Mr Bell Scott
> Said 'Ah, this is not
> A hobby I share with Sylvester.'

Mildred went on sitting for Rossetti. (Even in that there were danger signals: Rossetti 'gave her a distaff- embroidery frame- but she wouldn't work'.) In 1867 Herringham went to Paris 'to see a savant' about his scientific work. Mildred, accompanying him, was delighted with Paris, but Herringham found Haussmann's new boulevards 'inexpressibly vulgar'. Paris was the scene of their disaster— though even now, in 1905, Herringham believes 'she was not to blame- Scoundrel who marked her down as his prey- He and I were the guilty men- and Howell.'

The 'scoundrel' was 'a young man of 25- sprig of nobility- or rather a monstrous bulb'. They were introduced by Charles Augustus Howell:

'Howell was most amusing [Sylvester says]- always talked to me- irresistible- He took me away to see some furniture- I believe on purpose for Runcorn to be with Mildred- a precious pair of villains.'

'Runcorn?'

'Runcorn, yes- This is the first time his name has passed my lips for 30 years.'

'Runcorn. Lord Runcorn. Isn't that the title of Lord Bostingdale's eldest son?'

'Yes. This was the eldest surviving son of the late Lord Bostingdale.'

'The—late? Then . . . You don't mean that the present Lord—the Lord Bostingdale—was the man who—'

'Yes, I mean the present Lord.'

Shock quickens our faculties, and in that moment all that since boyhood I had read about Lord Bostingdale in newspapers—all the Tenniel cartoons in which I had seen him limned so respectfully—seemed to pass in a rush before my eyes. I felt as one who sees a pillar {of the state} topple, crumble, collapse in dust.

You, my reader, suffer no such shock. The name Bostingdale suggests nothing to you. You look it up in Debrett, and it isn't there; nor is Runcorn. Exactly. Both these names are inventions of my own. Why did I invent them? Because I prefer not to give the real ones. The nobleman who in '67 came into the lives of Sylvester and Mildred Herringham is still, in 1916, living, full of years and honours, and still, despite his age, an influence for good in our public life. I will not revive against him now an inconspicuous scandal which he lived down.

The crisis occurred back in London: Herringham discovers Mildred in the drawing-room reading Runcorn's love letter. In the manuscript Beerbohm did the scene twice: first, in numbered sequence as it would have been lodged in the mirror, then in reversed sequence as it would appear years later when the mirror gave up its stacked images. As Max and the reader were to experience it, then, the novel's melodramatic crisis has the absurd disconnections of a movie running backwards.

Between the event (1867) and its reappearance in the mirror (1911) comes Herringham's narration. 'I was furious- told her to go- I ought to have implored forgiveness.' He wanted to strike out—at Mildred, at Runcorn. Instead he took the only revenge he could find: he destroyed Mildred's image, that is, Rossetti's painting of her. And in losing a wife he lost also a friend: Rossetti, seeing the empty wall, asks after his painting. Herringham says to the artist who had buried his poems with his dead wife, 'I should have thought you of all men would understand.' And Rossetti: 'No. A man may sacrifice his work for a woman. Not another man's, Sylvester. And the sacrifice must be made in love, in sorrow, in remorse. Not in spite.' He never came to Bell House again.

In his loneliness Herringham closed his house and became a traveller. And the mirror began reflecting his dark and empty drawing-room. He returned and, in an effort to lighten his mind, became the host at his famous 'Mondays'. Eventually his experiments with the mirror engrossed his attention. 'He ceased to think of anything but this spectral meeting-again.' Beerbohm continues the account in his letter to the Editor of the *Century*:

Not 'spectral' to him, in 1906 this re-union. For him, as he brooded over it, it appeared now as something real. Night and day, moment by moment, the mirror was shedding off its innumerable films. And there, in the mirror, waiting—or rather, *coming*, actually *on the way*—was the very Mildred. 'She is on the way', was the phrase that Herringham used often to me in the last years of his life; and his one thought was whether he would be spared to be there to meet her. It was because of the maddening thought that he might die too soon, and because he could not bear to think of her coming and finding *no one* to meet her, that he confided to me the story of his life with her. In case he died, he wanted *me* to meet her.

Herringham died in 1909. In 1910 Beerbohm married and moved to Rapallo, 'taking of course my dear old friend's bequest with me'. At the appointed time—the mirror's 9:00 A.M., which in the *Villino* is 3:00 A.M.—he sat up to wait, fortified with chianti and sandwiches. The first sight of Sylvester is a shock: he is 'a boy!- I realized much younger than I- he 30, I 37! Made me feel strangely old.' What Beerbohm sees is Herringham's final look-round the drawing-room before starting his travels. He had imagined Sylvester re-entering his life, 'returning gladly, coming close to mirror and facing me'. He had forgotten the mirror's reversals: 'I was slightly *froissé*, as at my first meeting.'

The mirror-image remains sealed in its perfect *rondure*, indifferent to the world of chianti and sandwiches and people who only grow older. After that first disappointment Beerbohm could look forward to the excitement of seeing Herringham's wife. Because he had never set eyes on her, Mildred's appearance in the mirror was unlikely to disappoint him, as Herringham's had done. But what the mirror showed him first was not, in fact, Sylvester's Mildred but Rossetti's— the portrait of 'the Lady Mildred' in 'Lilies that Fester'. And thus he was set up for his next lesson in the discontinuity between image and substance. He sees Mildred in her prospect of lilies 'tall- she fighting her way- browned- grey- perpendicularly drooping'. Instead of describing her face he quotes Rossetti's poem 'Jenny': 'The shadows where the cheeks are thin, And pure wide curve from ear to chin'.[16] He notices her hands: 'lovely- as Rossetti loved them, and early

---

[16] Rossetti's poem is about a restful night with a prostitute.

renaissance men- those very long slim supple spatulate fingers, every one with a separate life'. Herringham had told Max that 'Rossetti had not at all idealised her face'. But when in time Max saw in the mirror the veritable Mrs Herringham—the woman now, not the portrait—'it seemed to [him] that Rossetti *had* idealised her. She seemed to [him] splendid but coarse.' He noticed especially her 'terrible hands- White plump of the kind admired- dimpled- smallish- fingers thick at base'. In life Herringham had seen a Rossetti woman; the mirror presents her to Max as mere Mildred Crump, a living caricature of her own portrait.

Mildred was to disappoint him further.

But this scenario [he wrote to the editor of the *Century*], bald though it is, is already over long, and therefore I will skip all details as to how it came about that presently, as I watched the mirror, hour by hour, I found absolute evidence that Mrs Herringham was not, as her husband in later years thought her, a sweet-natured and pathetic being who had gone astray by reason of his failure to appreciate her, and that Lord Runcorn was not by any means the villain I had supposed him to be.

And the mirror goes on, showing now the old drawing-room in happier days: 'There it is, strangely far away from our modern world. Rossetti is very often there—and oh if I could but hear what he says as he lounges there on the sofa!' The manuscript describes the scene and others like it, which resemble scenes actually drawn for *Rossetti and his Circle*:

See Rossetti sitting on sofa- in the evenings- lethargic- gazing at 'the Lady Mildred'- wonderful eyes- sometimes talking, laughing- everyone laughs *before* he speaks- maddening not to hear- Swinburne on one leg- noble head once- great emotion- Meredith chaffing 'Crumpisba'- roaring . . . In Italian sunshine, these Chelsea evenings of early 'sixties.

Beerbohm is telling the story in 1916, when the mirror has reached back to 1862. In 1918 it will begin reflecting its first English home, in Cavendish Square, where Sir Alfred Herringham brought it from France. Eventually it will show:

The 'thirties- Sylvester coming down to dessert- In 1950, if I live, shall see him as an infant in arms- I shall be 78! I who was 24 when I first saw him- he 58! Then lose him altogether- I hope I shall not- Let me die before he was born.

Then the mirror will show Paris, where it was made, in the *ancien régime*; and so on and on:

Giving off- up its dead- without hasting, without resting- day and night- till the day when all shall be done, and it becomes again a normal mirror. An inanimate Ariel obeying the commands of a dead Prospero-

There are alternative endings in the manuscript, of which the briefer is the better:

Bequeath to South Kensington [Museum]- furniture department- if they will accept- In 1978 (?) open- will reflect curator's face- Thereafter the visitors to that rather depressing place- Ordinary mirror- but romantic because they will think of all it has reflected- twice.

When Beerbohm had in fact become an old man, he told S. N. Behrman that he gave up work on *The Mirror of the Past* because 'it became too involved, you know, too complicated. I couldn't understand it myself.'[17] The manuscript abounds in small chronological inconsistencies despite the several calendars and schemes he invented to guide him. The physical appearance of the pages shows that he was tempted to keep on filling in times past with more and more apocryphal incidents. I have left out several of the looser strands: the story, for instance, of Herringham's servant Javes, whose own drawing-room comedy occupied the mirror while Herringham was on his travels; and the story, murkier still, of how Mildred did *not* die but, unbeknown to her Chelsea friends, became the famous entertainer Kate Carisbrooke. There were other problems. Rossetti is at the centre of Beerbohm's interest, but the exfoliating chronology makes Rossetti's appearance come late in the story, so that while the mirror is showing the 'seventies, for instance, anecdotes about the Rossetti circle in the 'sixties would have to be supplied out of order from Herringham's memories and his album-diary. The greatest challenge, though, is the one Beerbohm mentions in his letter to the editor of the *Century*: 'The book consists, to some extent, of what [Herringham] told me about his friends. These apocryphal memoirs are an integral and important part of this book about the past; but I must be careful that they don't overwhelm the actual dramatic side of the story—the personal, sentimental side of Herringham's life.' He needed to balance the latter

[17] Berhman, *Portrait of Max* (New York: Random House, 1960), 41.

narrative with the opportunities it provided for parody, satire, and caricature.

I have already cited some of the moments when he was successful. Others were mined for 'Hethway Speaking'. I have reserved a few more to show what Beerbohm was trying to achieve through his multiple narrative perspectives: the perspective of satire versus that of sentimental recollection; the perspective of the mirror and of the paintings it reveals; and the perspectives of its watchers—themselves incessant givers-off of images—the genteel old Herringham and the ironic Max.

For instance, the story of Herringham's encounter with his Chelsea neighbour Carlyle, shortly after Mildred's elopement, is recorded first from Herringham's sentimental perspective: 'It was', he told Max, 'one of the beautiful things that have happened to me.'

A walk along Cheyne Walk at night- September- Dark night- but in light of a lamp saw a familiar figure coming, leaning on a stick- It was Carlyle.

'I had been used to go there in days of dear Mrs Carlyle. It was more for her that I used to go. She was always very civil. And he—well, he was not. When she died—April '66—I gave up going- though I wrote to him- She had been dead — years- As you know, he was much broken by her death. He never ceased to mourn her—poor old rugged tender-hearted man! I raised my hat and was passing on- but he stopped, peering at me out of his wonderful eyes—the saddest, tenderest eyes I have ever known—and laid a hand on my shoulder-

'"And so ye've lost y'r woman." I could say nothing. "They're given to us, and they're taken from us; that's the way of it. And we've to plod on as we may." Pause. "Come in and see me sometimes." Passed on into the night.'

'Did you go?'

'Yes, several times.'

'Did he ever speak again to you of your wife—or of his own?'

'No. But now there was always something between us. There was the bond of bereavement.'

Immediately after this Beerbohm adds a note about an imaginary recent book, *Talks with Carlyle*:

I was distressed to find that he spoke of Herringham as 'a feeble, pernickety, infinitesimal man—one H., a dabbler with numerals and the like, who comes and pesters me with his kickle-kackle'. But this sort of thing was a mannerism, after all, and as we learn from many sources, he always finished his invectives with a laugh, thus robbing them of their sting and turning the laugh against himself.

Part of the joke is Beerbohm's own retreat to the limited perspective of his self-caricature, for in that version he too softens and sentiment- alizes Chelsea's angry sage. The *Talks with Carlyle* give an image, as the mirror gives its images; but every image requires an interpreter and in Beerbohm's narrative the gap between image and interpretation is never closed. And there is an edge to the joke, of the sort found in the artist stories of *Seven Men*. There is the intimation that, for all our endless broadcasting of images, we are threatened with virtual invis- ibility. In *The Mirror of the Past*, as in *Seven Men*, to be perceived is to exist—but tenuously, even with the mirror's second chance.

Herringham's last meeting with Rossetti—after their estrangement, in the artist's 'last sad days'—is another comedy of limited perspect- ives and incompatible styles, and another essay on the alienation of imagery. It will conclude my reconstruction of the unfinished novel. The year was 1881. Herringham recalls:

> In my worldly days- walking home from some party- *Ballads and Sonnets* just published- saw him coming along- leaning heavily on arm of a small man- I was not sure whether he would see me- or would wish to see me-
> 'Well, Sylvester, aren't you going to speak to me?'
> 'Oh, my dear friend.'
> We stood looking at each other, I holding his hand, and thinking of all that he had been to me. I stood there with a heart full of love and {reverence} and sorrow- I don't know what *he* felt; perhaps he was past all feeling. But I know he knew what was in *me*. And I think he would have spoken—of things; but you see, we were not alone. There was the small man- I forget his name, but I gathered he was acting as a sort of companion or nurse- bright red hair- and I remember hearing later that he became a very popular novelist- I spoke of *Ballads and Sonnets*- Small man- he had a particularly sonorous voice- said it must be gratifying to all Mr Rossetti's old friends to note the magnificent reception accorded this volume by the Press- He said something about Mr Rossetti's work now appealing to a wider and ever wider public. He said something about 'phenomenal sales' and something about 'the heart of every man and every woman in the English-speaking world'-
> I caught Rossetti's eye, and I thought I saw there for an instant a gleam of the great old laughter- 'Well, good night, Sylvester', he said- I never saw him again.

The small man with the bright red hair did indeed become a popular novelist. He is Hall Caine, a frequent early favourite for

Beerbohm's satire and caricature; and he was one of the first of Rossetti's self-seeking hagiographers (Plate 26).[18] In this vignette, Hall Caine is the keeper of Rossetti's image—which may be all of him there is. Here, as in *Rossetti and his Circle*, Beerbohm makes the massive Rossetti eerily passive, the still centre for the more wildly eccentric performances of his keepers and copiers, Hall Caine and Theodore Watts, and for the more vociferously projective Swinburne, Morris, and Meredith. Rossetti the image-maker had become in his lifetime a prisoner of his art's images. Literally he was copied by well-intentioned disciples like Treffry Dunn and by outright forgers like Howell; more pathetically, he became his own forger, creating Rossetti pastiches 'for Howell to sell to merchant princes'. Anyone, it seems, even Mildred Crump, could become a Rossetti woman. In Beerbohm's vignette, Rossetti himself is becoming the stuff for a best seller. *The Mirror of the Past* comments on and continues the process Rossetti himself had started. In parody and caricature Beerbohm embraces the tenuousness of the artist's existence and makes it his equivocal strength.

---

[18] Sir Thomas Henry Hall Caine (1853–1931): his *Recollections of Dante Gabriel Rossetti* appeared in 1882, less than a year after Rossetti's death. Beerbohm's satiric review of his hugely successful novel *The Christian* appeared in the *Daily Mail*, 11 August 1897. Of Caine's efforts at self-promotion he wrote, 'One should be grateful to any man who makes himself ridiculous'—and he never ceased being grateful to Hall Caine. In the essay 'Nat Goodwin—and Another' (1912), describing their awkward first meeting at the home of Herbert Tree, he writes: 'There had come a time when he got himself interviewed too much, photographed too much, seen too much, advertised in every way too much. I think this lust for publicity may have been a result of residence with Dante Gabriel Rossetti. Conceive: a raw and excitable stripling, caught suddenly from Liverpool into still more vital London, to live incessantly apart for almost two years with a man of genius who suffered from agoraphobia in an acute form. It was thought that Hall Caine lost too little time after Rossetti's death in bringing out a book about him. Poor young man!—I think it was natural that he should desire to lose not a moment. Light! air! publicity at any price and at once!—such was the quite inevitable and excusable reaction' (*Mainly on the Air*, pp. 76–7).

Conclusion: The Amber and the Flies

HONOURING Beerbohm on the occasion of his eightieth birthday, his future biographer, Lord David Cecil, wrote that 'there is no bitter grain of powder in the delicious spoonful of jam he offers us; he is out, not to unburden his soul, but only to delight'.[1] The nursery image applied to the old artist would be grotesque except that it does respond to aspects of Max's self-creation. It is part of the received lore, dictated largely by Beerbohm himself. One of the virtues of S. N. Behrman's *Portrait of Max* is that it adds to the Beerbohm canon a wealth of anecdotes which enroll Max in the school of conversational wits with his early models Whistler and Wilde. But it too is part of the condition Auden referred to when he called Beerbohm a sacred cow.[2] Behrman says that he likes best to contemplate Beerbohm as he appears in Will Rothenstein's pastel portrait, 'a diaphanous slight figure . . . who cherishes too intensely this evanescence . . . to replace it with the vulgar self-assertion of work'.[3] Yet self-assertion to an extraordinary degree is what Beerbohm practised in his art of ostensible effacement. The aloofness in Rapallo is at odds with his choice, in writing and drawing, to be frequently topical, autobiographical, and downright offensive to the victims of his mimetic witchery. 'Diaphanous' is not the word to describe the tormenter of Clement Scott, Hall Caine, George Moore, Bernard Shaw, H. G. Wells, the Royal Family, and the Labour Party.

Reversing the hagiographic procedure does not guarantee better results. Cyril Connolly, for instance, reacting to Behrman's memoir, demanded to know 'What terrific inner force or whirlpool kept

---

[1] In the MS Birthday Book at Merton College, Oxford.
[2] Auden, 'One of the Family', in J. G. Riewald, ed., *Surprise of Excellence: Modern Essays on Max Beerbohm* (Hamden, Conn.: Archon, 1974), 173.
[3] Behrman, *Portrait of Max* (New York: Random House, 1960) 5–6.

[Beerbohm] from unleashing his talents and egotism in proper competition with his fellows . . . ?'[4] The image of terrific whirlpools is less damning, insofar as pathology seems preferable to preciosity, but no more accurate than Lord David's nursery image. And Connolly's implied notion of 'proper competition' is crudely schoolboyish compared to Beerbohm's own strategies, which make him so hard to place, hard to define, despite memoirs, biography, volumes of letters, and critical studies like this one.

He derived some of that elusiveness from humour's anomalous cultural status: Max's first diversionary tactic was to make himself a funny man in a world that expected its artists to take themselves seriously. The cultural anomaly is the one Lamb exposed when he dared to compare Hogarth favourably with Reynolds. On the one hand, Max is a sophisticated, learned taste. The history of modern literature and art could be written, and usually is, without mentioning Max Beerbohm, but the audience he retains, fit though few, certifies his position among the culturally favoured. On the other hand, the forms he practised—the occasional and familiar essay, cartoons and caricatures—are the province of the glossy uppercrust of popular magazine culture. As a satirist or, as I have preferred to call it, a parodist, he won or condemned himself to a sort of privileged marginality.

In this he resembles another great comic artist, Saul Steinberg. In May 1952 the two major art exhibits in London were by the eighty-year-old Beerbohm, at the Leicester Galleries, and the young Steinberg, at the I.C.A. Critics recognized similarities as well as obvious differences. M. H. Middleton in *The Spectator* wrote that 'Steinberg is something of a dandy, too, but his wit is savage, anarchic and profoundly disquieting.'[5] Eric Newton in *The Listener* called Steinberg 'In one sense . . . Max's successor':

He too sees the world—the world of modern America—as a queer place, more surprising than lovable. Steinberg's line has far more surface vitality, but so also does the world he looks at. Steinberg is funny where Max is witty. Steinberg himself is part of the fun, while Max is aloof. Steinberg is interested

---

[4] 'Tea on the Terrace with Max Beerbohm', *Sunday Times*, 6 November 1960, magazine section, p. 32. Connolly calls Beerbohm 'a psychological case, a supreme egotist masquerading as a detached onlooker'.
[5] *The Spectator*, 9 May 1952, p. 612.

in behaviour, Max in character. But both build up a picture of a genuine world and both worlds are equally human.[6]

'Human' is in fact a weak descriptor for either artist's vision. Steinberg has drawn his self-portrait as a rabbit or a cat or a man with a brown paper bag over his head. Beerbohm's self-portrait as the dandy Max is only slightly more lifelike. Steinberg never draws caricatures in the technical sense; he is less interested in the particular human form than in its generic representations, of which he is the satiric representer. Steinberg's world is one of signs and symbols, resymbolized in his scribbles, rubber stamps, and parodies of a host of art-historical styles including the American vernacular. But if Max's apparent fidelity to the superficies of character locates him in a more recognizable tradition of caricaturing, it also disguises the fact that he too, like Steinberg, inhabits a world in which the 'human' is the product of its cultural works and art is a paradoxical means for creating true originals on the ground of the previously inscribed.

Such originality is not easily won or maintained. Artists are unusual in the extent of their awareness of the problems; politicians and other public figures in the extent of their liabilities. But all are at risk. We are each, as Sylvester Herringham tells Max, the headquarters from which our images go forth; but the images are captured in a variety of distorting mirrors which give them out again in alienated forms. We appear in the world as caricatures of ourselves even as we struggle to assert our authentic personalities. That struggle, comically perceived, provides a unifying subtext for much of Beerbohm's writing, not only in the strict parodies but also in the aggressive mockery of *The Works*, the clashing narrative styles of *Zuleika Dobson*, the uncanny relationships of the doubles in *Seven Men*, the threatened images in *The Mirror of the Past*. Of course it is the burden of his work as a caricaturist as well—work or, as he made it seem, play—that will briefly be the subject of my conclusion to this long essay on Beerbohm's writing.

'. . . [I]n London, in the great days of a deep, smug, thick, rich, drab, industrial complacency, Rossetti shone, for the men and women who knew him, with the ambiguous light of a red torch somewhere in a dense fog', Beerbohm writes in the 'Note' to *Rossetti and his Circle*.

[6] *The Listener*, 15 May 1952, p. 796.

'And so he still shines for me.'[7] Like the Duke of Dorset at Oxford, Rossetti in London is the observed of all observers; Max treats this doomed king among artists with the same comic detachment he had treated his king among dandies. The drawings capture moments in a struggle for personal distinction enacted in that mysterious time— compound of absurdity and grace—just before his own.

The Rossetti of Max's caricatures is a silent, still point in the world of human and animal specimens that surrounds him. We see him first in childhood, quietly drawing under a table in a room full of gesticulating Italian expatriates; he is 'precociously manifesting, among the exiled patriots who frequented his father's house in Charlotte Street, that queer indifference to politics which marked him in his prime and decline'. In his prime he leans against a tree in his back garden, indifferent to the circle of admirers—Burne-Jones and Pater, Swinburne kneeling in reverence, Morris expansively introducing him to a kangaroo—as well as to the outsider, 'Mr William Bell Scott[,] wondering what it is those fellows seem to see in Gabriel'. The comic vision softens aspects of the last days at 16 Cheyne Walk: in the drawing called 'Quis Custodiet Ipsum Custodem?', the horror of Rossetti's drug addiction is secondary to the jockeying for position among his friends (Plate 27). In the foreground Watts-Dunton, supported by Frederick Shields, lectures the eager Hall Caine:

Mr Caine, a word with you! Shields and I have been talking matters over, and we are agreed that to-night and henceforth you *must* not and *shall* not read any more of your literary efforts to our friend. They are too—what shall I say?—too luridly arresting, and are the allies of insomnia.

Rossetti slumps on a settee at the back of the room. However brightly Rossetti may have shone in Max's imagination, here he is nearly extinguished by the circling figures who cancel what they seek to support.

The threat of extinction had existed even in Rossetti's younger and happier days. Sylvester Herringham needed only one look at the Oxford Union frescoes to know they couldn't last; and indeed they are 'gone as surely as speeches by undergraduates- the work [Rossetti] will be most remembered by'. In *Rossetti and his Circle* Max recreates the vanished masterpiece, but he puts the exotic artist and his romantic

[7] *Rossetti and his Circle*, ed. N. John Hall (New Haven, Conn.: Yale Univ. Press, 1987), 48. I am indebted to Hall's commentary.

artwork in the presence of a complacent native questioner. Rossetti's foot is on the bottom rung of a ladder leading to his fresco; Benjamin Jowett's question, 'And what were they going to do with the Grail when they found it, Mr Rossetti?', seems to arrest his ascent (Plate 24). Not even death liberates Rossetti from the 'circle' of battening personalities. The penultimate plate shows 'Mr ———— and Miss ———— nervously perpetuating the touch of a vanished hand'. This is the forger (and, in *The Mirror of the Past*, procurer) Charles Augustus Howell, assisted by Rosa Corder; they are in the process of copying a Rossetti portrait of Fanny Cornforth. In his 'Note' to the volume, Beerbohm writes that 'Rossetti had invented a type of beauty'; the images he gave to life returned in the shapes of well-meant homage as well as forgery and caricature. (Max's caption echoes Tennyson: no artist is immune.) In the last plate, 'The name of Dante Gabriel Rossetti is heard for the first time in the western states of America. Time: 1882. Lecturer: Mr Oscar Wilde.' The elegant Oscar, in breeches and velvet tie, a lily in his hand, cries out the aesthetic gospel of a morose master who in Max's caricatures always dresses in shapeless black.

Rossetti and his Circle is a comic drama of competing personalities. Ebullient George Meredith insistently exhorts Rossetti 'to come forth into the glorious sun and wind for a walk to Hendon and beyond', while the heavy, scowling Rossetti sits painting a languid female model. 'Mr Browning brings a lady of rank and fashion to see Mr Rossetti': the painter, in black smock, looks contemptuously over the head of the sociable poet at a vision of Victorian bosom and bustle; the maid who opens the door to 16 Cheyne Walk is a Rossetti woman, and unimpressed by her starchy rival. 'Rossetti in his worldlier days (*circa* 1866–1868) leav[es] the Arundel Club with George Augustus Sala': the successful hack-journalist Sala, with cigar, diamond stick-pin, cane, and flashy blue coat, walks jauntily arm-in-arm with the black-clad, depressed Rossetti and confides to him:

You and I, Rossetti, we like and we understand each other. Bohemians, both of us, to the core, we take the world as we find it. *I* give Mr Levy what *he* wants, and *you* give Mr Rae and Mr Leyland what *they* want, and glad we are to pocket the cash and foregather at the Arundel.

In the next plate, a 'Riverside Scene', an odd little figure with a cascade of orange hair eagerly leads a stiff, reluctant taller man; this is

'Algernon Swinburne taking his great new friend Gosse to see Gabriel Rossetti'.

Among the comically mismatched pairs none clashes more discordantly than Carlyle and Whistler. Max puts them together in the drawing 'Blue China', where the dandified little painter points out the charms of porcelain to the unimpressed Scotsman (Plate 17). Art history puts them together by virtue of Whistler's portrait of Carlyle (*Arrangement in Gray and Black II*). It was painted shortly after the famous portrait of Whistler's mother (*Arrangement in Gray and Black*), and looks remarkably like it. In *The Mirror of the Past*, Herringham asks Carlyle how this odd conjunction of Carlyle, Whistler, and Whistler's mother came about. Carlyle says they met at the house of Jane Carlyle's old friend Madame Venturi. Here is the version Beerbohm revised for 'Hethway Speaking':

'And one day', [Carlyle] told [Herringham], 'there was a wee young man with a mop of black ringlets and a quizzing-glass—a sor-rt of pocket D'Israeli by the looks of him, but American in his talk, of which there was much. When he was gone, Mrs Venturi asked me what I thought of him; and I told her without cir-r-rcumlocution. Said she, But he's going to be a verra great painter, and he wants to paint *you*; and he's verra poor, she said: and he's verra guid to his Mither-r. She's a most per-rtinaceous crittur, is Mrs Venturi, and the next day I found myself with her at a house alongside the river, there to see this Mr Whistler's paintings. The Mither-r received us—a dainty-sad little auld silvery dame, gentle of speech and shy-authoritative. Presently in comes son, and we all go into his wor-rk-room, and there, propped up on a bit of wooden stand, is a picture of the Mither-r, with a frame to it. There she sat, side-face, a sad figure, all in black, lonesome and shy-authoritative, against plain grey wall of parlour. I canna count how many sittings I gave that slow-working son. One day he said finis and showed me his handiwork. There I sat, side-face, all in black, lonesome and meditative-gentle, against pale grey wall of parlour. Painter stood by me sharp-expectant. "Well, young man", I said at last, "ye're verra filial, verra filial indeed." ' (*Mainly on the Air*, pp. 123–4)

The fiercely independent Carlyle is recreated in the family of Whistler. And all Whistlers (as Beerbohm says) project 'the clean-cut image . . . of himself'. It is another comic version of the contest for self-possession. On more than one occasion Max himself appropriated the pose in which Whistler placed both his mother and the impatient Carlyle. He caricatured Whistler's biographer, the engraver Joseph

Pennell, 'thinking of the old 'un', sitting as Whistler made his mother and Carlyle sit (Plate 28). And once he sat that way for his own portrait: he had himself photographed in Carlylean dress and Whist-lerian pose, 'side-face, all in black, lonesome and meditative-gentle, against pale grey wall of parlour' (Plate 29). The wall is hung with Beerbohm forgeries. He signed the mount of the original photo 'Max—with apologies to all concerned'; and the 'all' would include not only Whistler, his mother, Carlyle, and Joseph Pennell but anyone whose image had ever been reinscribed by MAX. (The photograph once belonged to Shaw.)[8] It shows Max making 'a Whistler' into 'a Beerbohm' and in the process supplanting Carlyle as well. It is a self-portrait of the parodist as another artist's portrait.

The more 'original' the personality, the greater Beerbohm's competit-ive interest in its efforts at self-possession. Hence, in part, his fondness for the combative little Jimmy Whistler. Long before he was photographed in Whistlerian pose he published an essay on 'Whistler's Writing' (1904, *Yet Again*, pp. 99–111). It, too, like the caricaturing photograph, is self-referential: honouring a model, he creates a form for himself. He praises Whistler as that rarest of artists whose abilities transcend the limits of a single medium, or even of what is normally considered an artistic medium at all:

. . . Whistler was great, not merely in painting, not merely as a wit and dandy in social life. He had, also, an extraordinary talent for writing. He was a born writer. He wrote, in his way, perfectly; and his way was his own, and the secret of it has died with him. (*Yet Again*, p. 102)

But no one, he says, has (until now) done justice to *The Gentle Art of Making Enemies*. Hero-worshipping art lovers find the book 'painful' because the squabbles it records are 'incongruous with a great hero'. Yet Beerbohm hears in every sentence of Whistler's writing 'a clear vocal cadence'; and 'There, after all, in that vocal quality, is the chief test of good writing': 'Whistler was that rare phenomenon, the good talker who could write as well as he talked. Read any page of *The Gentle Art of Making Enemies*, and you will hear a voice in it, and see a face in it, and see gestures in it.' The essay that contains this praise

<hr />

[8] Original photograph at the Humanities Research Center, Austin, Texas; reprinted in *To-day* (July 1971), i, no. 5. Information provided by John O. Kirkpatrick, who also reprints the photograph in his *Max on View*.

25. 'Dante Gabriel Rossetti, in his back garden' (printed in *The Poets' Corner*, with additions and annotations by Max: Tortoise, Swinburne, Whistler, D. G. Rossetti, Theodore Watts-Dunton, Kangaroo, George Meredith, Portrait of 'Stunner', Ned Jones, Penguin [*sic*], 'Stunner', William Morris, Snake, Reginald Turner [barely visible above wall], Hall Caine, Holly Hunt, Ruskin) [*c*.1904]

26. 'Mr. Hall Caine' [unsigned 1898]

27. '*Quis Custodiet Ipsum Custodem?* Theodore Watts: "Mr. Caine, a word with you! Shields and I have been talking matters over, and we are agreed that this evening and henceforth you *must* not and *shall* not read any more of your literary efforts to our friend. They are too—what shall I say?—too luridly arresting and are the allies of insomnia."'

1916

28. 'Mr. Joseph Pennell thinking of the old 'un' 1913

29. Photograph of Max in Whistlerian pose—'with apologies to all' on mount [n.d.]

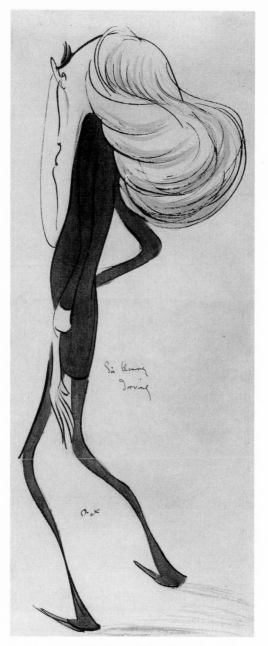

30. 'Sir Henry Irving' [1901]

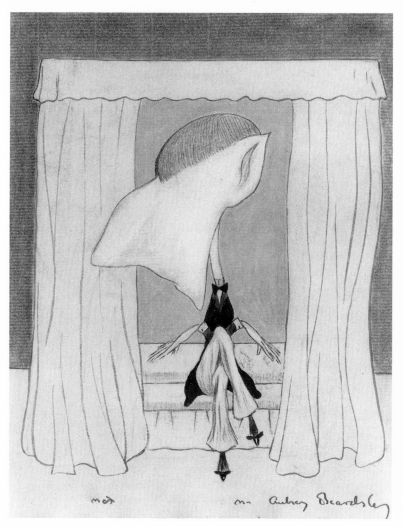

31. 'Mr. Aubrey Beardsley' [1896]

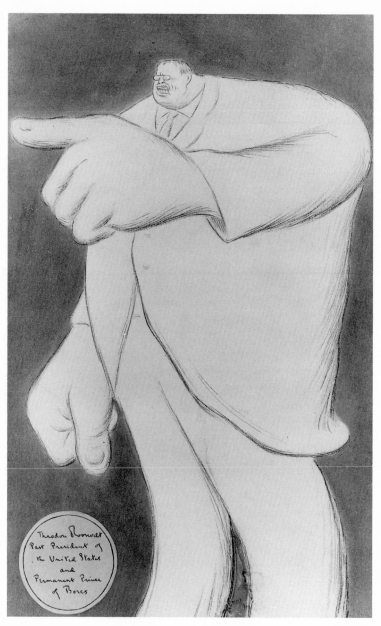

32. 'Theodore Roosevelt, Past President of the United States and Permanent Prince of Bores' [1912]

does in Max's way what it claims Whistler did in his—for though Whistler's 'meaning was ever ferocious . . . his method, how delicate and tender!' The voice we hear, the face and gestures we see in the essay on Whistler all belong to Max Beerbohm.

So Max begins, 'No book-lover, I. Give me an uninterrupted view of my fellow-creatures'; and he continues his essay on self-creativity by conjuring a picture of himself in the acts of writing and reading. As a reader, Max is indifferent to rare books; his thumb, in prizing open uncut edges, has mutilated many volumes, 'and I hope that in the sale-rooms of a sentimental posterity they may fetch higher prices than their duly uncut duplicates'. A First Folio Shakespeare would not be safe if he were reading it by his fireside and needed a spill to light his cigarette. We remember, reading this confession, the book-burning recorded in 'A Crime' and the whole criminal career of Max Beerbohm in which that defacement counts as a mere peccadillo. As it is, however, he is reading Whistler's volume: 'The book lies open before me, as I write. I must be careful of my pen's transit from inkpot to MS.'

Thus self-conjured, the reading writer who in his drawings has so often 'done' Whistler explains the chief bar to our appreciation of Whistler's writing. Whistler's very facility stands in the way of a just estimate: 'When a man can express himself through two media, people tend to take him lightly in his use of the medium to which he devoted the lesser time and energy . . .' Max acknowledges that as a writer Whistler was an 'amateur', but his writing was the better for it; his writing has 'that especial quality which the Muse grants only to them who approach her timidly, bashfully, as suitors'. Even as a painter Whistler lacked 'the professional touch' in matters of technique:

It was often said that his art was an art of evasion. But the reason of the evasion was reverence. He kept himself reverently at a distance. He knew how much he could not do, nor was he ever confident even of the things that he could do; and these things, therefore, he did superlatively well, having to grope for the means in the recesses of his soul. . . . He was a master through his lack of mastery. (*Yet Again*, p. 105)

Like the rest of the criticism in 'Whistler's Writing', the point, which may or may not be true of its ostensible subject, is suggestively true of Max Beerbohm.

With Beerbohm, though, it is impossible to say in which of the two media, writing or drawing, he can more properly claim amateur status. 'Did you ever learn to draw, Mr Beerbohm?': the question, which sounds like the caption to a cartoon by Max, was recorded in a hostile essay by Rebecca West.[9] It's a reasonable question, to which the answer is yes and no. Beerbohm learned to draw as he learned to write, by imitation; but prominent among his first unaugust models were Thackeray and Edward Lear—artists who could 'express [them-selves] through two media'; which is to say that Max learned to draw by schooling himself on 'amateurs'. He learned a little from Phil May in *Punch*, more from 'Ape' in *Vanity Fair*. But in any more technical sense he never learned to draw. And so it can be said, as he said of Whistler, that he learned an art of evasion, mastering a small area defined by the larger area he 'reverently' avoided.

Drawing came easier than writing; the syntax of line was more yielding than the syntax of words. His best drawings have the exuberance of a line triumphing over discursiveness or the need for explanation; so that his most inventive lines are not always in his most polished, elaborately captioned cartoons. The drawings in *Rossetti and his Circle*, which can be read as a loosely linked series of visual story-essays, seem to me constrained by their narrative logic, slight though it is. I find the same limitation in many of the situational caricatures, even the best, like the series on 'The Old and the Young Self' in *Observations*. Such caricatures tend to illustrate a joke; they bring out, as it were, rather than create their absurdities, as for instance that the sociable Edmund Gosse was brought up among the other-worldly Plymouth Brethren. In drawings where Max's bodies have to act some relatively plausible scene we see that bone beneath flesh is an embarrassment to his technical ability; his people's arms have a limited repertory of gestures. But those awkward appendages can become amazingly supple when they are independent of discursive wit and serve only the flowing lines of Max's invention, as they do for instance in a drawing of Sir Henry Irving (Plate 30) or in an early fantasy around the form of Aubrey Beardsley (Plate 31). In such drawings Max's line is most potent at that melting down and fashioning anew of its subject that he says is essential to 'The Spirit of Caricature'.

Many of his cartoons present an odd contrast between form and content. They are soft in overall appearance; the line is feeble; the

<hr />

[9] See above, Chapter 1, p. 13.

water-colour wash literally fades into the background. An exhibit of Max's drawings is a muted visual pleasure. But if the method is in some cases almost too 'delicate and tender', the 'meaning'—as Beerbohm writes of Whistler's—is often surprisingly 'ferocious'. As with much topical art, the ferocity becomes less apparent with the passage of time: 'the past is a work of art', he says in *The Mirror of the Past*, 'it is filtered- has style', and therefore a later generation may see in Max's drawings of (say) Kipling or Edward VII only art-upon-art and miss the shock they originally gave when they could be seen as violent wrenchings of living forms or as iconoclastic commentaries on contemporary pieties.

The fifteen drawings called 'The Second Childhood of John Bull' are unusual in this respect because the ferocity remains unmistakable. They were exhibited in 1901, during the Boer War; John Bull is a fat, bulbous-nosed drunkard, vulgar, stupid, alternately bullying and wheedling, a hatefully cruel monster of undeserved self-satisfaction. The drawings and captions are saturated with loathing, not only for English policy on the war and on the Irish question but for the ugliness of a whole bloated age. D. S. M[acColl], reviewing the 1901 exhibition for The *Saturday Review*, contrasted Max's drawings with Tenniel's 'heroic compositions': ' "Max" disturbs a general consen. to the suppression of caricature', he writes. 'Here it is mercilessly at work, the weapon used not to conciliate with gentle taps of the flat blade, but to do the killing work of wit':

A little germ that a hundred photographs might miss is isolated, is cultivated till it flowers into an awful plausible monster. Thus the vision of some harmless young gentleman [Arthur Balfour] in a stiff collar turns to a nightmare of a tall chimney-pot tube up through which a weak tendril of a neck straggles and tumbles over in a head.

The deadly weapon is a drawn line improvising in a way that neither words nor photographs can do. The reviewer concludes that ' "Max" has a formidable eye'.[10]

Again, the most politically explicit drawings most obviously retain that 'formidable' quality—the drawing, for instance, of 'Theodore Roosevelt, Past President of the United States and Permanent Prince of Bores' (Plate 32), with his tiny head and hugely threatening hand.

[10] *Saturday Review*, 14 December 1901, p. 739.

But it is not only in political caricatures or even in caricatures of people he hated that we see another way in which Max's drawing resembles Whistler's writing. Of Whistler as a controversialist, Beerbohm says:

They who were so foolish as to oppose him really did have their souls required of them. After an encounter with him they never again were quite the same men in the eyes of their fellows. Whistler's insults always stuck—stuck and spread round the insulted, who found themselves at length encased in them, like flies in amber. (*Yet Again*, p. 111)

And he concludes his essay: 'You may shed a tear over the flies if you will. For myself I am content to laud the amber.' Max's insulting lines also stuck and spread, but so deftly that many of the flies joined in lauding the amber.

But who opposed Max? And why was he bent on insulting them? Why did he require the souls of friends and enemies and bare acquaintances alike? In some cases the reason for his animus is obvious, but in just as many it seems morally causeless, a spontaneous product of the 'Spirit of Caricature'. A drawing of 1908 shows 'Mr Max Beerbohm receiv[ing] an influential, though biassed, deputation, urging him, in the cause of our common humanity, and of good taste, to give over' (Hart-Davis, *Catalogue*, no. 1423). Here are the old familiar faces of the published caricatures, the faces that would later decorate the walls of the Villino and its 'improved' books. The Portuguese ambassador, the Marquis de Soveral (always the best-dressed of Max's men), leads the deputation, speaking on behalf of a group that includes such diverse personalities as Kipling, James, Moore, Rothenstein, Hall Caine, Zangwill, Pinero, Lord Burnham, Edward Carson, Sargent, Shaw, Chesterton. Max receives them in an elegant library; on niches atop the bookcases are small busts of Lord Burnham, Hall Caine, and Chesterton. Seated at his desk, like a bureaucrat in the Office of Caricature, Max listens attentively to Soveral's plea. The petitioners stand deferentially, hat in hand. They seem oblivious of one another, as though powerless to free themselves from the forms in which Max has fixed them. Max is serious and sympathetic, but he will probably tell them that the matter is out of his hands.

In 'The Spirit of Caricature' (*Variety of Things*, pp. 119–30) he claims, in a subdued Wildean vein, that 'Caricature implies no moral judgment on its subject'. It is purely 'The delicious art of exaggerating, without fear or favour, the peculiarities of this or that human body, for the mere sake of exaggeration'. Neither liking nor loathing plays a part, nor is there any question of the artist's culpability: '... the caricaturist, though he may feel the deepest reverence for the man whom he is drawing, will not make him one jot less ridiculous than he has made another man whom he despises. To make the latter ridiculous gives him no moral pleasure: why should it give him any moral pain to make ridiculous the former?' Indeed the apparently destructive aspect of the art converts, by a witty application of aesthetic theory, to positive benefit: 'Tragedy, said Aristotle, purges us of superfluous awe, by evocation, and comedy likewise purges us of superfluous contempt. Even so might idealism of a subject purge us of superfluous awe for it, and caricature purge us of superfluous contempt.'

Max's humourous attempt to make caricature seem a salutary art stands in a good tradition of defences. Annibale Carracci was probably the first to take this aesthetic high road:

Is not the caricaturist's task exactly the same as the classical artist's? Both see the lasting truth beneath the surface of mere outward appearance. Both try to help nature accomplish its plan. [Carracci here sounds like Baudelaire or Wilde on cosmetics.] The one may strive to visualise the perfect form and to realise it in his work, the other to grasp the perfect deformity, and thus to reveal the very essence of a personality. A good caricature, like every work of art, is more true to life than life itself.[11]

But in Beerbohm's essay this sort of explanation, which justifies caricature by ignoring much of what makes it interesting, alternates with another sort. Beerbohm contrasts the political cartoonist, whose drawing arises from 'a normal impulse', with the true caricaturist who draws because of 'the sheer desire and irresponsible lust for bedevilling this or that human body ...' The vocabulary of desire, lust, and bedevilling is assimilated to the vocabulary of aesthetic objectivity in the paragraph where Max makes the caricaturist a sort of mad scientist who melts down the whole man 'as in a crucible' and fashions him anew from the solution; who tampers with every line and curve, and changes every particle 'scientifically, for the worse', until the subject

---

[11] Carracci, quoted by Richard Godfrey, intro. to *English Caricature 1620 to the Present* (London: Victoria and Albert Museum, 1984), 11.

stands 'wholly transformed, the joy of his creator, the joy of those who are privy to the art of caricature'. Here Beerbohm expresses both the mystic power and the sheer mischief that we actually find in his caricatures. They may remind us—as Whistler's writing reminds Beerbohm—of 'An urchin scribbling insults upon someone's garden wall' as well as of that other 'writing on the wall' that requires the souls of those who dwell within.

But no 'urchin', certainly not Whistler, ever had Max Beerbohm's delicate self-censoring mechanism. As caricaturist and parodist, from the time of his suppressed satire on Wilde, he cultivated that knowledge of strict limits that makes transgression such a powerful pleasure. He presented himself at the front of *The Works* as 'seem[ing] still to be saying, before all things, from first to last, "I am utterly purposed that I will not offend."' He had lapses, like the cartoons of royalty withdrawn from exhibition in 1923 and now owned by the Crown. Individuals protested, though seldom publicly ('Max Beerbohm has caricatured everyone ferociously' said George Moore; 'his representation of me hardly resembles a human being; I have never complained'[12]). But the large number of repressed, altered, or privately circulated drawings shows that between the self-liberating act of drawing and the self-assertive moment of showing came the anxiety of 'taste'.

It was the same in writing. In 1912 he composed a *Ballade Tragique à Double Refrain* about the stupefying boredom of life at Windsor Castle. He circulated manuscript copies to friends but threatened legal action when Harold Monro wanted to publish the poem: 'One can't call a harmless and estimable lady "duller than the King" in print. In MS one can. It is just a matter of taste that makes all the difference.'[13] The famous caricature of 'Mr Tennyson reading "In Memoriam" to his Sovereign' (Hart-Davis, *Catalogue*, no. 1656) shows the expansive poet and the diminutive Queen Victoria alone and lost in a vast room: the walls of the room, in the version published in *The Poets' Corner* (1904), are decorated with flowers, but in the (presumably) original drawing the flowers are skulls and cross bones. Why did

[12] Moore in Joseph Hone, *The Life of George Moore* (1936), p. 287, quoted by John Felstiner, *Lies of Art: Max Beerbohm's Parody and Caricature* (New York: Knopf, 1972), 103, whose excellent discussion includes other examples of protesting victims.

[13] 22 May 1913, in the Taylor Collection, Princeton University. The poem is published in *Max in Verse*. ed. J. G. Riewald (Battleboro, Vt.: Stephen Greene, 1963).

he alter the drawing? Desire of knighthood is one possibility, but I doubt it. 'It is just a matter of taste that makes all the difference', as he wrote to Harold Monro: without a sure sense of good taste, bad taste has no meaning. Max the caricaturist inhabited the narrow, dangerous space between the two.

Both the tactful dandy and the aggressive urchin in Max conformed to late Victorian standards. The protocols can be hard to recover. He exhibited some of his caricatures of Lord Burnham, for instance, but he kept others for private viewing; yet both kinds may offend a modern sensibility, and neither is more obviously actionable than the other. Lord Burnham, formally Sir Edward Lawson but originally Edward Levy, was a newspaper magnate and also, putatively, Reggie Turner's father. His rise in the gentile world interested Max, possibly because it looked like a vulgar parody of his own self-parodic act. In a drawing captioned 'Are we as welcome as ever?' (exhibited 1911, published in *Fifty Caricatures*, 1913; Hart-Davis, *Catalogue*, no. 198) Lord Burnham enters Buckingham Palace in a group which also includes Sir Ernest Cassel, Alfred and Leopold Rothschild, and Arthur Sassoon. Beerbohm explained the drawing to S. N. Behrman: 'These five men, all of them Jewish financiers, are friends of [the late] Edward [the Seventh] coming for the first time to see the new King George the Fifth and being somewhat apprehensive, don't you know.'[14] This drawing may seem in reasonably good taste compared to an unpublished drawing of Lord Burnham: it shows him clinging to a crucifix, his large nose hooked over the cross-bar, his eyes like a vulture's, his high-domed head visually echoing the skull at the foot of the cross. Presumably he is trying to claim the title scrolled above his nose, 'INRI' (no. 196A). But the published drawing of the apprehensive Jews paying court to a new monarch is just as 'ferocious' in its implications—or just as offensive, if we reject the excuse offered by the label 'satire'—as the unpublished drawing. The more tactful drawing is if anything more subversive because it makes the viewer complicit; we create, by reading into it, the offence of which Max is ostensibly innocent. The published caricature's power to offend depends on the suppressions it makes in the interest of 'good taste'.

Such drawings add a dram of eale to that sweetness David Cecil found in Max's spoonful of jam. His apparently disinterested devotion

[14] Behrman, *Portrait of Max*, p. 220.

to the art of insult, both in drawing and in words, secures him from the charge of partisan bias: some of his best friends were flies in his amber; but it also makes his motives more questionable. Not that Max's caricatures, any more than his essays and parodies, fail to express his own real values; but to be in favour of intelligence over stupidity, kindness over meanness, good taste over bad is to adopt a platform that still leaves plenty of room for the caricaturist to work. A caricature of King Edward VIII, called 'Long choosing and beginning late' (no. 528), is one of many that combine caricature and parody— distinct arts which in Beerbohm nonetheless clearly arise from the same impulse. This is the drawing that gave the most offence in the group of caricatures that had to be withdrawn from exhibition in 1923. Its political point is clear enough, yet it is also oddly non-partisan. It includes a long mock-extract from *The Times*, dated 10 November 1972, headed 'Ex-"Prince" Weds':

An interesting wedding was quietly celebrated yesterday at the Ealing Registry Office, when Mr Edward Windsor was united to Miss Flossie Pearson. The bridegroom, as many of our elder readers will recall, was at one time well-known as the 'heir-apparent' of the late 'King' George. He has for some years been residing at 'Balmoral', 85 Acacia Terrace, Lenin Avenue, Ealing; and his bride is the only daughter of his landlady. Immediately after the ceremony the happy pair travelled to Ramsgate, where the honeymoon will be spent. Interviewed later in the day by a *Times* man, the aged mother-in-law confessed that she had all along been opposed to the match, because of the disparity between the ages of the two parties—the bride being still on the sunny side of forty. 'I had always', she said, 'hoped that my Flossie was destined to make a brilliant match.' Now that the knot was tied, however, the old lady was evidently resigned to the *fait accompli*. 'I believe', she said, 'that Mr Windsor will make a good husband for my girl, for I must say that a nicer, quieter gentleman, or a more pleasant-spoken, never lodged under my roof.'

From this elaborate concoction of parody and caricature one might conclude that Beerbohm dislikes the Royal Family, or that he dislikes socialism, or that he dislikes the style of *The Times*, or the style of landladies, or all of the above. The opinions are of less interest than the distinct sense the reader/viewer takes of the caricaturist/writer in the act of hatching his impudent joke. Every detail, from the geography that links Balmoral, Ramsgate, and Ealing, down to the quotation marks that surround the words 'Prince', 'heir-apparent', and 'King', invites us to enjoy the seemingly disinterested exercise of insulting wit. The impudence dethrones Edward Windsor and empowers Max Beerbohm. In effect, the subject of such a caricature is its signature, MAX.

Who opposed Max? Potentially, any personality that competed with his, the 'distinct' as well as the 'dim'. His caricatures, like his parodies, inscribe his own image. Literally he is the most frequent subject of his drawing; and all his writing, even in strict parody, pictures him in the act of writing. But none of this makes Beerbohm a study in mental pathology. The parodist and the paranoid are alike in only one essential respect: they are intensely keen observers of other people. In two media Beerbohm found a single comic mode for rescuing civility from the disruptive demands of the imperialistic personality. His parodic art recreates but also defuses the threat that personality poses to personality as each becomes the mirror capturing and distorting the images projected by the other. It was an odd, personal accommodation. It made him an eternal on-looker and a scribbler in other men's margins, but it also made him, despite his own disclaimers, an authentic moral presence and a greatly original comic artist.

Index